Thoughts About Prophetic Subjects

JAMES C. MORRIS

Copyright © 2022 by James C. Morris

the author may be contacted at:
20 Spring Drive Place
Ocala, FL 34472-3008

author's e-mail address:
james-morris@sbcglobal.net

All rights reserved. No part of this publication may be reproduced, stored in a retrieval system, or transmitted in any way by any means, electronic, mechanical, photocopy, recording, or otherwise, without the prior permission of the copyright owner, except as provided by USA copyright law.

Scripture taken from the New King James Version.
Copyright © 1979, 1980, 1982 by Thomas Nelson, Inc.
Used by permission. All rights reserved.

Bible text from the New King James Version is not to be reproduced in copies or otherwise by any means except as permitted in writing by Thomas Nelson, Inc., Attn: Bible Rights and Permissions, P.O. Box 141000, Nashville, TN 37214-1000.

TABLE OF CONTENTS

Introduction 5
Thy Maker's Grief.. 7
The Absolute Certainty of Bible Prophecy 12
Why Even Conditional Prophecy Is Certain 19
Understanding Context in Bible Prophecy 25
Dispensations in the Bible... 28
Understanding the Prophecy of the Seventy Weeks........ 37
Who Will Be In the Land During the Seventieth Week. 51
The Neglected Character in End Time Prophecy............ 61
The Path of the Assyrian.. 70
The Lands of the Kings of the North and South
With the Assyrian Empire.. 73
The Five End Time Individuals of Bible Prophecy 83
The Scriptural Doctrine of Imminence 87
How We Know the Lord's Coming Is Near 89
The Rapture of the Church.. 101
Itemized Proof that the Rapture
Will Be Before the Tribulation 112
A Scriptural Precedent 116
A Widely Circulated Error About the Greek
Word Apantesis and the Pre-tribulation Rapture............ 129
Eight Scriptural Proofs that the Lord
Will Return Twice 136

The Scriptures Describe Different Gatherings
of God's People, Into Different Places, In Different
Ways, and at Different Times 138
How We Know the Gathering of His Elect
By the Angels Is Not the Rapture 150
Ten Greek Words Used For the Lord's Coming 158
The Four Formal Judgments of Scripture 185
A Note On the Meaning of the Word All 197
Who Are the Seed of Abraham? 201
The Ancient Promises 212
New Testament Prophecies of the Restoration of Israel . 259
The Promises to the Church 268
The Church Is Not Israel 273
The Millennium 280
The Worship During the Millennium 289
The New Heavens and the New Earth 296
When Will Israel Be Brought Back to the Land? 302
The Timing of Ezekiel 38-39 310
The Timing of the Sheep and Goats Judgment 320
The Letters to the Seven Churches 322
The Pseudo-science of Hermeneutics 336
The Errors of Amillennialism 348
The Errors of Replacement Theology 357
The Errors of Preterism 363
The Errors of Historicism 374
The Errors of British Israelism 381

Introduction

This is a collection of independent articles written over a number of years, concerning subjects relating to Bible prophecy. These have been arranged in a logical order and edited to suit publication together as a single volume. As these are independent articles, there is some repetition, because the same scriptures often apply to different subjects. Some of the material presented here is adapted from my previous book, "Keys to Bible Prophecy," by James C. Morris, published by Dispensational Publishing House, ISBN # 978-1-945774-33-1.

As positive ministry is generally superior to negative ministry, articles teaching important truths are given first, followed by articles exposing serious error.

The opening poem, "Thy Maker's Grief," is one of the first things I ever wrote about Bible prophecy. But that is not why it is first here. It presents an extremely important concept for a saint of God to understand. After that, come articles about how we can be certain that the prophecies in the Bible will most certainly be fulfilled. These are followed by articles critical to a general understanding of Bible prophecy. And then come articles dealing with our Lord's coming. These are followed by articles about the promises Our God made to the ancient nation of Israel, first in the Old Testament, and then in the New Testament. These are followed by a series of articles about various details of Bible prophecy. And then comes a series of articles about the timing of various events. The timing of the rapture had been discussed previously. But these articles trace the Lord's statements about other times.

Then, in the negative ministry section, comes first an article dealing with a seriously false approach to the study of the scriptures, that, unfortunately, is even subscribed to by many serious students of the scriptures. This article demonstrates that many of its concepts are contrary to explicitly stated scripture. This is followed by a series of articles demonstrating the errors involved in various systems of interpretation of the prophetic scriptures.

As with all of my books, this volume is based on the truth that the Bible is the very word of an almighty God, who cannot lie and who never makes a mistake. Since our God is almighty, nothing can stop Him from doing whatever He has determined to do. Since He cannot lie, He has bound Himself to do everything that He has declared He will do. And since He never makes a mistake, none of His plans can ever fail. So we can absolutely rely upon His complete keeping of every promise He ever made.

This book is sent forth with the prayer that it might be helpful to the church, the beloved bride of Christ, who shed His precious blood for us.

JAMES C. MORRIS

THOUGHTS ABOUT PROPHETIC SUBJECTS

Thy Maker's Grief

I. 1. See the earth with darkness covered,
Form without, and void o'er all.
See the waves of mighty waters
In one endless ocean roll.

2. See the mighty God of heaven
Move in spirit o'er the waste.
See Him form this worthless nothing
To a home for those He'll make.

3. See Him now with care unmeasured
Take the dust by wondrous plan,
Form it to His satisfaction,
Give it life, and call it man.

4. Share with Him in His rejoicing!
Couldst thou ought but do this when
God, thy God, hath thee created
Takes His joy in sons of men?

II. 1. See the man in new creation
Joy in fellowship with Him.
In this blessed place called Eden,
With a soul unmarred by sin.

2. See the foe in subtle cruelty
Tempt the man to turn to sin,
Make him doubt the God of heaven,
Spoil him for his own foul end!

3. See him now in fullest mastery
Drive mankind to depths of sin
Till their hearts can not imagine
Ought but deeper forms of sin.

4. Keep thee silence now before Him.
Now His grief's too deep to name.
Those He loves beyond a measure
Take their joy in their own shame!

III. 1. See the whole creation groaning,
Travailing in pain untold!
While the mighty foe abuses
All his own, though young or old.

2. See in flesh now come among them
(Wondrous plan) the Son of God!
See Him bear their griefs and sorrows
As foretold in His own word.

3. See Him now twixt earth and heaven
Hung upon a tree of shame.
See Him bear the sin of others.
Jesus (Savior) is His name!

THOUGHTS ABOUT PROPHETIC SUBJECTS

4. Oh! 'Tis now with joy and sorrow
Thou must watch this scene of shame.
Much rejoice that He hath saved thee;
Sorrow at His untold pain.

IV. 1. See His church in blessed newness
Come together, break the bread;
Every thought and every action
In accord with its great Head.

2. See the foe in fullest hatred
Sow his tares among the wheat;
Grievous wolves send in among them
With intent to slay the sheep.

3. See him now in ghastly triumph
Place his men in full control.
See the leaven, deftly scattered
Grow and swell to fill the whole.

4. Deeply mourn thy guilt before Him.
Thou art part of this sad whole.
Thine the guilt and His the sorrow
Feel this in thy deepest soul!

V. 1. See the church (thus He still calls it).
See Him stand without the door.
Though He waits in patience, knocking,
See it now Him full ignore.

2. See Him call His own out from it.
See Him rise and shut the door.
See Him now, and full upon it
All His wrath and fury pour.

3. See Him now in fullest fury
Pour His wrath creation o'er.
Weep and mourn, 'tis His great sorrow
That He now can spare no more.

4. Sob and weep, ye sons of heaven!
These are those thy God has loved;
Yet He now must vent His fury.
For their hatred they have proved.

VI. 1. This is anguish to thy Maker.
Sit with Him and weep awhile.
Share with Him His awful sorrow.
He has loved them all the while.

2. This His work, His awful strange work;
How could He, whose self is love,
Find but sorrow, deep, unspoken,
Over such an awful move.

3. Feel His sorrow! Oh! Rejoice not.
This is not thy Maker's joy.
Tis His sorrow, second only
To that when He gave His son.

4. This His sorrow is not spoken.
Yet tis there between the lines,
Hidden in the Revelation. [1]
Read it not, oh saint, with joy.

---

1. This is a reference to the **"silence in heaven for about half an hour"** that is stated in Revelation 8:1, **"When He had opened the seventh seal."** Others have suggested that here, the God of heaven is expressing His sorrow at what He must now do. The time for judgment has come, and justice must now be done. So God - sits there and does nothing. But God is not just a God of Love, He is also a God of Righteousness, so, after an expressive pause, He takes action. Do we share His sorrow at what He must now do? This also refers to Revelation 10:9-10, where John **"ate" "the little book,"** (studied Bible prophecy it until it became a part of himself) and it **"was as sweet as honey"** in his mouth. (It was delightful to begin to understand it.) But when he had eaten it, his **"stomach became bitter."** (When he had understood what God must do, it made him sick.) "Read it not, oh saint, with joy."

JAMES C. MORRIS

The Absolute Certainty of Bible Prophecy

Jesus said, "**assuredly, I say to you, till heaven and earth pass away, one jot or one tittle will by no means pass from the law till all is fulfilled.**" (Matthew 5:18) And the Holy Spirit, speaking through Paul, said that "**the gifts and the calling of God *are* irrevocable.**" (Romans 11:28-29)

We are told that God began His promise to Abraham by saying, "**By Myself I have sworn, says the Lord.**" (Genesis 22:16) The Holy Spirit said of this, "**For when God made a promise to Abraham, because He could swear by no one greater, He swore by Himself, saying, *Surely blessing I will bless you, and multiplying I will multiply you.' For men indeed swear by the greater, and an oath for confirmation is for them an end of all dispute. Thus God, determining to show more abundantly to the heirs of promise the immutability of His counsel, confirmed it by an oath, that by two immutable things, in which it is impossible for God to lie, we might have strong consolation, who have fled for refuge to lay hold of the hope set before us. This hope we have as an anchor of the soul, both sure and steadfast.*"(Hebrews 6:13-19)

We see several critically important things in this passage. The first, and most obvious, part of it is the stressing that this promise involved "**two immutable things, in which it is impossible for God to lie.**" This is closely related to what God said through Balaam, "**God is not a man, that He should lie.**" (And we note in passing that both of these two passages point out that, if God were not going to actually keep His promises, He would have been lying when He made them.) And we are explicitly told that God "**cannot lie.**" (Titus 1:2)

THOUGHTS ABOUT PROPHETIC SUBJECTS

But what was the other **"immutable"** thing? **"Because He could swear by no one greater,"** God **"swore by Himself."** Then the Holy Spirit pointed out that **"men indeed swear by the greater, and an oath for confirmation is for them an end of all dispute."** So whenever God swore by Himself, He was putting **"an end of all dispute"** about what He was saying.

And God did not just do this in regard to Abraham. He also did it concerning **"the Assyrian,"** saying:

> **"The LORD of hosts has sworn, saying, 'Surely, as I have thought, so it shall come to pass, And as I have purposed, so it shall stand.' That I will break the Assyrian in My land, And on My mountains tread him underfoot. Then his yoke shall be removed from them, And his burden removed from their shoulders. This is the purpose that is purposed against the whole earth, And this is the hand that is stretched out over all the nations. For the LORD of hosts has purposed, And who will annul it? His hand is stretched out, And who will turn it back?'"** (Isaiah 14:24-27)

And He said concerning everyone:

> **"I have sworn by Myself;**
> **The word has gone out of My mouth** *in* **righteousness,**
> **And shall not return.**
> **That to Me every knee shall bow,**
> **Every tongue shall take an oath."** (Isaiah 45:23)

And again, God said concerning **"Edom,"** (see verse 7) **" 'For I have sworn by Myself,'** says the LORD, **'that Bozrah shall** become a desolation, a reproach, a waste, and a curse. And all its cities shall be perpetual wastes.'" (Jeremiah 49:13)

But even when our God did not "swear by Himself," He often stressed the absolute immutability of His counsel in different words, saying things like, "**Thus says the LORD: 'If you can break My covenant with the day and My covenant with the night, so that there will not be day and night in their season, then My covenant may also be broken with David My servant, so that he shall not have a son to reign on his throne, and with the Levites, the priests, My ministers.'**" (Jeremiah 33:20-21) And, "**Thus says the LORD: 'If My covenant is not with day and night, *and if* I have not appointed the ordinances of heaven and earth, then I will cast away the descendants of Jacob and David My servant, so that I will not take *any* of his descendants *to be* rulers over the descendants of Abraham, Isaac, and Jacob. For I will cause their captives to return, and will have mercy on them.'**" (Jeremiah 33:25-26)

Earlier, He had said concerning His promises to David:
> "**My covenant I will not break,**
> **Nor alter the word that has gone out of My lips.**
> **Once I have sworn by My holiness;**
> **I will not lie to David:**
> **His seed shall endure forever,**
> **And his throne as the sun before Me;**
> **It shall be established forever like the moon,**
> **Even *like* the faithful witness in the sky.**" (Psalm 89:34)

Earlier in the same psalm He had said of this covenant,
> "**If his sons forsake My law**
> **And do not walk in My judgments,**
> **If they break My statutes**

> And do not keep My commandments,
> Then I will punish their transgression with the rod,
> And their iniquity with stripes.
> Nevertheless My lovingkindness
> I will not utterly take from him,
> Nor allow My faithfulness to fail."
> (Psalm 89:30-33)

Indeed, it would have been difficult to make this language more absolute. But yet again, He said:

> "Thus says the Lord GOD: 'On the day that I cleanse you from all your iniquities, I will also enable *you* to dwell in the cities, and the ruins shall be rebuilt. The desolate land shall be tilled instead of lying desolate in the sight of all who pass by. So they will say, "This land that was desolate has become like the garden of Eden; and the wasted, desolate, and ruined cities *are now* fortified *and* inhabited." Then the nations which are left all around you shall know that I, the LORD, have rebuilt the ruined places *and* planted what was desolate. I, the LORD, have spoken *it*, and I will do *it*.'"
> (Ezekiel 36:33-36)

And God was not only insistent that He would keep His word about His promises of blessing. He was similarly insistent concerning His pronouncements of coming judgments, saying things like:

> "Remember the former things of old,
> For I *am* God, and *there is* no other;
> I *am* God, and *there is* none like Me,
> Declaring the end from the beginning,
> And from ancient times *things* that are not *yet* done,
> Saying, 'My counsel shall stand,

And I will do all My pleasure,'
Calling a bird of prey from the east,
The man who executes My counsel, from a far country.
Indeed I have spoken *it*;
I will also bring it to pass.
I have purposed *it*;
I will also do it." (Isaiah 46:9-11)

Again, He said, "I, the LORD, have spoken, and will do *it*. I will scatter you among the nations, disperse you throughout the countries, and remove your filthiness completely from you. You shall defile yourself in the sight of the nations; then you shall know that I am the LORD." (Ezekiel 22:14-16)

And:

" 'I, the LORD, have spoken *it*;
It shall come to pass, and I will do *it*;
I will not hold back,
Nor will I spare,
Nor will I relent;
According to your ways
And according to your deeds
They will judge you,' Says the Lord GOD."
(Ezekiel 24:14)

But now we need to ask, why is this such an important concept? Why was God so insistent about the absolute nature of His pronouncements? We have already noticed that the purpose of His oath to Abraham was that we might understand that **"it is impossible for God to lie."** And we have already noticed that this is similar to what He had said much earlier through the prophet Balaam:

> "**God is not a man, that He should lie,**
> **Nor a son of man, that He should repent.**
> **Has He said, and will He not do?**
> **Or has He spoken, and will He not make it good?"**
> (Numbers 23:19)

And we have already noticed that here, our God was pointing out that He would have been lying when He made these promises, if He was not going to actually keep them. But again, why is this so important? To see why, we need to go back to something we skipped over previously.

We were explicitly told that the reason that God made His oath to Abraham was that **"we might have strong consolation, who have fled for refuge to lay hold of the hope set before us."** How did **"we"** get into the picture? What does this have to do with us? Actually, *everything*. It has *everything* to do with us. For if God could cancel *any* promise He ever made, He could also cancel any *other* promise He ever made. And that would include even His promises to save us and make is His own forever. And that is why it refers to **"the hope set before us,"** adding, **"This *hope* we have as an anchor of the soul, both sure and steadfast."**

We are also told something similar about the promises made to David. For we are told:

> "**Ho! Everyone who thirsts,**
> **Come to the waters;**
> **And you who have no money,**
> **Come, buy and eat.**
> **Yes, come, buy wine and milk**
> **Without money and without price.**

> **Why do you spend money for *what is* not bread,**
> **And your wages for *what* does not satisfy?**
> **Listen carefully to Me, and eat *what is* good,**
> **And let your soul delight itself in abundance.**
> **Incline your ear, and come to Me.**
> **Hear, and your soul shall live;**
> **And I will make an everlasting covenant with you--**
> **The sure mercies of David."**
> (Isaiah 55:1-3)

So the scriptures explicitly teach us to apply to ourselves the *absolutely unconditional* nature of the *sure* promises that God made to both **"Abraham"** and **"David."** And that is why this subject is so *critically* important. We need to realize that this is one of the *foundation* doctrines of our faith. If the promises of God are not *absolutely* reliable, we have *no* basis for our faith. If there is even *one* prophecy in the entire Bible that will not *actually* be fulfilled, we cannot be certain that our own sins have been forgiven, and we cannot be certain that we will be in heaven. In short, if Bible prophecy is not *absolutely* reliable, then we have trusted in an unreliable God, and we can be confident of nothing.

THOUGHTS ABOUT PROPHETIC SUBJECTS

Why Even Conditional Prophecy Is Certain

Much of Bible prophecy is stated in absolute terms. One of the more pronounced examples is:

> **"Remember the former things of old,**
> **For I *am* God, and *there is* no other;**
> **I *am* God, and *there is* none like Me,**
> **Declaring the end from the beginning,**
> **And from ancient times *things* that are not yet done,**
> **Saying, 'My counsel shall stand,**
> **And I will do all My pleasure,'"**
> (Isaiah 46:9-10)

This is not the only place where we find such absolute language in Bible prophecy. Two others are:

> **"Seek ye out of the book of the LORD, and read: no one of these shall fail, none shall want her mate: for my mouth it hath commanded, and his spirit it hath gathered them."** (Isaiah 34:16)

> **"'For I *am* the Lord. I speak, and the word which I speak will come to pass; it will no more be postponed; for in your days, O rebellious house, I will say the word and perform it,' says the Lord GOD."** (Ezekiel 12:25).

But there are other places in the Bible that seem to cast a doubt on the absolute certainty of such things.

> "The instant I speak concerning a nation and concerning a kingdom, to pluck up, to pull down, and to destroy *it*, if that nation against whom I have spoken turns from its evil, I will relent of the disaster that I thought to bring upon it. And the instant I speak concerning a nation and concerning a kingdom, to build and to plant *it*, if it does evil in My sight so that it does not obey My voice, then I will relent concerning the good with which I said I would benefit it." (Jeremiah 18:7-10)

And:

> "When I say to the righteous *that* he shall surely live, but he trusts in his own righteousness and commits iniquity, none of his righteous works shall be remembered; but because of the iniquity that he has committed, he shall die. Again, when I say to the wicked, 'You shall surely die,' if he turns from his sin and does what is lawful and right, *if* the wicked restores the pledge, gives back what he has stolen, and walks in the statutes of life without committing iniquity, he shall surely live; he shall not die. None of his sins which he has committed shall be remembered against him; he has done what is lawful and right; he shall surely live." (Ezekiel 33:13-16)

We also have one example in scripture where this actually happened:

> "Then God saw their works, that they turned from their evil way; and God relented from the disaster that He had said He would bring upon them, and He did not do it." (Jonah 3:10)

Are these contradictions? Is the prophetic word certain and sure? Or is it conditional? How can we know? Can we be certain

THOUGHTS ABOUT PROPHETIC SUBJECTS

of what will come to pass? There are many subjects in the Bible concerning which one set of passages says one thing, and another set says something that seems to contradict what the first set says. But whenever this happens in the Bible, there is always a third set of passages that clears up the apparent contradiction.

The conditions are always there, whether stated or not. If man repents of his evil, God will repent of the punishment He had pronounced upon him. And if man presumes upon a promised blessing and turns to sin, God will withhold the blessing. These things are always true. But God is all knowing, and this knowledge includes the future. In certain cases, He has specifically told us that certain people will not repent. We find this explicitly stated four times in the book of Revelation alone:

> **"And I gave her time to repent of her sexual immorality, and she did not repent."** (Revelation 2:21)

> **"But the rest of mankind, who were not killed by these plagues, did not repent of the works of their hands, that they should not worship demons, and idols of gold, silver, brass, stone, and wood, which can neither see nor hear nor walk. And they did not repent of their murders or their sorceries or their sexual immorality or their thefts."** (Revelation 9:20-21)

> **"And men were scorched with great heat, and they blasphemed the name of God who has power over these plagues; and they did not repent and give Him glory."** (Revelation 16:9)

> **"They blasphemed the God of heaven because of their pains and their sores, and did not repent of their deeds."** (Revelation 16:11)

The wickedness of man is so great that he is unable to repent unless God first does a work in his heart. We remember that Jesus said **"No one can come to Me unless the Father who** sent Me draws him." (John 6:44) and again that "**by grace you have been saved through faith, and that not of yourselves;** *it is* **the gift of God, not of works, lest anyone should boast.**" (Ephesians 2:8-9) And, "**Or do you despise the riches of His goodness, forbearance, and longsuffering, not knowing that the goodness of God leads you to repentance?**" (Romans 2:4) When men have rebelled too greatly against God, he will finally turn away from them, as we read in 2 Chronicles 36:16: "**But they mocked the messengers of God, despised His words, and scoffed at His prophets, until the wrath of the Lord arose against His people, till** *there was* **no remedy.**" So when God finally turns away from a man, or a nation, there is no longer a remedy, because he will no longer offer it.

In such cases God will sometimes do more than simply withhold the gift of repentance. He will in certain cases inflict what we call "judicial blindness." We read in Isaiah 6:9-10, "**Go, and tell this people: 'Keep on hearing, but do not understand; Keep on seeing, but do not perceive.' Make the heart of this people dull, And their ears heavy, And shut their eyes; Lest they see with their eyes, And hear with their ears, And understand with their heart, And return and be healed.**" John 12:39-40 specifically tells us that this is why the bulk of the men of Judah "**could not believe**" in Him when He came.

But more that this, He will actually go so far as to inflict delusion upon certain hardened rebels. This is specifically stated several times in the Bible. It is said concerning the coming "**Antichrist:**"

> "**The coming of the** *lawless one* **is according to the working of Satan, with all power, signs, and lying wonders, and with all unrighteous deception among those who perish, because they did not receive the love of the truth, that they might be saved. And for this reason God will send them strong delusion, that they should believe the lie, that they all may be condemned who**

did not believe the truth but had pleasure in unrighteousness." (2 Thessalonians 2:9-12)

It is also said concerning the wickedness of Israel at that same time: **"Just as they have chosen their own ways, And their soul delights in their abominations, So will I choose their delusions, And bring their fears on them; Because, when I called, no one answered, When I spoke they did not hear; But they did evil before My eyes, And chose *that* in which I do not delight."** (Isaiah 66:3-4)

But even as the Bible tells us that some will not repent, it also expressly says that Israel will repent. When Israel finally sees their long awaited messiah, " '*one* shall say unto him, What are these wounds in thine hands?' Then he shall answer, 'Those with which I was wounded in the house of my friends.' " (Zechariah 13:6 KJV[2]) The result is that **"In that day there shall be a great mourning in Jerusalem, like the mourning at Hadad Rimmon in the plain of Megiddo. And the land shall mourn, every family by itself: the family of the house of David by itself, and their wives by themselves; the family of the house of Nathan by itself, and their wives by themselves; the family of the house of Levi by itself, and their wives by themselves; the family of Shimei by itself, and their wives by themselves; all the families that remain, every family by itself, and their wives by themselves."** (Zechariah 12:11-14) This repentance will not be temporary, for after Israel's great deliverance from Gog, the Lord says, **"So will I make my holy name known in the midst of my people Israel; and I will not let them pollute my holy name any more."** (Ezekiel 39:7)

---

2. I have used the KJV reading here, rather than the NKJV, which we are using, because it seems to me that in this case the KJV reading better conveys the true sense of the passage.

This is like the eternal security of present-day believers, which is based, not on *their* faithfulness, but on the faithfulness of their Lord. We read in Philippians 1:6 that **"He who has begun a good work in you will complete *it* until the day of Jesus Christ."** As Paul said, **"I know whom I have believed and am persuaded that He is able to keep what I have committed to Him until that Day."** (2 Timothy 1:12)

And as Jude said:

> **"Now to Him who is able to keep you from stumbling,**
> **And to present *you* faultless**
> **Before the presence of His glory with exceeding joy,**
> **To God our Savior,**
> **Who alone is wise,**
> ***Be* glory and majesty,**
> **Dominion and power,**
> **Both now and forever.**
> **Amen."** (Jude 24-25)

Thus we understand how Bible prophecy can still be unconditional, even though God himself has said that His promises, both of blessing and of punishment, would no longer apply if people changed. For He has also promised that He will bring about repentance in those He intends to bless. And He has declared that He will inflict "judicial blindness" upon those He intends to punish, rendering them unable to repent.

Understanding Context in Bible Prophecy

In interpreting the scriptures generally, as in interpreting almost all communication, context is critical. For without considering the context it is possible to make almost anything *seem* to mean something entirely different from what the original writer or speaker *meant*. But in Bible prophecy, the normal rules of context do not always apply. For at times, even very short statements speak of events that are widely separated in time, as well as in subject.

We can see many examples of this in the Bible. For instance, we read in Revelation 12:

> "... **the dragon stood before the woman who was ready to give birth, to devour her Child as soon as it was born. She bore a male Child who was to rule all nations with a rod of iron. And her Child was caught up to God and His throne. Then the woman fled into the wilderness, where she has a place prepared by God, that they should feed her there one thousand two hundred and sixty days.**" (Revelation 12:4-6)

In this prophecy, the last part of the sentence in verse 4 and the first part of the sentence in verse 5 are clearly speaking of the birth of Christ. Then the last part of verse 5 just as clearly speaks of our Lord's ascension into heaven, which took place more than thirty years later, with even His crucifixion omitted. But then the next sentence jumps forward thousands of years to the seventieth week of Daniel, the time we call **"the great tribulation."**

This is just one of many such cases in Bible prophecy. Another one is the prophecy about our Lord's virgin birth, where we read, "**Therefore the Lord Himself will give you a sign: Behold, the virgin shall conceive and bear a Son, and shall call His name Immanuel.**" (Isaiah 7:14) This prophecy is tucked in just after a prophecy about the destruction of the northern sub-kingdom of "**Ephraim,**" which says "**Within sixty-five years Ephraim will be broken, So that it will not be a people.**" (Isaiah 7:8) And it is just before a prophecy about the coming attack of the dreaded "**Assyrian,**" not upon the kingdom of "**Ephraim,**" but upon king "**Ahaz,**" (verse 10) who was a king of "**Judah.**" For God told him, "**The LORD will bring the king of Assyria upon you and your people and your father's house.**" (Isaiah 7:17)

And who among us has not pondered over the many places where the New Testament says that such-and-such an event is a fulfillment of such-and-such a prophecy. But when you look at that prophecy, your reaction has been that the only way you could have known that prophecy spoke of that event is that the Holy Spirit explicitly said so.

Hosea 11:1-4 is a touching commentary on the Lord's bringing the children of Israel out from Egypt, saying:

> "**When Israel was a child,**
> **I loved him,**
> **And out of Egypt I called My son.**
> **As they called them,**
> **So they went from them;**
> **They sacrificed to the Baals,**
> **And burned incense to carved images.**
> **:I taught Ephraim to walk,**
> **Taking them by their arms;**
> **But they did not know that I healed them.**

> **I drew them with gentle cords,**
> **With bands of love,**
> **And I was to them as those**
> **who take the yoke from their neck.**
> **I stooped and fed them."**

But in Matthew 2:15 the Holy Spirit explicitly told us that the second sentence of this paragraph was a prophecy about our Lord being called back from Egypt.

Again, in Exodus 12 we have the instructions for the observance of the Passover. And among these we find an instruction that **"you shall not carry any of the flesh outside the house, nor shall you break one of its bones."** (Verse 46)

Unless the Holy Spirit had explicitly told us in John 18:36 that this was a prophecy that none of our Lord's bones would be broken when He was crucified, how many of us would have realized that detail?

So we see that the normal rules of focusing almost exclusively on the immediate context do not necessarily apply when interpreting prophecies in the Bible, but rather, the broader context of the rest of what God said in other places must also be considered.

Dispensations in the Bible

Dispensationalism is simply the doctrine that God interacts with mankind in different ways at different times. Detractors of this doctrine see it as God "trying" different things. But that is not the doctrine at all. Rather than imagining that God is "trying" different things, Dispensationalists realize that God is running a series of tests. But these are not tests in the sense of finding out what will happen. Instead, this series of tests is designed to demonstrate what God already knew, that mankind will fail under any conceivable circumstance.

God's first test of mankind was to leave him innocent, without any knowledge of good or evil. For **"they were both naked, the man and his wife, and were not ashamed."** (Genesis 2:25) In this test, God gave mankind only one law. **"Of the tree of the knowledge of good and evil you shall not eat."** (Genesis 2:17)

God warned them of the result of breaking this one law, that they would surely die. But they broke that one law, because they chose to believe Satan's lie that God did not have their own best interests in mind. This brought about the first change in God's dealings. **"And the eyes of them both were opened, and they knew that they *were* naked."** (Genesis 3:7) Here is a distinct change, a condition that had not existed before. They were naked before, but so what? That was just what they looked like. But now they knew that they were naked.

This dispensation, though short, ended with mankind being sent out of the garden of Eden, where everything for which they could wish had been provided for them. But now they had to work for a living.

THOUGHTS ABOUT PROPHETIC SUBJECTS

After expelling mankind from the garden, God left them more or less up to their own devices, with no guide (at least, with no guide that is recorded in the scriptures) except their consciences. And what was the result of this test? **"And GOD saw that the wickedness of man *was* great in the earth, and *that* every imagination of the thoughts of his heart *was* only evil continually."** (Genesis 6:5) **"The earth also was corrupt before God, and the earth was filled with violence."** (Genesis 6:11) So God sent the great flood, destroying all of mankind except Noah and his family.

So even as the first dispensation had ended with **"a flaming sword which turned every way,"** (Genesis 3:24) keeping mankind out of the garden, this one ended with all of mankind except one family being put to death.

After the flood, God made a new law, something that had not existed before. He said, **"Surely for your lifeblood I will demand *a reckoning;* from the hand of every beast I will require it, and from the hand of man. From the hand of every man's brother I will require the life of man.**

"Whoever sheds man's blood,
By man his blood shall be shed;
For in the image of God He made man." (Genesis 9:5-6)

This was again a change, something that had not existed before. And mankind went out, and began to establish kingdoms. And they began to rebel against God, building a tower to reach his heaven. (Of course, God knew, as we do today, that this would not work. But they did not know that.) Up to this time **"the whole earth had one language, and one speech."** (Genesis 11:1) But **"the LORD confused the language of all the earth; and from there the LORD scattered them abroad over the face of all the earth."** (Genesis 11:9)

So this dispensation, in which God first held man responsible to administer justice, ended with their single language confounded, so they were scattered abroad upon the face of the earth.

After this, God "**said to Abram:**

'Get out of your country,

From your family

And from your father's house,

To a land that I will show you.

I will make you a great nation;

I will bless you

And make your name great;

And you shall be a blessing.

I will bless those who bless you,

And I will curse him who curses you;

And in you all the families of the earth shall be blessed.'" (Genesis 12:1-3)

This, again, was something new. Something that God had never done before. He took a single man and gave him a great promise. Later on, He expanded that promise, saying, "**Lift your eyes now and look from the place where you are--northward, southward, eastward, and westward; for all the land which you see I give to you and your descendants forever. And I will make your descendants as the dust of the earth; so that if a man could number the dust of the earth, *then* your descendants also could be numbered.**" (Genesis 13:14-16) Later, He clarified this, "**saying: 'To your descendants I have given this land, from the river of Egypt to the great river, the River Euphrates:'**" (Genesis 15:18-21) And "**He said to Abram: 'Know certainly that your descendants will be strangers in a land that is not theirs, and will serve them, and they will afflict them four hundred years. And also**

THOUGHTS ABOUT PROPHETIC SUBJECTS

the nation whom they serve I will judge; afterward they shall come out with great possessions." (Genesis 15:13-14) Abraham's descendants forgot the promises and descended into the hopelessness of slavery, so hopeless that when God sent **"Moses and Aaron"** to deliver them, they said to them, **"Let the LORD look on you and judge, because you have made us abhorrent in the sight of Pharaoh and in the sight of his servants, to put a sword in their hand to kill us."** (Exodus 5:21)

So this dispensation ended with the promise forgotten, and even the hope of deliverance scorned.

But God indeed brought them out, and gave them a long and detailed law, with promises of blessing for those who kept it and curses for those who did not. This, again, was something God had never done before. It was new and different. But none of them kept this law. And they finally nailed the only one who ever kept it to a tree.

So this dispensation ended with the only truly righteous man who ever lived, hanging on a tree.

When Jesus died, God offered salvation to whoever would believe in Him. This was something God had never done before. Scripture calls this **"the dispensation of the grace of God."** (Ephesians 3:2) But scripture also tells us how this dispensation will end, saying **"evil men and impostors will grow worse and worse, deceiving and being deceived."** (2 Timothy 3:13) And Jesus himself asked the rhetorical question **"when the Son of Man comes, will He really find faith on the earth?"** (Luke 18:8) The answer, from other scriptures, is plainly, no. For we are told, **"Let no one deceive you by any means; for *that Day will not come* unless the falling away comes first, and the man of sin is revealed, the son of perdition, who opposes and exalts himself above all that is called God or that is worshiped, so that he sits as God in the temple of God, showing himself that he is God."** (2 Thessalonians 2:3-4) And **"The coming of** the *lawless one* is according to the working of Satan, with all power, signs, and lying wonders, and with all unrighteous deception among those who perish, because they did not receive the love of the truth, that they might be saved. And for this reason God will send them strong delusion, that they should believe the lie, that they all may be condemned who did not believe the truth but had pleasure in unrighteousness."** (2 Thessalonians 2:9-12)

So we are explicitly told that this dispensation will end with a punitive blindness imposed by God because men **"did not love the truth, but had pleasure in unrighteousness."**

Finally, we are explicitly told that there is a new dispensation coming. The worship during that dispensation is clearly described in Ezekiel. In Ezekiel 40:1-43:5, the prophet was shown a highly detailed vision of a temple, unlike anything that has ever been built. And then, in Ezekiel 43:7, the Lord said, **"this is the place of My throne and the place of the soles of My feet, where I will dwell in the midst of the children of Israel forever."** Then, a few verses later, the Lord said, **"These are the ordinances for the altar on the day when it is made."** (Ezekiel 43:18)

This is followed by a long series of detailed instructions for a form of worship unlike anything that God had ever specified in the past. This is not a description of a return to the law of Moses, but of a new system of worship, similar to that under the law of Moses, yet distinctly different from it. Both the sacrifices and the ordinances are distinctly different from those given through Moses. This runs from Ezekiel 43:18 through Ezekiel 46:24. Worship in this form would have carried the death penalty under the law of Moses, and would be blasphemous today. But our God has explicitly instructed the people of that future age to worship in this way.

And God has described that age in glowing germs.

"The wolf also shall dwell with the lamb,

THOUGHTS ABOUT PROPHETIC SUBJECTS

> The leopard shall lie down with the young goat,
> The calf and the young lion and the fatling together;
> And a little child shall lead them.
> The cow and the bear shall graze;
> Their young ones shall lie down together;
> And the lion shall eat straw like the ox.
> The nursing child shall play by the cobra's hole,
> And the weaned child shall put his hand in the viper's den.
> They shall not hurt nor destroy in all My holy mountain,
> For the earth shall be full of the knowledge of the LORD
> As the waters cover the sea." (Isaiah 11:6-9)

And again,

> "No more shall every man teach his neighbor, and every man his brother, saying, 'Know the LORD,' for they all shall know Me, from the least of them to the greatest of them, says the LORD. For I will forgive their iniquity, and their sin I will remember no more." (Jeremiah 31:34)

But our God has also plainly told us how that future dispensation will end.

> "Now when the thousand years have expired, Satan will be released from his prison and will go out to deceive the nations which are in the four corners of the earth, Gog and Magog, to gather them together to battle, whose number *is* as the sand of the sea. They went up on the breadth of the earth and surrounded the camp of the saints and the beloved city. And fire came down from God out of heaven and devoured them." (Revelation 20:7-9)

So the future dispensation will end with fire coming "**down from God out of heaven,**" and burning up the rebels.

As we consider these distinct changes in God's dealing with mankind, and the result of every one of these different periods of testing, we realize, first, that this is not just some kind of a fantasy, invented by mere mortals, but that this is indeed what the Bible actually says. And we further notice that every one of these periods of testing ended with a complete failure of mankind. But we also notice one other detail that is not *stated* in scripture, but which is nonetheless there. And that is that the Bible reveals seven such periods of testing. And we remember that the number seven is a number that represents perfection. That is, that God is running a perfect number of tests. Now no number of tests would *absolutely* prove that mankind would *always* fail. But God has chosen to demonstrate this with a perfect number of tests.

Now what could be the reason for God to do this? Why would God want to prove that mankind would fail under any conceivable circumstance? In our human pride we tend to think only about ourselves. But the Bible very clearly says:

> "**Behold, the nations are as a drop in a bucket,**
> **And are counted as the small dust on the scales;**
> **Look, He lifts up the isles as a very little thing.**
> **And Lebanon is not sufficient to burn,**
> **Nor its beasts sufficient for a burnt offering.**
> **All nations before Him are as nothing,**
> **And they are counted by Him less than nothing**
> **and worthless.**" (Isaiah 40:15-17)

There is something much greater than all the nations of mankind put together. And we are explicitly told that God has an "**eternal purpose.**" And that "**eternal purpose**" is "**that in the dispensation of the fullness of the times He might gather to-**

gether in one all things in Christ, both which are in heaven and which are on earth--in Him." (Ephesians 1:10)

These "**all things**" are not just "**all things**" "**on earth,**" but "**all things**" "**both which are in heaven and which are on earth.**" and so, in speaking "**of the mystery, which from the beginning of the ages has been hidden in God who created all things through Jesus Christ;**" (Ephesians 3:9) our God said, "**to the intent that now the manifold wisdom of God might be made known by the church to the principalities and powers in the heavenly *places*, according to the eternal purpose which He accomplished in Christ Jesus our Lord.**" (Ephesians 3:10-11)

This scripture is not speaking of causing "**the church**" to know "**the manifold wisdom of God,**" but of using "**the church**" to make something known "**to the principalities and powers in the heavenly *places*.**" And what is God making known to them? "**The manifold wisdom of God.**" And this is "**according to the eternal purpose which He accomplished in Christ Jesus our Lord.**" And that "**eternal purpose**" is "**that... He might gather together in one all things in Christ, both which are in heaven and which are on earth--in Him.**"

So God's grand "**eternal purpose**" is to "**gather together in one all things in Christ.**" and in the mean time, He is using what He is doing here on earth to demonstrate "**the manifold wisdom of God**" "**to the principalities and powers in the heavenly *places*.**"

So we see that God indeed has a purpose in making this demonstration, that mankind will fail under every conceivable circumstance. And why it is "**not by works of righteousness which we have done, but according to His mercy He saved us.**" (Titus 3:5) And why "**God so loved the world that He gave His only begotten Son, that whoever believes in Him should not perish but have everlasting life.**" (John 3:16)

But what are the results of this understanding of the dispensations laid out in the Bible? One of these is an understanding that there is another age coming in this earth, one that will be different from the present one. And simply believing the prophecies about this future age makes us understand that the many promises that God made to the ancient nation of Israel will most assuredly be kept.

But these promises that our God made to the ancient nation of Israel are entirely different from the promises He made to us. And this forces us to understand that **"the church"** and **"Israel"** are two entirely different entities. Many consider this understanding the essence of Dispensationalism. But that is an error, This difference is not the foundation of Dispensationalism, but a necessary result of understanding the dispensations of God.

Again, many say that a central part of dispensation is to maintain a "Literal-Grammatical-Historical hermeneutic." But that is nothing but using complicated words to say, simply believing the prophecies in the Bible. Simply believing that "God says what He means and means what He says." These beliefs will unlock the mysteries of the Bible. And these beliefs force the reverent and serious student of scripture into the understanding called Dispensationalism.

Understanding the Prophecy of the Seventy Weeks

Seventy weeks were revealed to Daniel in the following words:

> "**Seventy weeks are determined**
> **For your people and for your holy city,**
> **To finish the transgression,**
> **To make an end of sins,**
> **To make reconciliation for iniquity,**
> **To bring in everlasting righteousness,**
> **To seal up vision and prophecy,**
> **And to anoint the Most Holy."** (Daniel 9:24)

First, we need to understand that, although most of our English translations say seventy **"weeks,"** the Hebrew word translated **"weeks"** is שבוע, *shabuwa'* in our alphabet, in the plural, שבום, *shabwim* in our alphabet (word number 7620 in Strong's Hebrew Dictionary.) This word simply means "sevens," and is used in the Old Testament for both a period of seven days and a period of seven years.

This can be seen in the sabbath year of rest the LORD decreed for the land. He told Moses **"When you come into the land which I give you, then the land shall keep a sabbath to the LORD. Six years you shall sow your field, and six years you shall prune your vineyard, and gather its fruit; but in the seventh year there shall be a sabbath of solemn rest for the land, a sabbath to the LORD. You shall neither sow your field nor prune your vineyard."** (Leviticus 25:2-4) Compare this with the LORD'S command to **"Remember the Sabbath day, to keep it holy. Six days you shall labor and do all your work, but the seventh day *is* the Sabbath of the LORD your God. *In it* you shall do no work: you, nor your son, nor your daughter, nor your male servant, nor your female servant, nor your cattle, nor your stranger who *is* within your gates. For *in* six days the LORD made the heavens and the earth, the sea, and all that *is* in them, and rested the seventh day. Therefore the LORD blessed the Sabbath day and hallowed it."** (Exodus 20:8-11) The same word, **"sabbath,"** was used to describe both the seventh day and the seventh year.

This shows that in the Old Testament the concept of a **"week"** applied equally to periods of seven days and seven years. Only the context can show whether days or years was meant. And in this case, the context clearly shows that the meaning could not even possibly be days. So it is not simply interpretation to take seventy weeks as meaning 490 years. Nor is this an application of the so-called "day-year principle." This is a fully legitimate meaning of the Hebrew words used in this passage.

Next, we need to notice who these seventy weeks were **"determined"** for.

**"Seventy weeks are determined
For your people and for your holy city."** (Daniel 9:24a)

This was spoken to Daniel. And Daniel's people were unquestionably the Jews, and his holy city was unquestionably Jerusalem. Thus, these **"Seventy weeks are determined"** for the Jews and for Jerusalem. This means that any attempt to apply them to any other group or any other place is wresting scripture.

Next, we need to notice the purpose of these **"seventy weeks."** They **"are determined"**

"To finish the transgression,

To make an end of sins,
To make reconciliation for iniquity,
To bring in everlasting righteousness,
To seal up vision and prophecy,
And to anoint the Most Holy." (Daniel 9:24b)

First, there can be no doubt that **"the transgression"** of the Jews and of Jerusalem is not, even to this day, finished. So this goal of the **"seventy weeks"** has unquestionably not yet been accomplished.

The goal **"To make reconciliation for iniquity"** was unquestionably accomplished at Calvary. But most of the Jews and of Jerusalem have not yet repented, so, even to this time, **"everlasting righteous"** has not yet been brought in for the Jews and for Jerusalem.

But the scriptures plainly tell us that both of these will eventually be accomplished for the Jews and for Jerusalem. For the Lord plainly promised:

> **"In that day the Branch of the LORD shall be beautiful and glorious; And the fruit of the earth *shall be* excellent and appealing For those of Israel who have escaped. And it shall come to pass that *he who is* left in Zion and remains in Jerusalem will be called holy--everyone who is recorded among the living in Jerusalem. When the Lord has washed away the filth of the daughters of Zion, and purged the blood of Jerusalem from her midst, by the spirit of judgment and by the spirit of burning."** (Isaiah 4:2-4)

And again, He also promised:

> **"But this *is* the covenant that I will make with the house of Israel after those days, says the LORD: I will put My law in their minds, and write it on their**

> hearts; and I will be their God, and they shall be My people. No more shall every man teach his neighbor, and every man his brother, saying, 'Know the LORD,' for they all shall know Me, from the least of them to the greatest of them, says the LORD. For I will forgive their iniquity, and their sin I will remember no more." (Jeremiah 31:33-34)

So we see that the scriptures indeed tell us, and in explicit words, that in a future day the goals of making **"an end of sins"** and bringing in **"everlasting righteousness,"** will indeed be accomplished for the Jews and for Jerusalem.

Again, the goal **"To seal up vision and prophecy"** cannot have been accomplished for the Jews and for Jerusalem until everything prophesied for them has been accomplished.

But now we come to the goal **"To anoint the Most Holy."**

This term **"Most Holy"** is the Hebrew words קֹדֶשׁ קָדָשִׁים, *qodesh qodesh*, that is, the Hebrew word *qodesh*, which means holy, doubled. (This is word number 6944 in Strong's Hebrew dictionary.) This is not, as many have supposed, a reference to the Lord Jesus, but to the place behind the veil. The first time these words were used was in Exodus 26:33-34, where the Lord said concerning the tabernacle, **"you shall hang the veil from the clasps. Then you shall bring the ark of the Testimony in there, behind the veil. The veil shall be a divider for you between the holy *place* and the Most Holy. You shall put the mercy seat upon the ark of the Testimony in the Most Holy."** And the second time they were used was concerning the temple built by Solomon, as we read in 1 Kings 6:16, **"Then he built the twenty-cubit room at the rear of the temple, from floor to ceiling, with cedar boards; he built *it* inside as the inner sanctuary, as the Most Holy *Place*."** (Notice that in both of these passages, the word **"*place*"** is in italics, indicating that it was not in the Hebrew text.) This word is again used of that room of Solomon's temple in 1 Kings 7:50 and 8:6, in 2 Chronicles 4:22, and 5:7 and 11, and of the same room in the millennial temple as it is described in Ezekiel 41:4, 44:13, and 45:3.

This is distinguished from generic places that were holy, by calling those **"a holy place,"** using the Hebrew words קדוש במקום, *maqom quadosh* in our alphabet, (words number 6918 and 4725 in Strong's Hebrew dictionary.) This expression can be found in Leviticus 7:6 and 10:17.

And although the language is Greek instead of Hebrew, the term **"Most Holy"** is also used in the New Testament. It refers to the place behind the veil in Old Testament worship in Hebrews 9:25. And in verse 12 of the same chapter it refers to a similar place in heaven. And in Jude 20 it is used in regard to our faith.

The term **"most holy"** is also used of the **"altar of the burnt offering"** in Exodus 29:37 and 40:10, and of the offerings in Exodus 30:10, and 36, in Leviticus 2:3 and 10, 6:17, 25 and 29, 7:1, 6, 12 and 17, 14:13, 21:22, 24:9 and 27:28, in Numbers 18:9 and 10, in Ezra 2:63, in Nehemiah 7:65, and in Ezekiel 42:13.

So the **"Most Holy"** that was to be anointed in Daniel 9:24 cannot refer to the Lord Jesus because in the entire rest of the Bible, this term is never, even once, used of God himself. It has to refer to the **"Most Holy"** place of the future temple after it has been cleansed as described in Daniel 8:13-14, where we read, **"Then I heard a holy one speaking; and *another* holy one said to that certain *one* who was speaking, 'How long *will* the vision be, *concerning* the daily *sacrifices* and the transgression of desolation, the giving of both the sanctuary and the host to be trampled under foot?' And he said to me, 'For two thousand three hundred days; then the sanctuary shall be cleansed.' "**

But after this introductory part of the vision, in which Daniel was told both who these **"seventy weeks"** were **"determined"** for, and what was to be accomplished in them, Daniel was further told:

> "Know therefore and understand,
> *That* from the going forth of the command
> To restore and build Jerusalem
> Until Messiah the Prince,
> *There shall be* seven weeks and sixty-two weeks;
> The street shall be built again, and the wall,
> Even in troublesome times."
> (Daniel 9:25)

Here we have sixty-nine weeks, or 483 years, **"from the going forth of the command To restore and to build Jerusalem Until Messiah the Prince."** Some claim that there is historical evidence that our Lord's triumphal entry into Jerusalem occurred *exactly* 483 Hebrew years, *to the day*, after this order went forth. I cannot personally testify as to the accuracy of this claim. But history indeed confirms that it occurred at approximately that time.

But now the Divinely inspired account contains a break. We read:

> "And after the sixty-two weeks
> Messiah shall be cut off, but not for Himself;
> And the people of the prince who is to come
> Shall destroy the city and the sanctuary.
> The end of it *shall be* with a flood,
> And till the end of the war desolations are determined." (Daniel 9:26)

Two things were to happen after the sixty-two week second part of these pre-determined seventy weeks. **"Messiah"** would **"be cut off,"** and **"the people of the prince who is to come"** would **"destroy the city and the sanctuary."** And we know that both of these indeed happened exactly as prophesied. **"Messiah"** was indeed **"cut off,"** and **"the city and the sanctuary"** were indeed destroyed. The first of these plainly refers to our Lord's death at Calvary. The second was done by the ancient Romans under the leadership of Titus. Since Titus was a Roman, and Daniel was told this would be done by **"the people of the prince who is to come,"** this **"prince who is to come"** has to be, like Titus, a Roman. He cannot come from any other nation, for then **"the prince who is to come"** would not be **"the prince"** of **"the people"** who destroyed **"the city and the sanctuary."**

But we also know from history that these two events did not happen within a seven year period. Most historians feel that the errors in our calender make the actual date of Jesus' birth 4 BC. Since Jesus lived thirty-three years, that puts his death in 29 A.D. But according to history, the city was not destroyed until 70 A.D., forty-one years after that. So even if there are small errors in the accepted dates of history, we know that **"the city and the sanctuary"** were not destroyed in the same **"week"** (a seven year period) that our Lord was crucified. But we need to notice that both of these events are mentioned before the last week is even mentioned. So here we see that there is an undeniable break in the scriptural account of the **"seventy weeks."**

And the last **"week"** is treated differently. The prophecy does not even say that it is the seventieth **"week."** The only reason we know that it is the seventieth **"week"** is because all the rest of the **"weeks"** had already been used up. So this **"week"** has to be the seventieth one. We read:

> **"Then he shall confirm a covenant with many**
> **for one week;**
> **But in the middle of the week**
> **He shall bring an end to sacrifice and offering.**
> **And on the wing of abominations shall be**
> **one who makes desolate,**
> **Even until the consummation, which is determined,**

Is poured out on the desolate." (Daniel 9:27)

But in addition to this we need to notice a detail in each of these prophetic statements that almost everyone seems to have missed. For it has become almost standard for teachers of Bible prophecy to say that "the Antichrist," after making a seven year covenant with "the Jews," will break that covenant in the middle of the week and attack them in their land. But that is not what this prophecy says. For in this verse there is a distinct change in actors.

First, it says:

"Then he shall confirm a covenant with many for one week;

But in the middle of the week

He shall bring an end to sacrifice and offering."

Here the actor is distinctly called **"he"** two different times.

But then, suddenly, the actor changes. For the next stanza reads:

"And on the wing of abominations shall be one who makes desolate."

The actor, which had been **"he,"** suddenly changes to **"one."** This clearly identifies the **"one who makes desolate"** as someone different from the **"he"** who **"shall confirm a covenant with many for one week."** The identity of this **"one who makes desolate"** is not revealed in this prophecy. But he is identified in Isaiah 7, 10, 14, 30, and 31, in Micah 5, and in Nahum, as someone that the scriptures call **"the Assyrian."** The significance of these many prophecies has been missed because most scholars simply assume that they are only speaking of the ancient attack on Hezekiah by the Assyrian king Sennacherib. But these prophecies are filled with details that have most certainly never been fulfilled.

Now some imagine that the **"he"** in Daniel 9:27 is speaking of the Lord himself. They think that the almost unanimous opinion of the translators about this sentence is incorrect, and imagine that the words **"for one week"** should be translated "in one week." And imagine that the words **"in the middle of the week He shall bring an end to sacrifice and offering"** refer to our Lord. But that notion violates a rule of grammar that is the same in all languages. That rule is that whenever the word **"he"** is suddenly introduced, it refers to whoever is under discussion, which, unless the context indicates otherwise, is the last man mentioned. And in this case, the last man that had been mentioned was **"the prince that shall come,"** whose **"people"** were going to **"destroy the city and the sanctuary."** The interpretation that this refers to our Lord also makes the last part of this prophecy jump back in time, instead of being sequential, as is the rest of this entire prophecy.

And this wrested interpretation ignores what these **"seventy weeks are determined for."** We have already noticed that they were determined for Daniel's **"people"** (the Jews) and for Daniel's **"holy city."** (Jerusalem). But this wresting of the prophecy makes them for all mankind, not just for the Jews and for Jerusalem.

But the problem with this wresting of the word of God is not just a matter of misinterpreting the actual words of this prophecy. It does violence to the entirety of end time prophecy. For this is far from the only prophecy that speaks of an end time **"week."**

An end time covenant that will not be fulfilled is spoken of in another prophecy. Isaiah 28:14-18 says:

> **"Therefore hear the word of the LORD, you scornful men,**
> **Who rule this people who *are* in Jerusalem,**
> **Because you have said,**
> **'We have made a covenant with death,**
> **And with Sheol we are in agreement.**
> **When the overflowing scourge passes through,**
> **It will not come to us,**

> For we have made lies our refuge,
> And under falsehood we have hidden ourselves.'
> Therefore thus says the Lord GOD:
> 'Behold, I lay in Zion a stone for a foundation,
> A tried stone, a precious cornerstone,
> a sure foundation;
> Whoever believes will not act hastily.
> Also I will make justice the measuring line,
> And righteousness the plummet;
> The hail will sweep away the refuge of lies,
> And the waters will overflow the hiding place.
> Your covenant with death will be annulled,
> And your agreement with Sheol will not stand;
> When the overflowing scourge passes through,
> Then you will be trampled down by it.' "

So we see that a different prophecy clearly foretells such an end time ovenant that God will not allow to be fulfilled.

And in addition to this, there are no less than six other prophecies that mention an end time fulfillment of this last week. For the last verse of Daniel 9 clearly says that there would be a great event **"in the middle of the week."** This event divides the **"week"** into two half weeks. And one or the other of these two half weeks are seen in six other end time prophecies. They are spoken of as **"a time, times, and half a time,"** (three and a half years) as **"forty-two months,"** (again, three and a half years) and as **"one thousand two hundred and sixty days,"** (exactly three and a half Hebrew years, which were composed of twelve months of thirty days each.) So the two halves of this seventieth **"week"** are described in six other prophecies which have unquestionably never been fulfilled.

THOUGHTS ABOUT PROPHETIC SUBJECTS

The first half of this final **"week"** is first seen in Daniel 7, where in verse 25 **"the saints shall be given into"** the hand of the **"little" "horn"** of verse 8, which became **"greater than his fellows"** in verse 20, **"for a time and times and half a time."** It is also seen in the **"forty-two months"** for which **"the beast" "was given authority to continue"** in Revelation 13:5. It is again seen in Revelation 11:3, where God's **"two witnesses" "will prophesy one thousand two hundred and sixty days, clothed in sackcloth."**

The second half of this week is seen in Daniel 12, where **"the fulfillment of"** the **"wonders"** (verse 5) **"*shall be* for a time, times, and half *a time*; and when the power of the holy people has been completely shattered, all these *things* shall be finished."** (verse 7) We see it again in Revelation 12:7, where **"the woman was given two wings of a great eagle, that she might fly into the wilderness to her place, where she is nourished for a time and times and half a time, from the presence of the serpent."** And finally, it is seen in the **"forty two months"** during which **"the Gentiles" "will tread the holy city underfoot"** in Revelation 11:2.

So we see that the two halves of this final week are seen in six other prophecies about the end times. And this makes a grand total of eight prophecies that mention a future fulfillment of the last **"week"** of Daniel's prophecy of the **"seventy weeks."**

In conclusion, an understanding of three facts are fundamental to an understanding of end time prophecy. These three facts are:

That the **"seventy weeks are determined for"** the Jews and Jerusalem, not for the rest of the world.

That their seventieth week remains to be fulfilled in the end times.

And that it is divided into two halves by a signal event at its middle.

An additional note about the history of Christian understanding of this prophecy:

Some imagine that this understanding of a gap between the sixty-ninth week and the seventieth week is a relatively new concept, first developed by the dispensational teachers of the nineteenth century. But this is an error. The oldest Christian commentary on Bible prophecy of any significant length that has survived to the present day is the last twelve chapters of the famous work by Irenaeus titled "Against Heresies," which is believed to have been written between the years 186 and 188 A.D. In this work Irenaeus spoke of the reign of an evil ruler whom he taught would come in the end times, calling him "Antichrist," and saying:

"And then he points out the time that his tyranny shall last, during which the saints shall be put to flight, they who offer a pure sacrifice unto God: 'And in the midst of the week,' he says, 'the sacrifice and the libation shall be taken away, and the abomination of desolation [shall be brought] into the temple: even unto the consummation of the time shall the desolation be complete.' Now three years and six months constitute the half-week." (Against Heresies, by Irenaeus, book V, chapter XXV, section 4)

So there can be no rational debate that Irenaeus taught that the last of the seventy weeks revealed to Daniel would be fulfilled in his own future, not in his past.

Something on the order of twenty or so years after Irenaeus penned these words, a teacher named Hippolytus wrote the very oldest Christian commentary on scripture that has survived to the present day. His work was a commentary on Daniel which is thought to have been written sometime between the years 202 and 211. Hippolytus very clearly taught a gap in the prophecy of the seventy weeks, saying:

"For after sixty-two weeks was fulfilled and after Christ has come and the Gospel has been preached in every place, times having been spun out, the end remains one week *away*, in which

Elijah and Enoch shall be present and in its half the abomination of desolation, the Antichrist, shall appear who threatens desolation of the world. After he comes, sacrifice and drink offering, which now in every way is offered by the nations to God, shall be taken away." (Commentary on Daniel, by Hippolytus, book 4, 35.3, as rendered in the forthcoming translation by T. C. Schmidt.)

Later in this same work, Hippolytus said:

"Just as also he spoke to Daniel, "And he shall establish a covenant with many for one week and it will be *that* in the half of the week he shall take away my sacrifice and drink offering," so that the one week may be shown as divided into two, after the two witnesses will have preached for three and a half years, the Antichrist will wage war against the saints the remainder of the week and will desolate all the world so that what was spoken may be fulfilled, "And they will give the abomination of desolation one thousand two hundred ninety days. Blessed is he who endures to Christ and reaches the one thousand three hundred thirty-five days!" (Commentary on Daniel, by Hippolytus, book 4, 50.2, as above.)

Again, Clement of Alexandria whose work is believed to have "been given to the world in 194 A.D.," wrote, "That the temple accordingly was built in seven weeks, is evident; for it is written in Esdras. And thus Christ became King of the Jews, reigning in Jerusalem in the fulfilment of the seven weeks. And in the sixty and two weeks the whole of Judæa was quiet, and without wars. And Christ our Lord, 'the Holy of Holies,' having come and fulfilled the vision and the prophecy, was anointed in His flesh by the Holy Spirit of His Father. In those 'sixty and two weeks,' as the prophet said, and 'in the one week,' was He Lord. The half of the week Nero held sway, and in the holy city Jerusalem placed the abomination; and in the half of the week he was taken away, and Otho, and Galba, and Vitellius. And Vespasian rose to the supreme power, and destroyed Jerusalem, and desolated the holy place. And that such are the facts of the case, is clear to him that is able to understand, as the prophet said." ("The Stromata," by Clement of Alexandria, book 1, chapter 21.)

Here we see that Clement, though he did not see the gap in the seventy weeks extending into his own future, as did both Irenaeus, who wrote before him, and Hippolytus, who wrote after him, he also saw a short gap in the same prophecy, with the seventieth week in the time of Nero and Vespasian, nearly forty years after the end of the sixty-ninth week.

Since these are the only three surviving documents from that period that spoke of the subject, we see that this gap in the seventy weeks revealed to Daniel was not only indicated in the very text of the scriptures themselves, it was also taught by every Christian writer who commented on this prophecy during the first two centuries of the church. The early dating of these writers is significant because these were the only such writers who lived early enough to have personally known the dates involved. And *all* of them who wrote this early realized that the seventieth week was not fulfilled immediately after the sixty-ninth week.

Who Will Be In the Land During the Seventieth Week

The word of God is very precise. It means what it says. It means exactly what it says. And it does not mean what it does not say. This is particularly true of end time prophecy. So in studying Bible prophecy, it is important to pay careful attention to the fine details. For it is in them that we learn when and where many prophecies will be fulfilled. And Bible prophecy contains no synonyms. When different words are used in similar passages, those words were changed for a reason.

One detail we need to notice is a remarkable absence of the name "**Israel**" from prophecies about the people suffering during the seventieth "**week**" of the prophecy of the "**seventy weeks**" which was revealed through Daniel. The name "**Israel**" is used of the "**land**" where this suffering will take place, but not of the "**people**" who will be suffering. We often say that "**Israel**" does not mean "**the church**," and "**the church**" does not mean "Israel." But in the same way "**Israel**" does not mean "**Judah**," and "**Judah**" does not mean "**Israel**."

We remember that in the days of king "**Rehoboam**," son of "**Solomon**," the ten northern tribes revolted against the "**house of David**," choosing instead "**Jeroboam, the son of Nebat**" as their king. In that revolt, "**Israel**" was divided into two kingdoms. After that time, the inspired history usually called the northern kingdom "**Israel**" and the southern kingdom "**Judah**." But the northern kingdom was sometimes called "**Ephraim**" when the point was to stress its distinction from the southern kingdom. The name "**Israel**" continued to be used when referring to all twelve tribes.

The ten northern tribes were eventually carried away into **"Assyria,"** and have not, even yet, been restored to the land. A few generations later the two southern tribes were carried away into **"Babylon"** for **"seventy years."** After they were carried away, members of these two tribes were called **"Jews,"** both in the Old Testament and the New Testament. So in the Bible, as in modern times, the term **"Jew"** does not mean an **"Israelite,"** even though all **"Jews"** are **"Israelites."** The name **"Jew"** means a descendant of the southern kingdom of **"Judah,"** which was composed of tribes of **"Judah"** and **"Benjamin,"** and half of the priestly tribe of **"Levi."**

These distinctions were rigorously applied in end time prophecy. Prophecies about **"Israel"** are either about only the ten northern tribes or about the entire nation. Only the context can show which is meant. But prophecies about **"Judah"** concern only the two southern tribes.

We will first notice for whom the **"Seventy weeks are determined:"**

> **"Seventy weeks are determined**
> **For your people and for your holy city,**
> **To finish the transgression,**
> **To make an end of sins,**
> **To make reconciliation for iniquity,**
> **To bring in everlasting righteousness,**
> **To seal up vision and prophecy,**
> **And to anoint the Most Holy."** (Daniel 9:24)

Daniel's **"holy city"** is unquestionably **"Jerusalem,"** but who are Daniel's people? This is not left to our imagination. We are told in Daniel 1:9 that **"Daniel"** was **"of the sons of Judah,"** in Daniel 2:5 that he was **"of the captives of Judah,"** and twice (Daniel 5:3 and 6:3) that he was **"one of the captives from Judah."** Now since **"Daniel"** was **"of Judah,"** we know that he was also an **"Israelite."** But he was never called this in the inspired record. We find the reason for this in many other prophecies that speak of the troubles coming upon the God's earthly people. As we have already noticed, in these prophecies they are always called **"Judah,"** never **"Israel."**

We see this in Joel:

> **"Egypt shall be a desolation,**
> **And Edom a desolate wilderness,**
> **Because of violence against the people of Judah,**
> **For they have shed innocent blood in their land.**
> **But Judah shall abide forever,**
> **And Jerusalem from generation to generation.**
> **For I will acquit them of the guilt of bloodshed,**
> **whom I had not acquitted;**
> **For the Lord dwells in Zion."**
>
> (Joel 3:19-21)

We see this again in Obadiah where the Lord says concerning Edom: (see Obadiah 1:1)

> **"For violence against your brother Jacob,**
> **Shame shall cover you,**
> **And you shall be cut off forever.**
> **In the day that you stood on the other side?**
> **In the day that strangers carried captive his forces,**
> **When foreigners entered his gates**
> **And cast lots for Jerusalem?**
> **Even you were as one of them.**
> **"But you should not have gazed on the day of your brother**
> **In the day of his captivity;**

> Nor should you have rejoiced over the children of Judah
> In the day of their destruction;
> Nor should you have spoken proudly In the day of distress.
> You should not have entered the gate of My people In the day of their calamity.
> Indeed, you should not have gazed on their affliction
> In the day of their calamity,
> Nor laid hands on their substance
> In the day of their calamity.
> You should not have stood at the crossroads
> To cut off those among them who escaped;
> Nor should you have delivered up those among them who remained In the day of distress.
> "For the day of the Lord upon all the nations is near;
> As you have done, it shall be done to you;
> Your reprisal shall return upon your own head."
> (Obadiah 1:10-15)

We see it again in Zechariah, where the Lord addresses Israel generally, but specifically mentions a siege **"against Judah and Jerusalem"** and **"the house of Judah."**

> "The burden of the word of the Lord against Israel. Thus says the Lord, who stretches out the heavens, lays the foundation of the earth, and forms the spirit of man within him: 'Behold, I will make Jerusalem a cup of drunkenness to all the surrounding peoples, when they lay siege against Judah and Jerusalem. And it shall happen in that day that I will make Jerusalem a very heavy stone for all peoples; all who would heave it away will surely be cut in pieces, though all nations

of the earth are gathered against it. In that day,' says the Lord, 'I will strike every horse with confusion, and its rider with madness; I will open My eyes on the house of Judah, and will strike every horse of the peoples with blindness. And the governors of Judah shall say in their heart, "The inhabitants of Jerusalem are my strength in the Lord of hosts, their God." In that day I will make the governors of Judah like a firepan in the woodpile, and like a fiery torch in the sheaves; they shall devour all the surrounding peoples on the right hand and on the left, but Jerusalem shall be inhabited again in her own place' Jerusalem.

"The Lord will save the tents of Judah first, so that the glory of the house of David and the glory of the inhabitants of Jerusalem shall not become greater than that of Judah. In that day the Lord will defend the inhabitants of Jerusalem; the one who is feeble among them in that day shall be like David, and the house of David shall be like God, like the Angel of the Lord before them. It shall be in that day that I will seek to destroy all the nations that come against Jerusalem." (Zechariah 12:1-9)

And we see this again in Ezekiel 25, where we repeatedly find **"the land of Israel"** mentioned, but those who experience the trouble are **"the house of Judah."**

"The word of the Lord came to me, saying, 'Son of man, set your face against the Ammonites, and prophesy against them. Say to the Ammonites, "Hear the word of the Lord GOD! Thus says the Lord GOD: Because you said, "Aha!" against My sanctuary when it was profaned, and against the land of Israel when it was desolate, and against the house of Judah when they went into captivity, indeed, therefore, I will deliver you as a possession to the men of the East, and they shall set their encampments among you and make their dwellings among you; they shall eat your fruit, and they shall drink your milk. And I will make Rabbah a stable for camels and Ammon a resting place for flocks. Then you shall know that I am the Lord.'

"For thus says the Lord GOD: 'Because you clapped your hands, stamped your feet, and rejoiced in heart with all your disdain for the land of Israel, indeed, therefore, I will stretch out My hand against you, and give you as plunder to the nations; I will cut you off from the peoples, and I will cause you to perish from the countries; I will destroy you, and you shall know that I am the Lord.'

"Thus says the Lord GOD: 'Because Moab and Seir say, "Look! The house of Judah is like all the nations," therefore, behold, I will clear the territory of Moab of cities, of the cities on its frontier, the glory of the country, Beth Jeshimoth, Baal Meon, and Kirjathaim. To the men of the East I will give it as a possession, together with the Ammonites, that the Ammonites may not be remembered among the nations. And I will execute judgments upon Moab, and they shall know that I am the Lord.'

"Thus says the Lord GOD: 'Because of what Edom did against the house of Judah by taking vengeance, and has greatly offended by avenging itself on them,' therefore thus says the Lord GOD: 'I will also stretch out My hand against Edom, cut off man and beast from it, and make it desolate from Teman; Dedan shall fall by the sword. I will lay My vengeance on Edom by the hand of My people Israel, that they may do in Edom according to My anger and according to My fury; and they shall know My vengeance,' says the Lord GOD.

"Thus says the Lord GOD: 'Because the Philistines dealt vengefully and took vengeance with a spiteful heart,

> to destroy because of the old hatred,' therefore thus says the Lord GOD: 'I will stretch out My hand against the Philistines, and I will cut off the Cherethites and destroy the remnant of the seacoast. I will execute great vengeance on them with furious rebukes; and they shall know that I am the Lord, when I lay My vengeance upon them.'" (Ezekiel 25:1-17)

Even in Matthew and Mark, the scene of the coming trouble is called **"Judea,"** not **"Israel."**

Matthew 24:15-16 " **'Therefore when you see the** *"abomination of desolation,:* **spoken of by Daniel the prophet, standing in the holy place' (whoever reads, let him understand), 'then let those who are in Judea flee to the mountains.'"**

Mark 13:14 " **'So when you see the** *"abomination of desolation,"* **spoken of by Daniel the prophet, standing where it ought not' (let the reader understand), 'then let those who are in Judea flee to the mountains.'"**

Another detail we should notice is that end time prophecies about the Lord's people being brought back to the land always use the name **"Israel,"** and specifically say that this will involve **"all"** of **"Israel."** Even when **"Judah"** is mentioned in these prophecies, it is **"Judah and Israel."** There are too many of these to examine them all, but we will notice a typical one.

> "Therefore prophesy concerning the land of Israel, and say to the mountains, the hills, the rivers, and the valleys, 'Thus says the Lord GOD: "Behold, I have spoken in My jealousy and My fury, because you have borne the shame of the nations.' Therefore thus says the Lord GOD: 'I have raised My hand in an oath that surely the nations that are around you shall bear their own shame. But you, O mountains of Israel, you shall shoot forth your branches and yield your fruit to My people Israel, for they are about to come. For indeed I am for

you, and I will turn to you, and you shall be tilled and sown. I will multiply men upon you, all the house of Israel, all of it; and the cities shall be inhabited and the ruins rebuilt. I will multiply upon you man and beast; and they shall increase and bear young; I will make you inhabited as in former times, and do better for you than at your beginnings. Then you shall know that I am the Lord. Yes, I will cause men to walk on you, My people Israel; they shall take possession of you, and you shall be their inheritance; no more shall you bereave them of children.'" (Ezekiel 36:6-12)

This prophecy is addressed to a piece of real estate **"to the mountains, the hills, the rivers, and the valleys"** of "Israel." And tells them that **"I will multiply men upon you, all the house of Israel, all of it."** The repeating of the word **"all"** (כל, *kol* in our alphabet) in the Hebrew text stresses that this means *absolutely* **"all the house of Israel."**

Now why do we find only the name **"Judah"** in the details about the seventieth **"week,"** and only the name **"Israel,"** or both of the names, **"Judah and Israel"** in details about the restoration? We find the reason in the last chapter of Isaiah.

> **"The hand of the Lord shall be known to His servants,**
> **And His indignation to His enemies.**
> **For behold, the Lord will come with fire**
> **And with His chariots, like a whirlwind,**
> **To render His anger with fury,**
> **And His rebuke with flames of fire.**
> **For by fire and by His sword**
> **The Lord will judge all flesh;**
> **And the slain of the Lord shall be many**
> **'Those who sanctify themselves and purify themselves,**

> **To go to the gardens**
> **After an idol in the midst,**
> **Eating swine's flesh and the abomination and the mouse,**
> **Shall be consumed together,' says the Lord.**
>
> 'For I know their works and their thoughts. It shall be that I will gather all nations and tongues; and they shall come and see My glory. I will set a sign among them; and those among them who escape I will send to the nations: to Tarshish and Pul and Lud, who draw the bow, and Tubal and Javan, to the coastlands afar off who have not heard My fame nor seen My glory. And they shall declare My glory among the Gentiles. Then they shall bring all your brethren for an offering to the Lord out of all nations, on horses and in chariots and in litters, on mules and on camels, to My holy mountain Jerusalem,' says the Lord, 'as the children of Israel bring an offering in a clean vessel into the house of the Lord. And I will also take some of them for priests and Levites,' says the Lord." (Isaiah 66:14-21)

Here we see a plain reference to Armageddon. And then we read, **"and those among them who escape I will send to the nations... And they shall declare My glory among the Gentiles."** And **"Then they shall bring all your brethren for an offering to the Lord out of all nations, on horses and in chariots and in litters, on mules and on camels, to My holy mountain Jerusalem."**

Here we see the time specifically stated. The prophesied restoration will take *place after* **"Messiah"** comes, not *before*. The time of this return is again stated in Micah 5, where we read:

> **"Therefore He shall give them up,**
> **Until the time *that* she who is in labor has given birth;**

> **Then the remnant of His brethren**
> **Shall return to the children of Israel."** (Micah 5:3)

For more detail on this, see also Matthew 24:29-31, Jeremiah 16:14-18, and Ezekiel 34:11-16.

Now what is the point of all this? It is a simple concept that will open up an understanding of many prophecies. The return of **"the Jews"** to their **"land"** is not directly prophesied anywhere in scripture. It is prophesied indirectly, because we are plainly told that they will be in the **"land"** during Daniel's seventieth **"week."** But a return of **"Judah"** to the **"land,"** as such, is not mentioned in any end time prophecy. This is like the rebuilding of the **"temple"** and the resumption of animal **"sacrifices"** during the seventieth **"week."** Neither is directly prophesied, but both must happen. For both a **"temple"** and **"sacrifices"** are mentioned in prophecies concerning the seventieth **"week."**

When we understand this, we understand *when* many prophecies will be fulfilled. For prophecies that speak only of **"Judah"** are about the seventieth **"week,"** and those that speak of **"Israel,"** or about either **"Israel"** and **"Judah"** or **"Ephraim"** and **"Judah,"** are about the time after **"Messiah"** returns at the end of that seventieth **"week."**

THOUGHTS ABOUT PROPHETIC SUBJECTS

The Neglected Character in End Time Prophecy

Part one: **"The Assyrian"**

One of the best known prophecies in all of scripture is Micah 5:2.; **"But you, Bethlehem Ephrathah, *Though* you are little among the thousands of Judah, *Yet* out of you shall come forth to Me the One to be Ruler in Israel, Whose goings forth *are* from of old, From everlasting."** This prophecy is so well known because it is part of the so-called Christmas story. When the **"wise men from the East came to Jerusalem, saying, 'Where is He who has been born King of the Jews? For we have seen His star in the East and have come to worship Him.'"** Then **"Herod the king"** **"gathered all the chief priests and scribes of the people"** and **"inquired of them where the Christ was to be born."** In answer they quoted Micah 5:2. (Matthew 2:1-6)

But it seems amazing that so few prophetic scholars are aware of the rest of this prophecy. In the context of this verse we read:

> **"Now gather yourself in troops, O daughter of troops; He has laid siege against us; They will strike the judge of Israel with a rod on the cheek. 'But you, Bethlehem Ephrathah, *Though* you are little among the thousands of Judah, *Yet* out of you shall come forth to Me The One to be Ruler in Israel, Whose goings forth *are* from of old, From everlasting.' Therefore He shall give them up, Until the time *that* she who is in labor has given birth; Then the remnant of His brethren Shall return to the children of Israel.** (Micah 5:1-3)

Before we read of where Christ was to be born, we read that **"they will strike the judge of Israel with a rod on the cheek"** (verse 1) Then, in verse 3, we read that **"Therefore He shall give them up."** So this Old Testament prophecy clearly foretold the rejection of Christ by Judah, and of its consequence; the rejection of Judah by their God. But it also defined how long this rejection of Judah will last. It will last, **"Until the time *that* she who is in labor has given birth."** (verse 3)

This is an obvious reference to the last chapter of Isaiah, where we read,

> **"Before she was in labor, she gave birth; Before her pain came, She delivered a male child. Who has heard such a thing? Who has seen such things? Shall the earth be made to give birth in one day? *Or* shall a nation be born at once? For as soon as Zion was in labor, She gave birth to her children."** (Isaiah 66:7-8)

After "she who is in labor has given birth," **"Then the remnant of His brethren Shall return to the children of Israel."** (Micah 5:3) From this we see that the subject matter of this prophecy extends all the way from the birth and rejection of Christ to the future time of restoration for Israel. Indeed, the next verse of Micah 5 speaks of the majesty and greatness of the time when Judah's rejection has ended, saying, **"And he shall stand and feed in the strength of the LORD, in the majesty of the name of the LORD his God; and they shall abide: for now shall he be great unto the ends of the earth. And this *One* shall be peace."** (Micah 5:4-5) But this is followed by a passage that almost no one seems to have noticed. I can personally testify that I knew of this passage long before I even *began* to realize its significance.

> **"When the Assyrian comes into our land, And when he treads in our palaces, Then we will raise against him Seven shepherds and eight princely men. They shall**

THOUGHTS ABOUT PROPHETIC SUBJECTS

waste with the sword the land of Assyria, And the land of Nimrod at its entrances; Thus He shall deliver *us* from the Assyrian, When he comes into our land And when he treads within our borders." (Micah 5:5-6)

This passage should cause every serious student of Bible prophecy to sit up and take notice. Here we have a very simple statement of coming events. There is nothing in it that is hard to understand. Nothing in it requires deep interpretation.[3] But there is no way to even imagine that it has been fulfilled. This prophecy clearly refers to the future, but is totally missed in every system of prophetic interpretation that is widely accepted today. Something is clearly wrong.

Who is this person called **"the Assyrian"**? There are a number of prophecies about him. But like this one, they are almost universally missed. I believe this is because almost everyone simply assumes they only refer to Sennacherib, the Assyrian king who attacked Judea in the time of Hezekiah. But Micah 5:5-6 cannot refer to Sennacherib.

In 2 Kings 18:14-16, Hezekiah surrendered to Sennacherib. In the following chapter, (2 Kings 19) Sennacherib sent his army to Jerusalem anyway, under a commander called **"*the* Rabshakeh."** Hezekiah sent a message to Isaiah, saying, **"This day *is* a day of trouble, and rebuke, and blasphemy; for the children have come to birth, but *there is* no strength to bring them forth."**

---

3. The only way to make this prophecy even slightly difficult to interpret is to question the translation. But about 80% of all English translations render these two verses essentially as above. The Hebrew word translated *when* in this passage is *kiy*. (Strong's transliteration - word number 3588 in Strong's Hebrew Dictionary) In certain contexts, this word can also be translated if or should. This alternate translation is favored by some who find it inconceivable that a future Assyrian will again come **"into our land"** and tread **"in our palaces"** or **"within our borders."** They interpret this statement as a boast in what Messiah would do if such a thing were to happen. But if this were the Holy Spirit's meaning in these words, this would be the only place in the entire Bible where He even suggested such a concept. If, on the other hand, the intended meaning is that this will happen, this is only one of a number of similar prophecies. This article examines many unfulfilled details in the prophecies about an Assyrian invasion. Since these details have not been fulfilled, the prophecies containing them remain to be fulfilled in the future.

(2 Kings 19:3) We thus see that Hezekiah had no strength to resist the mighty Assyrian army, much less **"seven shepherds, and eight principal men."** And neither Judah nor Israel has ever invaded Assyria.

Sennacherib attacked Judah during the righteous reign of king Hezekiah, who **"trusted in the LORD God of Israel, so that after him was none like him among all the kings of Judah, nor who were before him. For he held fast to the LORD; he did not depart from following Him, but kept His commandments, which the LORD had commanded Moses."** (2 Kings 18:5-6) Nor was it only Hezekiah that was faithful, for **"Also the hand of God was on Judah to give them singleness of heart to obey the command of the king and the leaders, at the word of the LORD."** (2 Chronicles 30:12) But **"after these deeds of faithfulness, Sennacherib king of Assyria came and entered Judah; he encamped against the fortified cities, thinking to win them over to himself."** (2 Chronicles 32:1) Hezekiah cried out to the Lord, who answered him, **"I will defend this city, to save it For My own sake and for My servant David's sake."** (Isaiah: 37:35)

But in Isaiah 10:6, the Lord says of the king of Assyria that **"I will send him against an ungodly nation, And against the people of My wrath I will give him charge, To seize the spoil, to take the prey, And to tread them down like the mire of the streets."**[4]

In Hezekiah's day, both he and his people had been righteous and the Lord promised to save them from Sennacherib. But in the day described in Isaiah 10 the nation will have been ungodly and

---

4. Some might think this refers to Assyria's successful attack on Israel, but verse in 11 this evil king says, **"Shall I not, as I have done unto Samaria and her idols, so do to Jerusalem and her idols?"** This shows that at the time referred to in this prophecy the attack on Samaria (the capitol of ancient Israel) will have already taken place, while the attack on Jerusalem (the capitol of Judah) is still future.

He will send Assyria to punish them. The first Assyrian was an enemy of God, while the second will actually be His agent.

But this latter day Assyrian does not intend to serve God, **"nor does his heart think so."** (Isaiah 10:7) He will therefore be punished **"when the LORD has performed all His work on Mount Zion and on Jerusalem."** (verse 12) This clearly refers to the future, for the Lord's **"work on Mount Zion and on Jerusalem"** will not be finished until all prophecy concerning them has been fulfilled. Again, we read in the twentieth verse of this chapter, **"And it shall come to pass in that day that the remnant of Israel, And such as have escaped of the house of Jacob, Will never again depend on him who defeated them, But will depend on the LORD, the Holy One of Israel, in truth."** This is a clear reference to the last days, for even up to our own time Israel has still not learned to **" depend on the Lord, the Holy One of Israel, in truth."**

Again, in Isaiah 14, immediately after saying the Assyrian would be destroyed, (verses 24-27) the Lord added, **"do not rejoice, all you of Philistia, Because the rod that struck you is broken; For out of the serpent's roots will come forth a viper, And its offspring *will be* a fiery flying serpent... Wail, O gate! Cry, O city! All you of Philistia *are* dissolved; For smoke will come from the north, And no one *will be* alone in his appointed times."** (verses 29-31) In stating that **"out of the serpent's roots will come forth a viper"** and that **"its offspring *will be* a fiery flying serpent,"** this passage clearly sets forth two separate attacks, one in the past (relative to the time referred to) and one in the future. These two attacks are separated in time by an unspecified number of generations, as the second attacker is the **"offspring"** of the first.

Some assume that the words **"the rod that struck you is broken"** in this passage refer to the death of Judah's king Ahaz. This is because the preceding verse (Isaiah 14:28) says **"This is the burden which came in the year that King Ahaz died."**

But there are two reasons this cannot be correct. First, Ahaz could never be called **"the rod that struck"** Philistia. Indeed, the very opposite was true. We read in 2 Chronicles 28:18-19 that **"The Philistines also had invaded the cities of the lowland and of the South of Judah, and had taken Beth Shemesh, Aijalon, Gederoth, Sochoh with its villages, Timnah with its villages, and Gimzo with its villages; and they dwelt there. For the Lord brought Judah low because of Ahaz king of Israel, for he had encouraged moral decline in Judah and had been continually unfaithful to the Lord."** The last king of Judea that had defeated the Philistines was Uzziah, the grandfather of Ahaz. (see 2 Chronicles 26:6-7)

But there is another reason **"the rod that struck"** Philistia cannot be Ahaz. The second attack in this prophecy is referred to as **"smoke"** that **"will come from the north."** Judea, the land of Ahaz, was east of Philistia, not north of it. The significance of this detail will become plain in the next section of this study when we notice the prophecies about **"the king of the North."**

Shortly after this prophecy was given, Sennacherib attacked the land of the Philistines. Some might think this was the second attack mentioned in this prophecy. But this would require that the first attack be one that had been made by either Tiglath-Pileser III or Sargon II. Each of these previous Assyrian kings had been an ancestor of Sennacherib. Each of them had conquered Philistia. And both of them were dead. But the words **"the rod that struck you is broken"** could not realistically be applied to either of them. The power of Assyria had not been **"broken"** when either of these kings had died. On the other hand, both Isaiah 37:35 and 2 Kings 19:35 tell of a most remarkable destruction of Sennacherib's army by **"the angel of the Lord."** The words **"the rod that struck you is broken"** clearly fit this defeat. These facts make it clear that Sennacherib is the first attacker in this prophecy, not the second one. So the second one has to be future.

THOUGHTS ABOUT PROPHETIC SUBJECTS

In the first chapter of Nahum *"one* **Who plots evil against the LORD, A wicked counselor,"** (verse 11) comes forth from Nineveh,[5] the ancient capitol of Assyria. (Nahum 2:8, 3:7)

In the next to the last verse of the prophecy, this **"wicked counselor"** is expressly called the **"king of Assyria."** (Nahum 3:18) The Lord declares that He will make **"an utter end"** of this invasion, adding that **"affliction will not rise up a second time."** (Nahum 1:9) He then tells His people that **"though I have afflicted you, I will afflict you no more."** (verse 12) The Divine history and many prophecies clearly show that Judah's affliction did not end at the destruction of Sennacherib. The Assyrian invasion was only the beginning of her great and long affliction, which has not yet ended. Indeed, their greatest affliction is still future.

Both the severity and the long duration of this affliction are stressed in the fifth through the tenth chapters of Isaiah. The twenty-fifth verse of the fifth chapter tells us, **" Therefore the anger of the LORD is aroused against His people; He has stretched out His hand against them And stricken them."** Then follow the words; **"For all this His anger is not turned away, But His hand *is* stretched out still."** These last words are repeated over and over in the following chapters. (Isaiah 9:12, 9:17, 9:21, and 10:4) The significance of this doleful refrain finally appears in Isaiah 10:24-25: **"Therefore thus says the Lord GOD of hosts: 'O My people, who dwell in Zion, do not be afraid of the Assyrian. He shall strike you with a rod and lift up his staff against you, in the manner of Egypt. For yet a very little while and the indignation will cease, as will My anger in their destruction.'"**

The Lord's indignation against His people who dwell **"in Zion,"** that is, **"Jerusalem,"** (verse 32) will continue until **"the Assyrian"** is destroyed. When this takes place, however, the indignation will cease and His anger will finally be **"turned away."** How fitting it is

---

5. We often hear of the region of ancient Nineveh in the news by its modern name of Mosul. This major center of fighting in Iraq is the home of the world's largest surviving Assyrian community.

that the first of the gentile conquerors of God's people should also be the last; that Judah's thousands of years of suffering should finally be ended in the destruction of their first great oppressor.

We have already noticed the description of the Assyrian's attack in Isaiah 10. This account continues through verse 32, ending with this remarkable description of the Assyrian's approach on Jerusalem:

> **"He has come to Aiath, He has passed Migron; At Michmash he has attended to his equipment. They have gone along the ridge, They have taken up lodging at Geba. Ramah is afraid, Gibeah of Saul has fled. Lift up your voice, O daughter of Gallim! Cause it to be heard as far as Laish; O poor Anathoth! Madmenah has fled, The inhabitants of Gebim seek refuge. As yet he will remain at Nob that day; He will shake his fist at the mount of the daughter of Zion, The hill of Jerusalem."** (Isaiah 10:28-32)

Some assume this refers to Sennacherib's advance on Jerusalem, but that cannot be correct. The advance on Jerusalem described in this prophecy is from the north. But Isaiah 36:2, 2 Kings 18:17, and 2 Chronicles 32:9 all say Sennacherib's forces came to Jerusalem from Lachish, which was southwest of Jerusalem. Archeologists have found extensive evidence of Assyrian presence in this southern region, but not in any part of ancient Judea north of Jerusalem. That is, not along the path described in Isaiah 10:28-32.[6]

Others assume that this passage describes an army's approach on Armageddon. But this path leads away from Armageddon, not toward it.

---

6. The accuracy of this statement was personally confirmed to me in private conversation by Dr. Ibrham E'phal, the director of Antiquities at the Hebrew University in Jerusalem. This man is recognized as the world's foremost authority on the archeology of ancient Israel.

THOUGHTS ABOUT PROPHETIC SUBJECTS

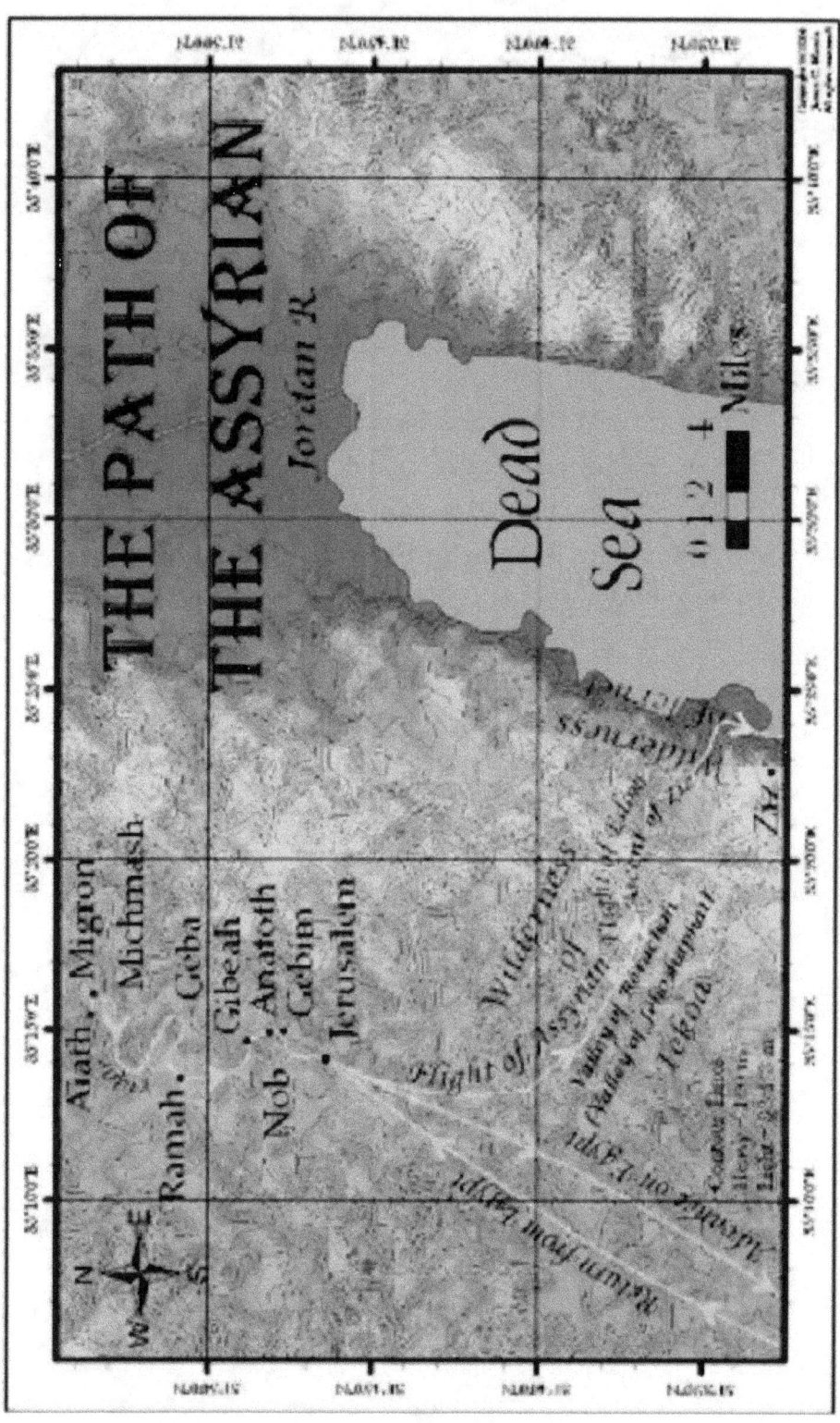

The Path of the Assyrian

The following details show the daily progress of this attack. Each stop specifically mentioned is marked by a red star in the map above.

Day 1:"**At Michmash he has attended to his equipment.**"
Day 2:"**They have taken up lodging at Geba.**"
Day 3:"**As yet he will remain at Nob that day.**"
Day 4:"**He will shake his fist at the mount of the daughter of Zion, The hill of Jerusalem.**"

This passage describes a defeat of ten cities in only four days. Even by modern standards, this is remarkable progress for an advancing army. There will be no strength to resist his advance, for "**he shall come against princes as *though* mortar, As the potter treads clay.**" (Isaiah 41:25)

Sennacherib boasted that he had conquered 46 of Hezekiah's fortified cities, with their neighboring small towns, by the use of siege ramps and battering rams, by boring holes and making breaches, as well as by relentlessly attacking with foot soldiers. Such a campaign would clearly take a long time. So it could not be the swift advance described in this prophecy.

Sennacherib left this boast on each of seven monuments known to modern scholars. [7]

---

[7]. These seven monuments are listed on page 10 and translated on page 129 of "Sennacherib's Campaign to Judah: new studies," by William R. Gallagher, Leiden; Boston; Köln: Brill, 1999. This authoritative book clearly presents the current state of historical scholarship on this subject. Working from a purely logical basis, it demonstrates the error in many objections to the historical reliability of Biblical accounts of

THOUGHTS ABOUT PROPHETIC SUBJECTS

The best known of these is a prism shaped monument. It is often called "The Oriental Institute Prism" because it is held by the Oriental Institute. As this institute is part of the University of Chicago, it is also called "The Chicago Prism." But the Oriental Institute simply calls it the "Clay Prism of Sennacherib."

This monument (and each of the others) lists the cities Sennacherib conquered in this campaign. These lists clearly show that as he invaded this area he came along the seacoast, not inland through the mountains.

This fact is so well established that A. T. Olmstead quoted Isaiah 10:28-32 in his monumental 650 page "History of Assyria," commenting on how badly Isaiah blew this prophecy; because this was not the path Sennacherib followed. [8] Of course, he failed to realize that Isaiah was not talking about Sennacherib.

Finally, it would seem the writers of the Dead Sea Scrolls would have known the route Sennacherib followed. But they plainly did not think Sennacherib followed this route, for one of them quoted this exact passage, (Isaiah 10:28-32) commenting that it referred to "the Last Days." [9]

This ends our discussion of this character as expressly called **"the Assyrian"** in the Holy Scriptures. But we are far from finished with the prophecies about him.

Part two: **"The king of the North"**

The king of the revived northern splinter of the empire of Alexander the Great, that is, the Selucid empire, in Daniel 11:40-45. The third verse of this chapter says that **"a mighty king"**

---

this campaign. It devotes well over a hundred pages to these accounts, but doesn't even mention any portion of Isaiah 10:28-32.

8. "History of Assyria," by A. T. Olmstead, Chicago: University of Chicago Press, 1951, pgs. 301 and 302.

9. From the commentary on Isaiah in "The Dead Sea Scrolls, a New Translation," by Michael Wise, Martin Abegg, Jr., and Edward Cook, New York: 1996, pg. 210. Scholars believe these scrolls were written between the first and third centuries B.C.

would arise. We then read that **"when he has arisen, his kingdom shall be broken up and divided toward the four winds of heaven, but not among his posterity nor according to his dominion with which he ruled; for his kingdom shall be uprooted, even for others besides these."** (Daniel 11:4) The next twenty-seven verses (Daniel 11:5-32) describe a long series of wars between **"the king of the North"** and **"the king of the South."** This account covers a number of generations, mentioning events which took place over a period of approximately 130 years. Every act of **"the king of the North"** in this account was actually committed by one of the Selucids, a family that ruled out of Antioch in Syria. And every act of **"the king of the South"** was actually committed by one of the Ptolemies, a family that ruled out of Alexandria in Egypt.

The Ptolemies ruled only over Egypt, but the Selucids, the kings of the North, ruled over a vast empire. The following map shows the area they ruled. This is compared to the area ruled by the previous Assyrian empire. The map clearly shows that aside from a few sections at the edges, these two empires covered the same area. [10] (The region of today's Syria and Iraq.) From this we understand that the prophetic character called **"the Assyrian"** is the same individual as the character called **"the King of the North."**

---

10. Since the Seleucids ruled out of Antioch in Syria, they are sometimes called the kings of Syria. While this is technically correct, referring to them in this way masks the true identity of **"the Assyrian."**

THOUGHTS ABOUT PROPHETIC SUBJECTS

The Lands of the Kings of the North and South With the Assyrian Empire

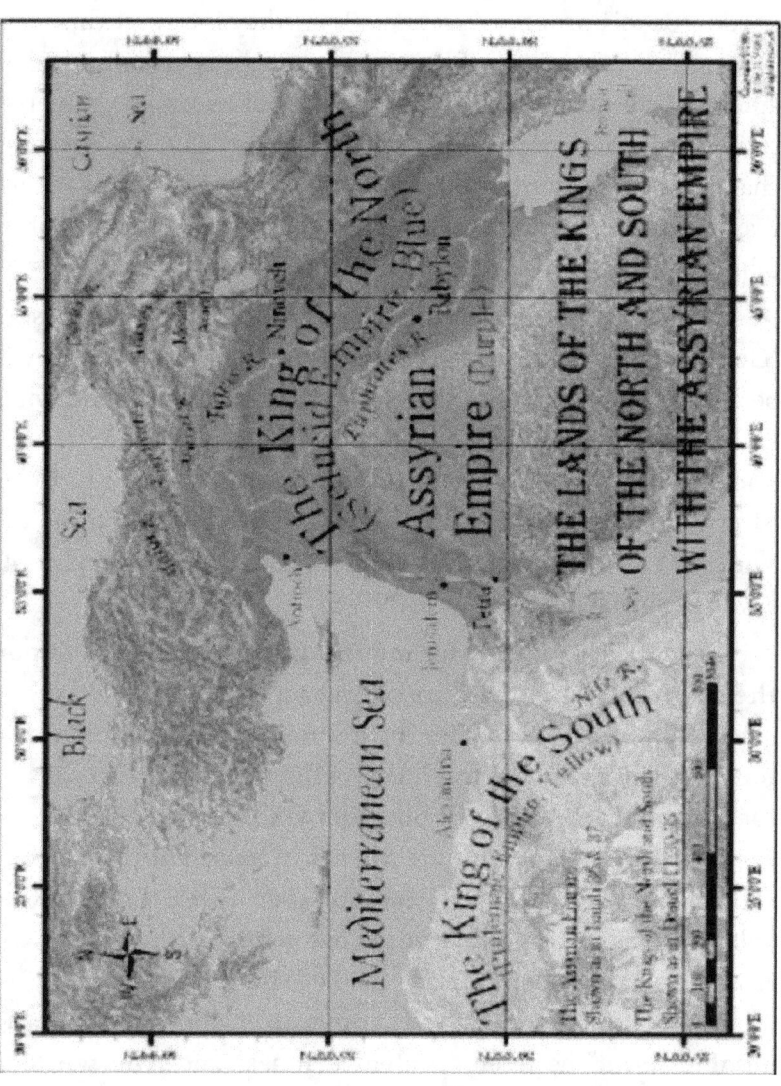

It is remarkable that many otherwise competent students of prophecy miss the plain testimony of Daniel 11. They recognize that in the first twenty-seven verses **"the king of the North"** in each generation is the current ruler of the Selucid empire. But then they say that in the last part of the chapter (the part that remains to be fulfilled) the meaning of this term changes. In the future portion of this prophecy (verses 40-45) they interpret this term to mean **"Gog,"** the king of Russia who attacks Israel in Ezekiel 38 and 39. Why would the Holy Spirit use a full twenty-seven verses to identify **"the king of the North,"** only to have the meaning change when He came to the application? This idea rebels against reason. But it is not only unreasonable, it twists the entire fabric of prophecy into a hopeless muddle.

There are significant differences between the attacks of **"Gog"** and **"the king of the North."** First, these attackers will be destroyed in different places. The Lord tells Gog **"'You shall fall upon the mountains of Israel, you and all your troops and the peoples who *are* with you; I will give you to birds of prey of every sort and *to* the beasts of the field to be devoured. You shall fall on the open field; for I have spoken,' says the Lord GOD."** (Ezekiel 39:3-5)

Gog will fall **"upon the mountains of Israel"** and **"upon the open field."** But these are only general. Specific detail is also given. **"It will come to pass in that day *that* I will give Gog a burial place there in Israel, the valley of those who pass by east of the sea; and it will obstruct travelers, because there they will bury Gog and all his multitude. Therefore they will call *it* the Valley of Hamon Gog."** (Ezekiel 39:11) Gog will be buried in **"the valley of those who pass by east of the sea."** This cannot be the place where **"the northern army"** is destroyed, for its **"stench will come up"** from **"a barren and desolate land"** between **"the eastern sea"** and **"the western sea."** (Joel 2:20)

A place in Israel between **"the eastern sea"** and **"the western sea"** and also **"east of the sea"**[11] would have to be on the Mediterranean Sea coast. But the coast of the Mediterranean between **"the eastern sea"** and **"the western sea"** is a fertile plain. No part of this plain is **"barren and desolate."**

Also, the attack in Daniel 11 ushers in **"a time of trouble, Such as never was since there was a nation, *Even* to that time."** (Daniel 12:1) But the attack in Ezekiel 38 and 39 ushers in a time when **"'I will not hide My face from them anymore; for I shall have poured out My Spirit on the house of Israel,' says the Lord GOD."** (Ezekiel 39:29) Again, this **"time of trouble, Such as never was since there was a nation, *Even* to that time."** (Daniel 12:1) corresponds exactly with the **"great tribulation, such as has not been since the beginning of the world until this time, no, nor ever shall be"** we read about in Matthew 24:21. This great tribulation will come upon **"those who are in Judea."** (Matthew 24:16) But Gog will attack **"My people Israel,"** (Ezekiel 38:14-16) not Judah. Some would consider this nit-picking about words, but in the Bible, every word is significant. This is particularly true in regard to end time prophecy. Every detail is significant. Every change in wording is significant. Even so, **"the North,"** the realm of **"the king of the North,"** is a different term than **"the far north,"** from which **"Gog"** will come. (Ezekiel 38:15) This is highlighted by the fact that in Daniel 11:44 the attacker is troubled by **"tidings,"** not only **"out of the east,"** but also **"out of the north."** This implies that there is another nation further north than that of **"the king of the North."**

Finally, **"the land of Egypt shall not escape"** from **"the king of the North,"** and **"the Libyans and the Ethiopians"**

---

11. Some translations, including the New Century Version, God's Word to the Nations, and the New Living Translation, read **"east of the Dead Sea"** instead of **"east of the sea."** This is based on a conclusion that the Hebrew text implies the Dead Sea, even though it is not named. Only a few scholars have come to this conclusion. But if correct, this is further proof that these places are different. For a valley east of the Dead Sea could not be between **"the eastern sea"** and **"the western sea."**

are listed among those he subdues. (Daniel 11:42-43) But we are not told that **"Gog"** will invade Egypt, and **"Ethiopia and Libya"** are listed among his allies. (Ezekiel 38:5) All this makes it plain that **"Gog"** and **"the king of the North"** are two different prophetic characters.

Returning now to Daniel 11, it is important to remember that when Alexander the Great died, his four generals divided his kingdom **"toward the four winds of heaven,"** as we read in Daniel 11:4. Two of these generals were Selucus and Ptolemy, the first kings of these warring dynasties. At the time of the division, Ptolemy took the southern portion of the kingdom and Selucus got the eastern portion. But soon after, Selucus also took over the northern portion and moved his throne there. When we remember this, we realize that **"the king of the North"** is not just the king of some northern land. He is the king of a particular northern land, that is, the northern splinter of Alexander's kingdom.

In Daniel 11:36-39 we read of a willful king who will arise. His wickedness is punished by a two pronged attack. **"At the time of the end the king of the South shall attack him; and the king of the North shall come against him like a whirlwind, with chariots, horsemen, and with many ships; and he shall enter the countries, overwhelm** *them,* **and pass through."** (Daniel 11:40) But **"the king of the South"** quickly drops out of the picture, and the rest of the account deals only with **"the king of the North." "He shall also enter the Glorious Land, and many** *countries* **shall be overthrown; but these shall escape from his hand: Edom, Moab, and the prominent people of Ammon. He shall stretch out his hand against the countries, and the land of Egypt shall not escape. He shall have power over the treasures of gold and silver, and over all the precious things of Egypt; also the Libyans and Ethiopians** *shall follow* **at his heels. But news from the east and the north shall trouble him; therefore** he shall go out with great fury to destroy and annihilate many. And he shall plant the tents of his palace between the seas and the glorious holy mountain; yet he shall come to his end, and no one will help him."** (Daniel 11:41-45) This passage begins with **"the king of the North"** entering **"the Glorious land,"** and ends with him **"between the seas and the glorious holy mountain."** This is the same area as the one **"the Assyrian"** will attack. As this takes place **"at the time of the end"** (verse 40), we realize that this attack takes place in the same general time as the attack by **"the Assyrian."**

But now we must concentrate on two other details of this account. In verse 40 we see the willful king being attacked by **"the king of the South"** and **"the king of the North,"** evidently at the same time. But then **"the king of the North"** subdues many other countries, including **"the land of Egypt"** and **"the Libyans and Ethiopians."** With reference to these details we now need to notice two other prophecies about **"the Assyrian."** The first of these is in Isaiah 7.

"The Lord will bring the king of Assyria upon you and your people and your father's house—days that have not come since the day that Ephraim departed from Judah. And it shall come to pass in that day That the Lord will whistle for the fly That *is* in the farthest part of the rivers of Egypt, And for the bee that is in the land of Assyria. They will come, and all of them will rest In the desolate valleys and in the clefts of the rocks, And on all thorns and in all pastures. In the same day the Lord will shave with a hired razor, With those from beyond the River, with the king of Assyria, The head and the hair of the legs, And will also remove the beard." (Isaiah 7:17-20) In verse 13 this prophecy had been specifically addressed to **"the house of David,"** so this prophecy specifically states that **"the king of Assyria"** will come against the land ruled by **"the house of David,"** that is, the land of Judea, which is now called Israel. But attached to this explicit prophecy is a very interesting detail.

This attack will be accompanied by swarms from **"Egypt"** and **"Assyria."** While the swarms in the prophecy are only swarms of insects, it seems obvious from the context that this is typical language. That the real meaning is swarms of soldiers, so many that they resemble swarms of insects. But they come from both of these distant lands at the same time, just as we read of **"the king of the south"** and **"the king of the North"** in Daniel 11:40.

But now we go to Isaiah 20 and read: **"the Lord spoke by Isaiah the son of Amoz, saying, 'Go, and remove the sackcloth from your body, and take your sandals off your feet.' And he did so, walking naked and barefoot. Then the Lord said, 'Just as My servant Isaiah has walked naked and barefoot three years *for* a sign and a wonder against Egypt and Ethiopia, so shall the king of Assyria lead away the Egyptians as prisoners and the Ethiopians as captives, young and old, naked and barefoot, with their buttocks uncovered, to the shame of Egypt.'"** (Isaiah 20:2-4) So we now read that **"the king of Assyria"** will **"lead away"** as **"captives"** both **"the Egyptians"** and **"the Ethiopians."** This is exactly what **"the king of the North"** does in Daniel 11:43, although the passage in Isaiah does not add that **"The king of Assyria"** will also lead away the Libyans as prisoners.

Thus we see that these two attackers, that is, **"the Assyrian"** and **"the king of the North"** are identified as future rulers over the same geographic area. They will both attack at approximately the same time. They will also both attack Judea, which is now called Israel. They will both do this at the same time that Egypt attacks. And both of them will also attack Egypt and Ethiopia. In view of this remarkable number of similarities, is it reasonable to doubt that these two prophetic designations represent the same future individual?

Part three: **The male goat's little horn.**

In Daniel 8, the prophet saw a male goat, which **"*had* a notable horn between his eyes."** (verse 5) But **"the large horn was broken, and in place of it four notable ones came up toward the four winds of heaven."** (verse 8) Daniel was then told that **"the male goat *is* the kingdom of Greece. The large horn that *is* between its eyes *is* the first king. As for the broken *horn* and the four that stood up in its place, four kingdoms shall arise out of that nation, but not with its power."** (verses 21-22) As we have already noticed, four kingdoms arose out of the empire of Alexander the Great, the first of the great Grecian kings. **"And out of one of them came a little horn which grew exceedingly great toward the south, toward the east, and toward the Glorious *Land*."** (verse 9) The detail that this little horn came **"out of one of"** the four kingdoms shows that it can not represent either the Roman leader or the Russian one; for Alexander's empire did not include Rome or any part of Russia. But Selucus, the first of the Selucid kings, that is, the first **"king of the North,"** was one of the four that rose out of Alexander's empire. So we see that this attacker will rise from a geographic area that includes the areas ruled by both **"the Assyrian"** and **"the king of the North."**

We are specifically told these things will happen **"in the latter time of their kingdom, When the transgressors have reached their fullness."** (verse 23) So we know this is an end time prophecy. That is, that this prophecy applies to the same general time period as those about **"the Assyrian"** and **"the king of the North."** We are also told that this will happen **"in the latter time of the indignation."** (verse 19) Other translations render this as **"at the final period of the indignation,"** (NASB) **"at the latter end of the indignation,"** (RSV) and **"in the last end of the indignation."** (KJV) Comparing this with Isaiah

10:25, which we have already examined, we again recognize **"the Assyrian,"** for **"the indignation"** will cease in his destruction.

Finally, we are specifically told that this evil attacker **"shall destroy the mighty, and *also* the holy people."** So we know that he will attack the same area as that attacked by **"the Assyrian"** and **"the king of the North."** So again, is it reasonable to doubt that this prophetic designation also represents the same future individual as **"the Assyrian"** and **"the king of the North?"**

Part four: **"one who makes desolate"**

In Daniel 9:27. **"the prince who is to come.""shall confirm a covenant with many for one week; But in the middle of the week He shall bring an end to sacrifice and offering."** But then **"on the wing of abominations shall be one who makes desolate, Even until the consummation, which is determined, Is poured out on the desolate."** It is important to noticed the change in actors that occurs in this prophecy. In the first part of Daniel 9:27 the actor is **"he,"** clearly meaning **"the prince who is to come."** But then the actor changes to **"one."** From this we see that at this point another character is introduced. This is more than just a matter of interpretation. It is a matter of the basic structure of language. The **"one who makes desolate"** is not the same person as **"the prince who is to come."** He is a different character.

According to Daniel 9:27, this **"one who makes desolate"** shall come **"on the wing of abominations."** We read in Jeremiah 10:22, **"Behold, the noise of the report has come, And a great commotion out of the north country, To make the cities of Judah desolate, a den of jackals."** This attack from the north will come **"Because of the evil of"** the doings of the **"men of Judah and inhabitants of Jerusalem."** (Jeremiah 4:4, see verses 6, 7, 10, and 14)

Remember that the Lord said of the Assyrian, **"I will send him against an ungodly nation, And against the people of**

THOUGHTS ABOUT PROPHETIC SUBJECTS

My wrath." (Isaiah 10:6) In Daniel 8:12 it is **"Because of transgression"** that **"an army was given over *to the horn* to oppose the daily *sacrifices.*"** The transgression mentioned in these passages is not just some kind of general evil, but a specific outrage. In Daniel 8:13 this outrage is called **"the transgression of desolation,"** and **"both the sanctuary and the host"** are given **"to be trampled under foot."**

Our Lord spoke of this in Matthew 24:15-21. **"Therefore when you see the** *'abomination of desolation,'* **spoken of by Daniel the prophet, standing in the holy place (whoever reads, let him understand), then let those who are in Judea flee to the mountains. Let him who is on the housetop not go down to take anything out of his house. And let him who is in the field not go back to get his clothes. But woe to those who are pregnant and to those who are nursing babies in those days! And pray that your flight may not be in winter or on the Sabbath. For then there will be great tribulation, such as has not been since the beginning of the world until this time, no, nor ever shall be."**

This is repeated in Mark 13:14-19. Can any serious student of prophecy doubt that the outrage which brings down the **"one who makes desolate"** is when **"the man of sin... the son of perdition" "sits as God in the temple of God, showing himself that he is God"**? (2 Thessalonians 2:4)

So we see that **"the Assyrian," "the king of the North,"** the male goat's **"little horn,"** and the **"one who makes desolate,"** all represent the same end time individual. This can further be seen in the details of his destruction. The prophecy about the **"one who makes desolate"** does not include his end, because the subject of that prophecy is God's discipline of His guilty people, not their eventual deliverance. But as **"the king of the North,"** he **"shall come to his end, and no one will help him."** (Daniel 11:45) **"But I will remove far from you the northern *army*, And will drive him away into a barren and desolate land,**

With his face toward the eastern sea And his back toward the western sea; His stench will come up, And his foul odor will rise, Because he has done monstrous things." (Joel 2:20) As the male goat's little horn, he **"shall be broken without human means."** (Daniel 8:25) As **"the Assyrian,"** he will be beaten down **"through the voice of the LORD."** (Isaiah 30:31) And finally, **"Assyria shall fall by a sword not of man, And a sword not of mankind shall devour him. But he shall flee from the sword, And his young men shall become forced labor."**[12] (Isaiah 31:8)

When we realize all this, we realize that this neglected character is the central (human) figure of end time Bible prophecy, occupying more space than any other two characters combined. Thus, it is most remarkable that this character has been totally missed by every well known teacher of Bible prophecy in the last hundred years. But, although it is not well known, this character figures largely in the writings of earlier dispensational teachers. Nineteenth century writers from the Plymouth brethren, such as J. N. Darby, William Kelly, and William Trotter, spoke often of him.

---

12. We should note in passing that although Sennacherib's army was destroyed without human means and he returned home, (2 Kings 19:35-36) neither scripture nor any ancient monument or record says anything about his young men having been made slaves.

THOUGHTS ABOUT PROPHETIC SUBJECTS

The Five End Time Individuals of Bible Prophecy

One of the most common errors in interpreting the prophetic scriptures is rolling various end time individuals into an imaginary single individual. And that imaginary composite character is usually called "the Antichrist."

There are five distinct end time individuals found in Bible prophecy.

The most widely known of these is the end time individual called **"the beast."** This is the end times ruler of Rome who will bring about a revival of the Roman Empire. He is the little horn of Daniel 7:8 that uproots three other horns, and has **"a mouth speaking pompous words."** And he is **"the prince who is to come"** of Daniel 9:26. We know he will be a ruler of Rome because he will be a ruler of the people that destroyed **"the city and the sanctuary."** (Again, Daniel 9:26) As this was done by the Romans, this **"prince who is to come"** has to be a Roman. A common error about this prophetic individual is that he will attack Judah, which is now called Israel, in the middle of the seventieth week. The scriptures indeed describe such an attack. But no scripture says, or even implies, that this attacker will be **"the beast."**

But an end time individual that is noticed much less often is called **"the king"** in Daniel 11:36-40. In considering **"the king,"** we need to remember that the language of scripture is very precise. God does not waste words. Every detail is significant. **"the king,"** of Daniel 11:36-40 (which in the Hebrew text is מלך, *melek* in our alphabet, word number 4428 in Strong's Hebrew Dictionary) is a wholly different word from **"the prince,"** of Daniel 9:26 (which in the Hebrew text is נגיד, *nagid* in our alphabet, word number 5057 in Strong's Hebrew Dictionary.)

This change in wording indicates two different persons. This evil **"king"** is the **"worthless shepherd"** whom God **"will raise up" "in the land," "who will not care for those who are cut off, nor seek the young, nor heal those that are broken, nor feed those that still stand. But he will eat the flesh of the fat and tear their hooves in pieces."** (Zechariah 11:16)

He will be punished for this by receiving wounds in his eye and his right arm. He cannot be the head of the seven headed beast that John saw **"as if it had been mortally wounded, and his deadly wound was healed."** (Revelation 13:3) For wounds to his eye and his right arm, though serious, are not **"deadly."** And the **"worthless shepherd"** will not recover from his wounds. Instead, **"His arm shall completely wither, And his right eye shall be totally blinded."** (Zechariah 11:17)

Our Lord contrasted himself to this shepherd, calling him **"a hireling,"** and again saying he **"leaves the sheep and flees."** (John 10:11-16) In so contrasting himself to this **"hireling,"** our Lord was pointing him out as the **"Antichrist,"** the great false Messiah. Again, our Lord said, **"I have come in My Father's name, and you do not receive Me; if another comes in his own name, him you will receive."** (John 5:43) Here, again, Jesus was referring to "the Antichrist." This individual appears in the Revelation as the **"beast"** that John saw **"coming up out of the earth"** in Revelation 13:11-18 and as **"the false prophet"** which is found in Revelation 16:13, 19:20, and 20:10.

Now many think **"the false prophet"** cannot be "the Antichrist" because he tells men to worship **"the beast."** (Revelation 14:12) But they forget that Jesus told men to worship God the Father. In imitating the true **"Messiah,"** the great false Messiah will in a similar way claim to be God, but will also tell men to worship another.

THOUGHTS ABOUT PROPHETIC SUBJECTS

Another end time individual found in the scriptures, but almost universally missed, is called **"the Assyrian."** He is clearly described in Isaiah 7, 10, 14, 30, and 31, in Micah 5, and in the whole book of Nahum. He is the great attacker that invades **"Judah,"** which is now called Israel, in the middle of the seventieth week. The daily progress of his attack is given in Isaiah 10:28-32. God will allow this attack as punishment because the leaders of the Jews will have allowed **"the man of sin,"** who is also called **"the son of perdition,"** to sit **"as God in the temple of God, showing himself that he is God."** (2 Thessalonians 2:3-4)

If you compare a map of the ancient Assyrian empire with a map of the Selucid empire, which is **"the king of the north"** of Daniel 11, you will see that these two ancient empires covered the same areas at different ancient times. The maps of their empires are identical except for a few sparsely settled areas around the edges. Because of this, I conclude that **"the Assyrian"** and **"the king of the north"** are two different designations for the same end time individual.

Another end time individual is **"the king of the south,"** of Daniel 11:5-40. which attacks **"Judah,"** which is now called Israel, at the same time as **"the king of the north."** (Daniel 11:40) But **"the king of the north"** turns on him and attacks his homeland, Egypt, (Daniel 11:42-43) causing him to pass out of the picture. The identity of **"the king of the north"** with **"the Assyrian"** is again shown by the fact that in Isaiah 7:17-19, the armies of **"Assyria"** and **"Egypt"** are depicted as swarms of insects, attacking **"Judah"** at the same time.

The other end time character is **"Gog,"** Who in Ezekiel 38:2 is identified as **"of the land of Magog,"** which is unquestionably Russia. He is there also stated to be the **"prince of Rosh,"** which is the name of the ancient tribe for which Russia is named, and the prince of **"Meshech and Tubal,"** two tribes which in ancient times lived in what is now Turkey, but in Medieval times migrated *en masse* to what is now Russia. Numerous markers in Ezekiel 38 and 39 make it plain that this attack comes *after*, not *before*, the time of "the Antichrist," and *before*, not *after*, the millennium. In Revelation 20:8-9, the nations that attack after the millennium are called **"Gog and Magog."** But that, being a thousand years later, is a completely different attack. And every detail we are given about that attack is different from the corresponding details given in Ezekiel 38 and 39.

So each of these five end time individuals is clearly set forth as being from a different country, and each of them does distinctly different things. So lumping all (or some) of them together as if they were a single individual throws all of the prophetic scriptures into an unintelligible mess.

THOUGHTS ABOUT PROPHETIC SUBJECTS

The Scriptural Doctrine of Imminence

Those who deny the doctrine of imminence often warn us to be watching for the coming of Antichrist. But there is not even one scripture that instructs us to be watching for him. Instead, the scriptures repeatedly teach us to be watching for our Lord's coming.

> **"For the grace of God that brings salvation has appeared to all men, teaching us that, denying ungodliness and worldly lusts, we should live soberly, righteously, and godly in the present age, looking for the blessed hope and glorious appearing of our great God and Savior Jesus Christ,"** (Titus 2:11-13)

> **"For they themselves declare concerning us what manner of entry we had to you, and how you turned to God from idols to serve the living and true God, and to wait for His Son from heaven, whom He raised from the dead, *even* Jesus who delivers us from the wrath to come."** (1 Thessalonians 1:9-10)

> **"I urge you in the sight of God who gives life to all things, and *before* Christ Jesus who witnessed the good confession before Pontius Pilate, that you keep *this* commandment without spot, blameless until our Lord Jesus Christ's appearing,"** (1 Timothy 6:13-14)

And they not only instruct us to be watching for our Lord's coming, but to be eagerly anticipating it.

> **"so that you come short in no gift, eagerly waiting for the revelation of our Lord Jesus Christ,"** (1 Corinthians 1:7)

So we see that our Lord's coming is continually presented, throughout the entire New Testament, as an immediate hope to be eagerly anticipated, not as something to come after a unparalleled period of intense persecution. And this is the basis of the scriptural doctrine of imminence.

THOUGHTS ABOUT PROPHETIC SUBJECTS

How We Know the Lord's Coming Is Near

There has been much discussion about whether or not we can actually know that the Lord's coming for us is near. We have all heard many Christians saying the time is near. But how do we know that? Is it really possible to know such a thing?

To answer this question, we need to begin with two scriptures that explicitly tell us that we should be able to know when the time is near. The first of these is: "**For you yourselves know perfectly that the day of the Lord so comes as a thief in the night. For when they say, 'Peace and safety!' then sudden destruction comes upon them, as labor pains upon a pregnant woman. And they shall not escape. But you, brethren, are not in darkness, so that this Day should overtake you as a thief.**" (1 Thessalonians 5:2-4) Here we find a coming day mentioned, which is called "**the day of the Lord.**" and we are explicitly told that it "**comes as a thief in the night.**" The Holy Spirit then goes on to explain that by this He means that it will catch the careless by surprise. He will just suddenly be there, without any warning that they will be aware of. But then the Holy Spirit very explicitly says, "**But you, brethren, are not in darkness, so that this Day should overtake you as a thief.**" Here we see, and clearly see, that if we understand the scriptures as well as our God expects us to, "**you, brethren**" will see "**this Day**" approaching, even though it catches "**them,**" that is, the unbelievers, by surprise.

The second place where we clearly see this is the passage, "**And let us consider one another in order to stir up love and good works, not forsaking the assembling of ourselves** together, as *is* the manner of some, but exhorting *one another*, and so much the more as you see the Day approaching." (Hebrews 10:24-25)

Like the first scripture we examined, this one explicitly says that we would be able to **"see the Day approaching."** Again, this is assuming that we have made ourselves as acquainted with the Holy Scriptures as our God intended we should be. For we are also told that **"All Scripture is given by inspiration of God, and is profitable for doctrine, for reproof, for correction, for instruction in righteousness, that the man of God may be complete, thoroughly equipped for every good work."** (2 Timothy 3:16-17) So if we do not personally know what the Bible actually teaches, we are spiritually incomplete, and we are not **"thoroughly equipped for every good work."**

But when we bring these scriptures up, someone often brings up two others. **"Watch therefore, for you know neither the day nor the hour in which the Son of Man is coming."** (Matthew 25:13) And **"But of that day and hour no one knows, not even the angels in heaven, nor the Son, but only the Father."** (Mark 13:32) And it is indeed absolutely correct that we cannot know **"the day nor the hour"** when our Lord will come. But that is a specific time. The other scriptures we examined speak of a general time, not a specific one. So there is zero contradiction between these scriptures. We indeed cannot know **"the day nor the hour."** But, if we know the scriptures as well as our God expects to know them, we will indeed be able to **"see the Day approaching."** And we will not be **"in darkness, so that this Day should overtake"** us **"as a thief."**

But what are the specific scriptures that make it plain that our Lord's coming for us is very near? We are told absolutely nothing that must take place before that time. Instead, we are told that **"We shall not all sleep, but we shall all be changed-- in a moment, in the twinkling of an eye, at the last trumpet. For**

THOUGHTS ABOUT PROPHETIC SUBJECTS

the trumpet will sound, and the dead will be raised incorruptible, and we shall be changed." (1 Corinthians 15:51-52) This coming of the Lord for His own has come to be called "the rapture," and is distinctly different from His coming to judge the world. And it also is the first of a long chain of events that the Bible tells us will take place.

The Bible repeatedly calls the period in which these things will happen, **"the time of the end."** (Daniel 8:17, 11:35 and 40, 12:4 and 9) And it says many things by which we can understand when it is getting near. Some of these things are stated in broad generalities. But others of them are stated in language that is very detailed and specific. And that very detailed and specific language includes both things that have actually come to pass recently, and other things that have recently become obviously possible as events that could easily happen in the near future. To understand what the Bible teaches on this subject, we need to examine all three of these classes of prophecies. We will begin by reviewing a few prophecies that are stated in broad generalities.

In Luke 17, Jesus **"was asked by the Pharisees when the kingdom of God would come."** (Luke 17:20) as part of His answer, Jesus said, **"as it was in the days of Noah, so it will be also in the days of the Son of Man: They ate, they drank, they married wives, they were given in marriage, until the day that Noah entered the ark, and the flood came and destroyed them all. Likewise as it was also in the days of Lot: They ate, they drank, they bought, they sold, they planted, they built; but on the day that Lot went out of Sodom it rained fire and brimstone from heaven and destroyed them all. Even so will it be in the day when the Son of Man is revealed."** (Luke 17:26-30)

Several things shine out brightly from this description. The first is, that His coming will be sudden, without any warning that the unbelievers would understand. But then two other things jump out at us. At that time, it will be **"as it was in the days of Noah,"** and **"as it was also in the days of Lot."**

What was it like **"in the days of Noah,"** and **"in the days of Lot"**? We read in Genesis 6:10-11, **"Noah begot three sons: Shem, Ham, and Japheth. The earth also was corrupt before God, and the earth was filled with violence."** So this comparison tells us that at that time the earth will be filled with corruption and violence. Then, we also read that **"Lot dwelt in the cities of the plain and pitched *his* tent even as far as Sodom. But the men of Sodom *were* exceedingly wicked and sinful against the LORD."** (Genesis 13:12-13) And a few chapters later we are explicitly told the nature of their wickedness, for **"before they lay down, the men of the city, the men of Sodom, both old and young, all the people from every quarter, surrounded the house. And they called to Lot and said to him, 'Where are the men who came to you tonight? Bring them out to us that we may know them *carnally*.'"** (Genesis 19:4-5) So, although they were **"exceedingly wicked and sinful,"** the specific nature of their wickedness was homosexuality.

Now who could deny that at the present time the earth is filled with corruption, violence, and wickedness. And sadly, we all know that homosexuality is now rampant on a worldwide scale. Now some would argue that these things have always been in the world. But those of us who are as old as myself *all* remember that, throughout most of history, up to the time of our own youth, such behavior was considered socially unacceptable. But in the mid 1960s, there came a sudden and dramatic change. Now, **"they declare their sin as Sodom, They do not hide *it*."** (Isaiah 3:9) And everyone knows that violence is increasing dramatically all over the world. So these things, though general in nature, are distinct signs that the Lord's coming is near.

Again, in Matthew 24:3-4, Jesus' **"disciples came to Him privately, saying, 'Tell us, when will these things be? And** what *will be* the sign of Your coming, and of the end of the age?' And Jesus answered and said to them:" (Matthew 24:3-4) His answer then included the following: "**For nation will rise against nation, and kingdom against kingdom. And there will be famines, pestilences, and earthquakes in various places. All these** *are* **the beginning of sorrows.**" (Matthew 24:7-8) So the beginning of this time of sorrow will be a time of many wars, along with "**famines, pestilences,** [that is, epidemics] **and earthquakes.**" Again, one would have to be blind and deaf to not realize that all these things have become commonplace in recent decades. Yet all of us that are older remember that it was different in our youth. But these things are still general.

But now we come to one more prophecy that, while general in scope, is specific in detail, bridging, as it were, the division between general prophecies and specific prophecies. At the end of his prophecy, Daniel was told, "**But you, Daniel, shut up the words, and seal the book until the time of the end; many shall run to and fro, and knowledge shall increase.**" (Daniel 12:4) Here we are told two very specific details about the end times. The first is that "**many shall run to and fro.**" The Hebrew word here translated "**run**" is an enhanced form of שׁוּט, *shut* in our alphabet, word number 7751 in Strong's Hebrew Dictionary. This enhanced form implies great speed. Remember that it was only about a generation ago when "a mile a minute" was an expression for the ultimate in speed. Yet today, ordinary people that is, the common people, or the "**many,**" travel on jet planes, which go on the order of eight to nine miles a minute. And even when only traveling in cars, most people consider "a mile a minute," that is, sixty miles an hour, as going rather slow. So who could deny that this is something that is uniquely different about our current generation.

Again, when my parents were young, the standard method of travel was to either ride on or be pulled by beasts, usually horses or oxen. So there was not very much travel. Some people indeed traveled far. But this was rare. But today even common people travel far and wide on a regular basis.

The second specific detail of the end times in this last passage is that **"knowledge shall increase."** And indeed, the sum total of all human knowledge, that is, the sum total of "facts" that are recorded and available for reference, is currently doubling every ten years or so. And half of all the true scientists that have ever lived are working today. So today, knowledge is increasing at a startling rate. So these two details again show, and very clearly show, that we are indeed near **"the time of the end."**

And in recent decades there has been a marked resurgence of openly practiced witchcraft. This has always been practiced in secret, but of late it has become open and flagrant on a very wide scale. This is explicitly mentioned in Bible prophecy, calling it **"sorceries"** in Isaiah 47:9 and 12, in Micah 5:12, in Nahum 3:4, and in Revelation 9:21, and **"sorcery"** in Revelation 18:23.

This covers the general descriptions of the end times. And these alone should be enough to make anyone realize that we are indeed near the end. But beyond these general things, the scriptures state a very large number of highly specific details of the world geopolitical situation that will exist in **"the time of the end."** Even as late as the early 1940s, *none* of these world geopolitical situations existed. But *all* of them exist today. These specific and explicit things that have already come to pass include:

The Jews are again in their ancient homeland, with their own rulers. This was not distinctly prophesied anywhere in the Bible. The return described in the Bible is a return of all Israel, which has not yet happened. But, although this return was not distinctly prophesied, the end time scenario in the Bible opens with Judah, that is, the Jews, in their land.

First, we need to realize that the often discussed seventieth **"week"** of Daniel's famous prophecy of the **"seventy weeks,"** (Daniel 9:24-27) is merely the unfulfilled last **"week"** of these "**seventy weeks.**" And we are explicitly told that these "**seventy weeks**" were "**determined for**" Daniel's "**people,**" who are the Jews, and his "**holy city,**" which is Jerusalem. (Daniel 9:24) So, in order for this prophecy to be fulfilled, it was absolutely necessary for the Jews to be in Jerusalem.

Jesus spoke of them being in that land at that time saying, "**When you see the 'abomination of desolation,' spoken of by Daniel the prophet, standing in the holy place**" (whoever reads, let him understand), **then let those who are in Judea flee to the mountains. Let him who is on the housetop not go down to take anything out of his house. And let him who is in the field not go back to get his clothes.**" (Matthew 24:15-18)

Again, we read of them being in Jerusalem in Isaiah 28:14-18, where we read, "**Therefore hear the word of the LORD, you scornful men, Who rule this people who are in Jerusalem, Because you have said, 'We have made a covenant with death, And with Sheol we are in agreement. When the overflowing scourge passes through, It will not come to us, For we have made lies our refuge, And under falsehood we have hidden ourselves.' Therefore thus says the Lord GOD:... 'Your covenant with death will be annulled, And your agreement with Sheol will not stand; When the overflowing scourge passes through, Then you will be trampled down by it.'**"

Again, we read of that day, "**Behold, I will make Jerusalem a cup of drunkenness to all the surrounding peoples, when they lay siege against Judah and Jerusalem. And it shall happen in that day that I will make Jerusalem a very heavy stone for all peoples; all who would heave it away will surely be cut in pieces, though all nations of the earth are gathered against it.**" (Zechariah 12:2-3) It would obviously be impossible to **"lay siege against Judah and Jerusalem"** unless Judah, that is, the Jewish nation, was in Jerusalem.

These, and other scriptures, made it very plain that Judah, that is, the Jews, would be in the land in the end times. As all Jews had been expelled from the land by a decree of the Roman Emperor Hadrian sometime around A.D. 130, and had never returned in any significant numbers, these prophecies could not be fulfilled until they had returned to the land and to the city. Because of this, students of Bible prophecy have always known that the Jews would return to their ancient homeland. This was explicitly stated in a "Commentary on Daniel" written by Hippolytus, which is thought to have been published between the years 202 and 211 A.D. This is the very oldest Christian commentary on scripture that has survived to the present day. (See "Ancient Dispensational Truth," by James C. Morris, pp 51-52.) This was also explicitly taught in the early 1700s by William Lowth, in the most widely circulated series of Bible commentaries of the 1700s. (See pp. 126-129 of the same volume.)

Simultaneous attacks from Egypt and Assyria are mentioned in Isaiah 7 and Daniel 11. Ancient Assyria was the northern half of present day Iraq, And present day Mosul, the center of Islamic extremism in that area, and the home of the world's largest surviving community of "Assyrians," is at the site of ancient Nineveh, the ancient capitol of Assyria. And the book of Nahum says that the **"king of Assyria"** (Nahum 3:18) will rise out of **"Nineveh."** (Nahum 1:1 and 11)

And Ezekiel 38 and 39 detail a great end time attack on Israel, led by Russia, and joined by many other nations, including Persia, (which is now called Iran) Ethiopia, and Libya. And all know the interest Russia has been showing in this region for the last 50 or so years.

Again, the nations surrounding Israel are filled with murderous hatred against the Jews, even to the point of desiring to annihilate them. This was explicitly stated in many end time prophe-

THOUGHTS ABOUT PROPHETIC SUBJECTS

cies of the Bible. One of the places where these nations are explicitly named in Psalm 83, where we read:

> "**They have taken crafty counsel against Your people,**
> **And consulted together against Your sheltered ones.**
> **They have said, 'Come, and let us cut them off from being a nation,**
> **That the name of Israel may be remembered no more.'**
> **For they have consulted together with one consent;**
> **They form a confederacy against You:**
> **The tents of Edom and the Ishmaelites;**
> **Moab and the Hagrites;**
> **Gebal, Ammon, and Amalek;**
> **Philistia with the inhabitants of Tyre;**
> **Assyria also has joined with them;**
> **They have helped the children of Lot.**" (Psalm 83:3-8)

It is well known that ancient **"Edom"** occupied the southern part of modern Jordan and the northeastern part of modern Saudi Arabia, and that **"the Ishmaelites"** occupied other parts of modern Saudi Arabia. And it is thought that **"Amalek"** and **"the children of Lot"** also lived in the northern parts of modern Saudi Arabia. It is also well known that ancient **"Moab"** lived in the central part of modern Jordan, and that the ancient nation of **"Ammon"** lived in the northern part of modern Jordan. Today's Palestinians proudly declare themselves to be ancient **"Philistia.** And, of course, it is well known that ancient **"Assyria"** was the northern part of today's Iraq. **"Tyre,"** being a city, is still exactly where it has always been. And this leaves only **"the Hagarites"** and **"Gebal"** whose modern identities are unknown today. These are the nations from which attacks against modern Israel are being continually launched. And of course, even though the governments of some of these nations are officially at peace with Israel, their people are not.

And finally, we need to examine the third class of these prophecies. Things that are specifically prophesied to take place in the end times, which, although they have not yet happened, have recently become obviously possible as events that are very likely to happen in the near future.

The first of these is that until our generation a war that would literally kill everyone, and everything, was unthinkable. But today it is common knowledge that an all out nuclear exchange would eradicate life on this planet. There can be no reasonable doubt that our Lord was referring to this threat when, in speaking about the time we call "the tribulation," He said that **"unless those days were shortened, no flesh would be saved."** (Matthew 24:22) But He also added the words **"but for the elect's sake those days will be shortened."** We can therefore safely conclude that the threat of nuclear annihilation is indeed real. In fact, it would definitely happen if our Lord did not step in. But He has promised to step in before it goes that far. The all out nuclear exchange that would end all life on this planet will not take place. But this does not mean there will not be a limited nuclear exchange.

Again, we are plainly taught that ten nations will unite to re-establish the Roman Empire. And we all know that today there is a movement toward a united Europe. (The European Common Market is not the union described in Bible prophecy, but is a move in that direction.)

Again, Revelation 9 speaks of an army of two hundred million men that will come from beyond the Euphrates river. And Red China has boasted that it can field this number of men at any time.

And yet again, we remember that the seventieth week of Daniel's prophecy of the seventy weeks will begin with the confirmation of **"a covenant with many for one week."** (Daniel 9:27) That is, there will be a temporary treaty confirmed for a

THOUGHTS ABOUT PROPHETIC SUBJECTS

period of seven years. And the concept of a temporary treaty "to allow things to stabilize" was introduced into international politics in the early 1990s in an attempt to bring an end the ethnic fighting in the former Yugoslavia. So we can easily conceive of such a seven year treaty being proposed in the near future as a solution to the fighting in the middle east.

But finally, and perhaps the most chilling of all these developments that we can see on the horizon, we are explicitly told that the second **"beast"** of Revelation 13 will cause **"all, both small and great, rich and poor, free and slave, to receive a mark on their right hand or on their foreheads, [17] and that no one may buy or sell except one who has the mark or the name of the beast, or the number of his name."** (Revelation 13:16b-17) And the world banking system is working hard toward bringing about what they call the "cashless society," in which all monies are reduced to simply credits in banks. This is being advocated as a way to eliminate the theft of money, because there will simply be no money to steal. But they point out that it would still be possible to steal the credit or debit cards that are currently used to access the banking system. So they propose replacing these cards with a tattoo, made in ink that is invisible to the naked eye, but which can be read by the scanners that have already been installed almost everywhere. And their proposed location for that tattoo is on a person's right hand, or, if that has been maimed, on their forehead! So if they are successful in their attempts to put this system into place, this will not be a matter of making a *law* that no one is *allowed* to buy of sell without the mark, but of making it *physically impossible* to buy or sell *anything* without the mark.

When we realize that all of these details of Bible prophecy have either actually come to pass or have become obvious near term possibilities within the lifetimes of the older people among us, we realize that **"the time of the end"** is indeed beginning to come to pass, and thus that the Lord's coming is indeed very near.

How this should affect the hearts and minds of **"all who have loved His appearing."** (1 Timothy 4:8) For **"we know that when He is revealed, we shall be like Him, for we shall see Him as He is. And everyone who has this hope in Him purifies himself, just as He is pure."** (1 John 3:2-3) And **"He who testifies to these things says, 'Surely I am coming quickly.' Amen. Even so, come, Lord Jesus!"** (Revelation 22:20)

THOUGHTS ABOUT PROPHETIC SUBJECTS

The Rapture of the Church

For Christians of the present time, all other prophetic events pale into nothingness beside this one great event, which the scriptures speak of in numerous places. Jesus spoke of it, saying, **"I go to prepare a place for you. And if I go and prepare a place for you, I will come again and receive you to Myself; that where I am,** *there* **you may be also."** (John 14:2-3) But we also read, **"that He may establish your hearts blameless in holiness before our God and Father at the coming of our Lord Jesus Christ with all His saints."** (1 Thessalonians 3:13)

In the first passage above our Lord says **"I will come again and receive you to Myself."** The second one speaks of **"the coming of our Lord Jesus Christ with all His saints."** It is obvious that His coming to receive us to Himself has to take place before His coming **"with all His saints."** The words used by the Holy Spirit do not allow any other conclusion. But how long before **"the coming of our Lord Jesus Christ with all His saints,"** will He **"come again and receive"** us to Himself?

The answer to this question begins with the promise, **"Because you have kept My command to persevere, I also will keep you from the hour of trial which shall come upon the whole world, to test those who dwell on the earth."** (Revelation 3:10)

The Greek word translated *from* in this verse is εκ, *ek* in our alphabet, word number 1537 in Strong's Greek Dictionary. This Greek word indeed means *from*, but in the sense of *away from* or *out of*. Some imagine that this only means *out of* the **"hour of trial"** after having been *in* it. But in this phrase, that interpretation is excluded by the word **"keep."** In the Greek, this word is τηρησσω, *teresso* in our alphabet, a future form of the Greek word τηρηο, *tereo* in our alphabet, word number 5083 in Strong's Greek Dictionary. This Greek word literally means *to guard*, but in the scriptures was usually used in the sense of our English word *keep*, and is so translated more than two-thirds of the times it occurs in the Greek text of the New Testament. So it is clear that the real meaning of this promise is to be *kept out of* "**the hour of trial.**" [13]

But what is this "**the hour of trial**" that they will be *kept out of*? The Greek word translated "**hour**" in this passage is ωρας, *horas* in our alphabet, a genitive singular form of the Greek word ωρα, *hora* in our alphabet, word number 5610 in Strong's Greek Dictionary. This Greek word literally means "**hour**," but is often used figuratively for a short period of time. As our Lord told

---

13. To really understand this, we need to consider another promise made concerning a similar time period. The Lord said to Israel, "**Ask now, and see, Whether a man is ever in labor with child? So why do I see every man *with* his hands on his loins Like a woman in labor, And all faces turned pale? Alas! For that day is great, So that none is like it; And it *is* the time of Jacob's trouble, But he shall be saved out of it.**" (Jeremiah 30:6-7) In this case, the Hebrew word translated *saved* is יושע, *yvsha* in our alphabet, which is an imperfect form of ישע, *yasha'* in our alphabet, word number 3467 in Strong's Hebrew Dictionary. This Hebrew word means *saved* in the sense of *succor*. In the KJV, this Hebrew word is rendered *save* 149 times, *deliver* 13 times, *help* 12 times, and once as *rescue*. We notice this to clearly understand that this Hebrew word carries an entirely different sense from the Greek word *tereo* used in Revelation 3:10. In one case, the Lord promised to help some of His own get through their designated time of trouble. In the other, He promised to keep others of His own out of a time of testing designed for others.

It is also significant to consider a third group mentioned concerning this period. In Revelation 7:9, John saw "**a great multitude which no one could number, of all nations, tribes, peoples, and tongues, standing before the throne and before the Lamb.**" Then, a few verses later, we read, "**Then one of the elders answered, saying to me, 'Who are these arrayed in white robes, and where did they come from?' And I said to him, 'Sir, you know.' So he said to me, 'These are the ones who come out of the great tribulation, and washed their robes and made them white in the blood of the Lamb.'**" (Revelation 7:13-14) Here the words "**come out of**" are a translation of the Greek word ερχομενοι εκ. The Greek word ερχομενοι, *erchomenoi* in our alphabet, is a present form of the Greek word ερχομαι, *erchomai* in out alphabet, word number 2064 in Strong's Greek Dictionary, which means to come or go, in a great variety of applications. And we have already seen the meaning of the Greek word εκ. So one group is promised that "**I will keep you**" (out of) "**the hour of trial.**" A second group was promised to be helped "**out of**" "**the time of Jacob's trouble.**" And a third group will "**come out of the great tribulation.**" Only the last two groups will go through this time.

those that came to arrest Him in the garden, "**this is your hour, and the power of darkness.**" (Luke 22:53) And as He had told His own a few hours earlier, "**Now My soul is troubled, and what shall I say? 'Father, save Me from this hour'? But for this purpose I came to this hour.**" (John 12:27)

But what **hour** are they promised to be *kept out of?* It is not just some general period of time. It is a specific one. It is "**the hour of trial.**" It is specifically called "**the hour,**" for the word "**the**" is in the Greek text, as the word της, *tes* in our alphabet. This is a genitive singular form of the Greek word ὁ, *ho* in our alphabet, [14] word number 3588 in Strong's Greek Dictionary, which literally means "**the.**" But what "**hour of trial**" is this specific time that they are they promised to be *kept out of?* It is "**the hour of trial which shall come upon the whole world, to test those who dwell on the earth.**"

There is a specific "**hour of trial**" coming "**to test those who dwell on the earth.**" When we see the reason this hour is coming we understand the term "**hour of trial.**" For the Greek word translated "**to test**" here is πειρασαι, *peirasai* in our alphabet. This is an infinitive form of the Greek word πειραξο, *peirazo* in our alphabet. This is word number 3985 in Strong's Greek Dictionary, and in the infinitive mood, it literally means exactly as it is translated, "**to test.**" So we see that this scripture explicitly tells us that there is a particular time of testing coming, and that the purpose of that time is "**to test those who dwell on the earth.**" Its purpose is not "**to test**" the saints of God, but "**those who dwell on the earth.**" This is a moral class, those whose hearts are on the earth, rather than on heaven. This moral class of people is mentioned in these words eight times in the Revelation, [15] and always negatively.

---

14. Unlike English, in both Biblical Greek and Hebrew, definite articles are *normally* used only for stress. If the word "the" is in the original text of any part of the Bible, it means the thing being referred to is a particular thing, not just something in general.

15. See Revelation 3:10, 11:10, 13:8, 13:12, 13:14 (twice) 14:6 and 17:8 Also see "**inhabitants of the earth**" in Revelation 12:12.

But we are also told where this time of testing will come. It **"shall come upon the whole world."** The Greek word translated **"whole"** in this clause is ολης, *holes* in our alphabet, a singular form of the Greek word ολος, *holos* in our alphabet, word number 3650 in Strong's Greek Dictionary. This Greek word literally means **"whole,"** or *all,* that is, *complete.* That is, there is no part of the world that will be exempted from this time of testing. So there is coming a specific time of testing, and it is coming **"upon the whole world."** But the Lord's own are promised that they will be *kept out of* that time of testing. Now if this time is coming upon the whole world, but the Lord's own will be *kept out of* it, they cannot be in the world during that time of testing. Thus we see that Revelation 3:10 tells us that the Lord's own will be removed from the earth before this time of testing begins.

We see this again in a passage about Noah and Lot. **"For if God did not spare the angels who sinned, but cast them down to hell and delivered them into chains of darkness, to be reserved for judgment; and did not spare the ancient world, but saved Noah, one of eight people, a preacher of righteousness, bringing in the flood on the world of the ungodly; and turning the cities of Sodom and Gomorrah into ashes, condemned them to destruction, making them an example to those who afterward would live ungodly; and delivered righteous Lot, who was oppressed by the filthy conduct of the wicked (for that righteous man, dwelling among them, tormented his righteous soul from day to day by seeing and hearing their lawless deeds)—*then* the Lord knows how to deliver the godly out of temptations and to reserve the unjust under punishment for the day of judgment."** (2 Peter 2:4-9)

Here the Holy Spirit gives us two specific examples, **"Noah"** and **"Lot,"** both of whom were physically removed from the scene of judgment before it took place. Then, in the context of these two examples, He said, **"*then* the Lord knows how to deliver the godly out of temptations and to reserve the unjust under punishment for the day of judgment."** (2 Peter 2:9)

Thus the Holy Spirit showed His intention to **"deliver the godly out of temptations"** by physically removing them from the scene **"of temptations"** before these **"temptations"** take place, just as He did for **"Noah"** and **"Lot."** The Greek word here translated **"out of"** is the same *ek*, that we saw translated as **"from"** in Revelation 3:10, whose normal meaning is *from* in the sense of *away from* or *out of*, and the Greek word translated **"temptations"** is *peirasmou*, the singular form of the *peirasmon* that we saw in Revelation 3:10 This Greek word does not mean, or even imply, trouble, but literally means *testing*. There are no accidents in the precise wording of scripture. The fact that the Holy Spirit used these same two Greek words in these two parallel passages is highly significant.

Again, we read of the coming of **"the man of sin."** The Holy Spirit said **"And now you know what is restraining, that he may be revealed in his own time. For the mystery of lawlessness is already at work; only He who now restrains *will do so* until He is taken out of the way. And then the lawless one will be revealed, whom the Lord will consume with the breath of His mouth and destroy with the brightness of His coming."** (2 Thessalonians 2:6-8) In this scripture the Holy Spirit said **"you know what is restraining."** He did not say "you should know," or "you ought to know." He said **"you know."** This makes it plain that he was speaking of Himself. No other possible restrainer could be so obvious He did not need to be named.

We are told that **"He who now restrains *will do so* until He is taken out of the way."** How can this be, when Jesus said, **"I will pray the Father, and He will give you another Helper, that He may abide with you forever—the Spirit of truth, whom the world cannot receive, because it neither sees**

Him nor knows Him; but you know Him, for He dwells with you and will be in you." (John 14:16-17) One scripture tells us "**the Spirit of truth**"is given "**that He may abide with you forever.**" The other says that **He** will be "**taken out of the way.**" How can one who will "**abide with you forever**" be "**taken out of the way?**"

We read in 1 Thessalonians 4:16-17 that "**the Lord Himself will descend from heaven with a shout, with the voice of an archangel, and with the trumpet of God. And the dead in Christ will rise first. Then we who are alive *and* remain shall be caught up together with them in the clouds to meet the Lord in the air. And thus we shall always be with the Lord.**" The Holy Spirit, "**the Spirit of truth,**"is truly given "**that He may abide with you forever.**" But Jesus, "**the Lord Himself,**" will also "**descend from heaven**" and catch us up "**to meet the Lord in the air. And thus we shall always be with the Lord.**"

This event has to be the time when the Holy Spirit is "**taken out of the way.**" This is because the saints of God will be removed from this earth, yet the Holy Spirit will be with them forever. It is therefore plain that the Holy Spirit will be "**taken out of the way**" at the same time the saints of God will be "**caught up... in the clouds to meet the Lord in the air.**" But it is only after that happens that "**the lawless one will be revealed.**" For we remember that "**the mystery of lawlessness is already at work; only He who now restrains *will do so* until He is taken out of the way. And then the lawless one will be revealed.**" (2 Thessalonians 2:6-8) So this scripture, which shows that the Holy Spirit will be "**taken out of the way**" before the Antichrist, "**the lawless one,**" will be revealed thereby shows that the rapture has to take place before that time.

We see this again in the parable of the ten virgins, where we read that "**the bridegroom came, and those who were ready** went in with him to the wedding; and the door was shut. Afterward the other virgins came also, saying, 'Lord, Lord, open to us!' But he answered and said, 'Assuredly, I say to you, I do not know you.'"** (Matthew 25:10-12) here we plainly see **"those who were ready"** taken into **"the wedding,"** while **"the other virgins"** are held outside a door that remains closed in spite of their pleading. The fact that the door remains closed for those that were not **"ready"** is highlighted in 2 Thessalonians 2:10-12, where we are told that **"they did not receive the love of the truth, that they might be saved. And for this reason God will send them strong delusion, that they should believe the lie, that they all may be condemned who did not believe the truth but had pleasure in unrighteousness."** But we need to remember that this is after **"those who were ready went in with him to the wedding."** That is, after the rapture.

This is again highlighted in Revelation 19, where we read of the marriage of the Lamb taking place in heaven, **" 'Let us be glad and rejoice and give Him glory, for the marriage of the Lamb has come, and His wife has made herself ready.' And to her it was granted to be arrayed in fine linen, clean and bright, for the fine linen is the righteous acts of the saints. Then he said to me, 'Write: "Blessed *are* those who are called to the marriage supper of the Lamb!" ' And he said to me, 'These are the true sayings of God.' "** (Revelation 19:7-9)

We need to notice that, in the order of the events described in Revelation 19, this comes immediately after the celebration in verses 1-6 of the judgment of **"the great harlot,"** the false bride of Christ, and just before the Lord goes forth from heaven in verses 11-16 as the **"KING OF KINGS AND LORD OF LORDS,"** followed by the armies of heaven, which are **"clothed in fine linen, white and clean."** (verse 14) But we had just been told (in verse 8) that **"the fine linen is the righteous acts of the saints."** This agrees perfectly with the statement from Matthew 25:10 that **"the bridegroom came, and those who were ready went in with him to the wedding." For "**the marriage of the Lamb**" could not take place in heaven until after "**His wife**" (Revelation 19:7) had arrived in heaven.

This is made even more plain in Luke 12:35-37, where we read, "**Let your waist be girded and** *your* **lamps burning; and you yourselves be like men who wait for their master, when he will return from the wedding, that when he comes and knocks they may open to him immediately. Blessed** *are* **those servants whom the master, when he comes, will find watching. Assuredly, I say to you that he will gird himself and have them sit down** *to eat,* **and will come and serve them.**" Here, we see that the "**master**" "**will return from the wedding.**" But He could not "**return from the wedding**" unless the wedding had already taken place before He returned. So this again shows that "**the marriage of the Lamb**" *has to* take place *before* the Lord comes as described in Luke 12.

But there is another reason for this understanding, found, not in the New Testament, but in the prophecies of the Old Testament. To understand this reason, we first need to notice Daniel 9:24, where we read:

"**Seventy weeks are determined**

For your people and for your holy city,

To finish the transgression,

To make an end of sins,

To make reconciliation for iniquity,

To bring in everlasting righteousness,

To seal up vision and prophecy,

And to anoint the Most Holy."

The next two verses describe sixty-nine of these "**weeks**" that will take place "**from the going forth of the command To restore and build Jerusalem Until Messiah the Prince.**"

(Daniel 9:25) Then in verse 27, we are explicitly told of a drastic event that will take place **"in the middle of the week."** This event divides the seventieth week into two half weeks, which are seen no less than six times in the prophetic scriptures. They are spoken of as **"a time, times, and half a time,"** (three and a half years) as **"forty-two months,"** (again, three and a half years) and as **"one thousand two hundred and sixty days,"** (exactly three and a half Hebrew years, which were composed of twelve months of thirty days each.) So his seventieth **"week"** is indeed a major theme of the prophetic scriptures, and has come to be generically called **"the tribulation."**

But who are these "seventy weeks **"determined For"**? We read that they are **"determined For your people and for your holy city."** These words were spoken to Daniel. And Daniel's **"people"** were unquestionably the Jews, and his **"holy city"** was unquestionably Jerusalem. So this seventieth week, which we generically call **"the tribulation,"** being one of the **"seventy weeks,"** was explicitly stated to be **"determined For"** the Jews and Jerusalem. This period, which is a central theme in Bible prophecy, was *not* **"determined For"** the church it was **"determined For"** the Jews and Jerusalem. And through the rest of the book of Daniel, as throughout the writings of the three major prophets that preceded him and the twelve minor prophets that came after him, the church is never mentioned, even once. And the same thing is seen in the book of Revelation. The period we generically call "the tribulation, along with its preparatory period, fills the book of Revelation from the end of chapter four until the beginning of chapter 20. And throughout this large block of Bible prophecy, the church is never mentioned, even once.

When we consider Daniel 9:24, we realize *why* the church is never mentioned in any of these many prophecies. It is because this period is not **"determined For"** the church. It is **"determined For"** the Jews and Jerusalem. And that is why the church is removed before this period begins. The purpose of this removal is not, as many imagine, to protect the church from persecution. It is because the central purpose of the seventieth **"week"** has nothing to do with the church. It is directed toward a different group. And that group is the Jews and Jerusalem, not the church.

Finally, in Revelation 4:4 we read, **"Around the throne *were* twenty-four thrones, and on the thrones I saw twenty-four elders sitting, clothed in white robes; and they had crowns of gold on their heads."** As there were twelve tribes in Israel and twelve apostles, this seems to indicate the presence of all the Old Testament and New Testament saints of God already in heaven before the beginning of the seal and trumpet visions of Revelation six through nine. And thus, it appears to indicate that the rapture will taken place before anything symbolized in those visions will take place.

Almost all objections to this conclusion are based on a rank assumption that our Lord will only return one time. No scripture *says* this, but they interpret numerous scriptures to *mean* it. The error of ths rank assumption is treated in the article titled **"A Scriptural Precedent."**

But there is one argument against this conclusion that we need to treat here. Many wrest the central message of 1 Thessalonians 4:16-17, where we read, **"For the Lord Himself will descend from heaven with a shout, with the voice of an archangel, and with the trumpet of God. And the dead in Christ will rise first. Then we who are alive and remain shall be caught up together with them in the clouds to meet the Lord in the air. And thus we shall always be with the Lord."** These people claim that the Greek word απαντησιν, *apantesin* in our alphabet, (a form of word number 529 in Strong's Greek Dictionary) which is translated **"to meet"** in this passage, referred to a formal reception in which people went out to greet a coming dignitary and escort him back into the city. But this claim about the meaning of this Greek word, although widely circulated among modern theologians, is incorrect. Its error is demonstrated at length in the article titled "**A Widely Circulated Error About the Greek Word *Apantesis* and the Pre-tribulation Rapture.**"

Further, this interpretation cannot be correct because, as we noted earlier, in John 14:2-3, we read, "**In my Father's house are many mansions: if *it were* not *so*, I would have told you. I go to prepare a place for you. And if I go and prepare a place for you, I will come again, and receive you unto myself; that where I am, *there* ye may be also.**" In this scripture, our Lord first refers to His Father's house, saying "**In my Father's house are many mansions.**" He then says that he is going "**to prepare a place for you.**" From this statement it is plain that the place to which He was going "**to prepare a place for you**" was His "**Father's house.**" So He said He was going to His "**Father's house,**" "**to prepare a place for you.**" So His "**Father's house**" is where He will "**prepare a place for you.**" And, as that is where He has prepared "**a place for**" us, it is where He take us when He "**will come again, and receive you unto**" Himself. "**That where I am, *there* ye may be also.**" This scripture does not present a picture of coming, picking us up along the way, and taking us with Himself to another place. It presents a picture of coming to get us and taking us back to where he came from, that is, His "**Father's house.**" That is where He has gone "**to prepare a place for**" us. That is where He is, and that is where he will take us, for the stated purpose of this coming is "**that where I am, *there* you may be also.**"

Itemized Proof that the Rapture Will Be Before the Tribulation

1. Many insist that the Bible clearly teaches that the Lord will only return one time, But no passage in the entire Bible says that. It is true that the New Testament only uses the singular in speaking of the Lord's future coming. But that is EXACTLY what the Old Testament did in speaking of His coming. It ALWAYS spoke of His coming in the singular, even though the New Testament EXPLICITLY says He will come again. So the fact that the New Testament does the same thing, in only speaking of His return in the singular does NOT indicate that He will only return one time.

2. John 14:2-3 clearly teaches that when the Lord comes again, He will take us to His **"Father's house,"** which obviously means heaven. So this cannot mean He picks us up as He descends from heaven to judge the wicked, as many imagine He will do.

3. Matthew 25:1-12 clearly teaches that when the Lord comes as **"the Bridegroom,"** He will take us **"IN" "TO" "the wedding."**

4. Revelation 19:7-9 clearly describes **"the marriage of the Lamb"** taking place in heaven, just before Revelation 19:11-16 describes the Lord going forth from heaven as **"KING OF KINGS AND LORD OF LORDS,"** and **"clothed in a robe dipped in blood."**

5. Luke 12:35-40 explicitly states that the Lord **"will RETURN FROM the wedding,"** coming this time, not as **"the bridegroom,"** but as **"their Master."** This CANNOT take place at the same time He takes us **"IN" "TO" "the wedding."**

6. 1 Thessalonians 4:16-17 explicitly says that it will be **"the Lord himself"** that comes for us, and that we will be **"caught up," "to meet the Lord in the air."**

7. 1 Corinthians 15:51-52 explicitly says that this will take place **"in a moment, in the twinkling of an eye."**

8. Revelation 3:10 explicitly states that the Lord will **"keep"** the faithful "out of the hour of testing," (that is the literal meaning of the Greek words used) And it says that this "hour of testing" **"shall come upon the whole world,"** and that its purpose is **"to test those who dwell on the earth."**

9. 2 Peter 2:4-11 explicitly says that **"the Lord knows how to deliver the godly"** "out of testing." (Here EXACTLY the same Greek words are used as are used in Revelation 3:10, not only the same words, but even the same forms of those words.)

10. Isaiah 66:15-20 clearly teaches that Israel will be brought back **"to My holy mountain Jerusalem"** after the Lord comes **"with fire," "to render His anger with fury and His rebuke with flames of fire."** This gathering is clearly completely different from the rapture.

11. Micah 5:3 clearly teaches that the remnant of Israel will **"return"** when **"she who is in labor has given birth,"** which clearly means when the tribulation has ended.

12. Ezekiel 20:33-38 explicitly says that, as Israel returns, to **"the land of Israel,"** the Lord will deal with them **"face to face,"** which clearly indicates that He will be physically present at that time.

13. Jeremiah 16:14-16 says that, in bringing Israel **"back into the land which I gave to their fathers,"** the Lord will send **"fishermen"** and **"hunters,"** to **"hunt them from every mountain and every hill, and out of the holes of the rocks."** Such a mission would appear to require angelic powers.

14. "The church" is often called **"the elect"** and often referred to as either **"elect"** or **"chosen."** And it is called **"God's elect"**

in Romans 8:33 and Titus 1:1. But in the entire Bible, there is not even one passage that is unquestionably speaking about **"the church,"** where a pronoun is attached to the Hebrew or Greek word that is alternately translated as **"chosen"** or **"elect."** But "Israel" is called **"His chosen"** in 1 Chronicles 16:13, Psalm 105:6, and Psalm 105:43, and is called either **"My chosen"** or **"My elect"** in Isaiah 43:20, Isaiah 45:4, Isaiah 65:9, Isaiah 65:15, and Isaiah 65:22. So the fact that both Matthew 24:31 and Mark 13:27 mention the Lord sending **"angels"** to **"gather"** **"His elect"** indicates a gathering of **"Israel,"** not of **"the church."** For no other passage in the entire Bible applies this term to **"the church."** And, as we have noticed, the time of that coming is the time when **"Israel"** will be gathered, and we are clearly told that it will be **"the Lord himself"** who comes for us, and not mere **"angels,"** whose usage is implied in Jeremiah 16:14-16 and stated Matthew 24:31 and Mark 13:27.

15. 2 Thessalonians 2:1-8 says that **"the man of sin"** will be revealed before **"the day of Christ."** this seems to be a reference to the day that other scriptures call **"the day of the Lord."** That would probably explain why some ancient manuscripts (and some modern translations) read "the day of the Lord" in this verse, But this passage most certainly does NOT say that **"the man of sin"** will be revealed before **"our gathering together to Him."** That had been mentioned as part of what this passage is about. But is NOT stated as the day before which **"the man of sin"** will be revealed.

16. 2 Thessalonians 2:7-8 says that **"the mystery of lawlessness is already at work; only He who now restrains *will do so* until He is taken out of the way. And then the lawless one will be revealed."**

Some interpret the restrainer in this passage to be the Roman Empire. But **"the lawless one"** was not **"revealed"** when the Roman Empire was **"taken out of the way."** Some defend this notion by interpreting **"the lawless one"** to be Popery. But Popery was **"revealed"** before the Roman Empire was **"taken out of the way,"** not after it was **"taken out of the way."**

Some interpret the restrainer to be Michael the Archangel. But Daniel 12:1 explicitly says that the **"time of trouble"** is when Michael will **"stand up,"** not when he will be **"taken out of the way."**

Some interpret the restrainer to be the church. But, although the Greek text does not contain the word **"He,"** The Greek word translated **"restrains"** is in a masculine singular form. And the Greek words translated **"taken"** and **"way"** are both in singular forms. So the translators were most certainly correct in inserting the word **"He"** in both places where we find it in this verse, without putting it in italics. For the Greek text most certainly indicates that the restrainer is a masculine individual. And the church is a feminine assembly. So the restrained cannot be the church.

This leaves the Holy Spirit as the only alternative to be the restrainer. And in truth, the Holy Spirit is the only masculine individual that has the power to restrain evil on a worldwide basis. And as our Lord promised that the Holy Spirit would **"abide with you forever,"** (John 14:16-17) the time when **"He"** is **"taken out of the way"** has to be the time when the church is taken to the **"Father's house,"** (John 14:2-3,) and when **"the bridegroom"** takes **"those who were ready"** **"in with him to the wedding."** (Matthew 25:10) Thus we see that this scripture teaches that the rapture will take place before **"the lawless one will be revealed."**

Some have objected to this by pointing out that many will turn to the Lord during the tribulation period. So they reason that the Holy Spirit has to still be in the world. But they forget that many came to repentance and turned to the Lord before the Holy Spirit descended on the day of Pentecost. (Acts 2:1-4) So people can be converted without the Holy Spirit being present in the way He is here now.

A Scriptural Precedent

There were many prophecies that foretold the first coming of Jesus. These prophecies included not only where He would be born, but even when He would come. But the vast bulk of the Biblical scholars of Jesus' day totally missed most of these prophecies. They missed them because they concentrated on passages that spoke of Him as the glorious conquering Messiah, such as:

> **"Gird Your sword upon *Your* thigh,**
> **O Mighty One,**
> **With Your glory and Your majesty.**
> **And in Your majesty ride prosperously**
> **because of truth, humility, and righteousness;**
> **And Your right hand shall teach You awesome things.**
> **Your arrows *are* sharp in the heart of the King's enemies;**
> **The peoples fall under You."** (Psalm 45:3-5)

Even though they were aware of other passages that spoke of Him in a completely different light, they neglected ones like:

> **"He was oppressed and He was afflicted,**
> **Yet He opened not His mouth;**
> **He was led as a lamb to the slaughter,**
> **And as a sheep before its shearers is silent,**
> **So He opened not His mouth.**
> **He was taken from prison and from judgment,**
> **And who will declare His generation?**
> **For He was cut off from the land of the living;**

THOUGHTS ABOUT PROPHETIC SUBJECTS

For the transgressions of My people He was stricken." (Isaiah 53:7-8)

They should have considered the contrast between such passages. The Holy Spirit told us that the prophets who uttered them considered it, saying, **"Of this salvation the prophets have inquired and searched carefully, who prophesied of the grace *that would come* to you, searching what, or what manner of time, the Spirit of Christ who was in them was indicating when He testified beforehand the sufferings of Christ and the glories that would follow."** (1 Peter 1:10-11)

The ancient Jewish scholars loved the prophecies about Israel's future glory, so they were looking for a Messiah to fulfill those prophecies. But they neglected the equally important prophecies about how their deliverer would suffer. So they failed to recognize their great Messiah when he arrived. Now that the suffering is over, and the rest of the Holy Scriptures have been given to us, we realize that these prophecies spoke of the same Messiah, but at different times.

Even so, many scholars of our own day neglect similar differences in various unfulfilled prophecies about our Lord's coming. Some of these prophecies speak of His coming as a wonderful thing, full of blessing. Others speak of it as a horrible thing, full of terror. Even as the ancient scholars missed the many differences between the prophecies about His suffering and those about His glory, many modern scholars miss similar differences between prophecies about His coming in blessing for His own, and prophecies about His coming in judgment on the wicked. Even as the earlier prophecies spoke of the same Messiah, but at different times, these unfulfilled prophecies also speak of the same Christ, but at different times.

Isaiah 13:9 describes **"the day of the Lord"** as **"Cruel, with both wrath and fierce anger."** Jeremiah 46:10 calls it **"A day of** vengeance, That He may avenge Himself on His adversaries." Joel 2:11 says that **"the day of the Lord *is* great and very terrible;"** adding, **"Who can endure it?"** Malachi 3:2 expands this by saying:

"But who can endure the day of His coming?

And who can stand when He appears?

For He *is* like a refiner's fire

And like launderers' soap."

And Amos 5:18-20 says:

"Woe to you who desire the day of the Lord!

For what good is the day of the Lord to you?

It *will* be darkness, and not light.

It *will* be as though a man fled from a lion,

And a bear met him!

Or *as though* he went into the house,

Leaned his hand on the wall,

And a serpent bit him!

Is not the day of the Lord darkness, and not light?

Is it not very dark, with no brightness in it?"

So we see that **"the day of the Lord"** is a **"cruel"** **"day of vengeance,"** a time so terrible that it can not be endured, that no one can stand when the Lord appears, and that there is **"no brightness"** in **"the day of the Lord."** This is reinforced by Joel 2:1-2, where we read:

"For the day of the LORD is coming,

For it is at hand:

A day of darkness and gloominess,

A day of clouds and thick darkness,

Like the morning clouds spread over the mountains."

THOUGHTS ABOUT PROPHETIC SUBJECTS

The statement, **"Woe to you who desire the day of the Lord"** (Amos 5:18) stands in stark contrast with the statement of 2 Timothy 4:8 that the Lord will give **"the crown of righteousness"** to all who **"have loved His appearing."** One scripture very clearly states God's displeasure with anyone desiring **"the day of the Lord,"** and another scripture just as clearly states his pleasure with those who **"have loved His appearing."** This, in and by itself, should show any serious student that these scriptures are speaking of two different events.

The first question in Malachi 3:2, **"who can endure the day of His coming?"** is radically different from the exhortation in 1 John 2:28, where we read, **"And now, little children, abide in Him, that when He appears, we may have confidence and not be ashamed before Him at His coming."** One scripture clearly shows that no one **"can endure the day of His coming,"** while another scripture just as clearly shows that it is possible to **"have confidence and not be ashamed before Him at His coming."** Again, these scriptures cannot be speaking of the same future event.

The second question in Malachi 3:2, **"who can stand when He appears?"** is radically different from the exhortation in Luke 21:36 to **"Watch therefore, and pray always that you may be counted worthy to escape all these things that will come to pass, and to stand before the Son of Man."** As we noticed before, one scripture clearly shows that no one **"can stand when He appears,"** while another tells us to **"pray that you may be counted worthy... to stand before the Son of Man."** Are we to imagine that our God exhorted us to pray for something that could not happen? Or do we realize that these two scriptures refer to two different future events.

Again, we have noticed that Joel 2:2 says that **"the day of the Lord"** is **"A day of darkness and gloominess, A day of clouds and thick darkness,"** and Amos 5:20 says, **"Is not the day of the Lord darkness, and not light? *Is it not* **very dark, with no brightness in it?"** These stand in stark contrast to the exhortation in Titus 2:13 that we should be **"looking for the blessed hope and glorious appearing of our great God and Savior Jesus Christ."** One scripture very clearly teaches that the gloominess of **"the day of the Lord"** will be so dark that there will be **"no brightness in it."** While another scripture says his **"glorious appearing"** is our **"blessed hope."** These scriptures cannot be describing the same event.

But these contrasts are not the only differences between the unfulfilled prophecies about our Lord's coming. There are also significant differences in the details contained in these prophecies. The best known of these is that Jesus said, **"Watch therefore, for you know neither the day nor the hour in which the Son of Man is coming."** (Matthew 25:13) He also said **"But of that day and hour no one knows, not even the angels in heaven, nor the Son, but only the Father."** (Mark 13:32) But in Daniel 12:9 we read, **"Then I said, 'My lord, what** *shall be* **the end of these** *things?'"* In answer, the prophet was told in Daniel 12:11 that **"from the time** *that* **the daily** *sacrifice* **is taken away, and the abomination of desolation is set up,** *there shall be* **one thousand two hundred and ninety days."** Now these are diametrically opposed concepts. Even the Lord Jesus Himself (speaking as a man) did not know the day or the hour of His coming. But even as a man He already had the scripture which specifically stated that He would come **"one thousand two hundred and ninety days"** after **"the time** *that* **the daily** *sacrifice* **is taken away, and the abomination of desolation is set up."** Thus we see that these two scriptures speak of different events that take place at different times.

The coming of the Lord in blessing for His own is described in the following words: **"For the Lord Himself will descend from heaven with a shout, with the voice of an archangel, and** with the trumpet of God. And the dead in Christ will rise first. Then we who are alive *and* remain shall be caught up together with them in the clouds to meet the Lord in the air. And thus we shall always be with the Lord. Therefore comfort one another with these words." (1 Thessalonians 4:16-18)

Although 1 Thessalonians 4:16 plainly says that it is "**the Lord Himself**" who will come for us, Matthew 24:31 just as plainly says that "**He will send His angels with a great sound of a trumpet, and they will gather together His elect from the four winds, from one end of heaven to the other.**" In one case, "**we**" are "**caught up**" by "**the Lord Himself**" and in the other "**His elect.**" are gathered by "**His angels.**"

To understand the significance of this contrast we need to look at Exodus 33, where we read in verses 1-4 that "**the LORD said to Moses, 'Depart and go up from here, you and the people whom you have brought out of the land of Egypt, to the land of which I swore to Abraham, Isaac, and Jacob, saying, "To your descendants I will give it." And I will send My Angel before you, and I will drive out the Canaanite and the Amorite and the Hittite and the Perizzite and the Hivite and the Jebusite. Go up to a land flowing with milk and honey; for I will not go up in your midst, lest I consume you on the way, for you are a stiff-necked people.' And when the people heard this bad news, they mourned, and no one put on his ornaments.**" But in verses 12-17 we read, "**Then Moses said to the LORD, 'See, You say to me, "Bring up this people." But You have not let me know whom You will send with me. Yet You have said, "I know you by name, and you have also found grace in My sight." Now therefore, I pray, if I have found grace in Your sight, show me now Your way, that I may know You and that I may find grace in Your sight. And consider that this nation is Your people." And He said, 'My Presence will go with you, and I will give you rest.' Then** he said to Him, 'If Your Presence does not go with us, do not bring us up from here. For how then will it be known that Your people and I have found grace in Your sight, except You go with us? So we shall be separate, Your people and I, from all the people who are upon the face of the earth.' So the LORD said to Moses, 'I will also do this thing that you have spoken; for you have found grace in My sight, and I know you by name.'"

Thus we see that the scriptures plainly show us that there is a significant difference between the presence of the Lord Himself and that of only a mere angel. But one scripture about the future plainly teaches that **"we"** will be **"caught up"** by **"the Lord Himself"** and another says **"His elect"** are gathered by **"His angels."** Again, these scriptures cannot be speaking of the same event.

Again, 1 Thessalonians 4:17 plainly states that when our Lord comes for us we **"shall be caught up together with them in the clouds to meet the Lord in the air."** But when he comes in judgment on the wicked **"His feet will stand on the Mount of Olives."** (Zechariah 14:4) In the first case, He meets His own **"in the air."** But in the second case we are expressly told that **"His feet will stand on the Mount of Olives."** Meeting us **"In the air"** is significantly different from standing **"on the Mount of Olives."**

Again, Revelation 1:7 says,**"Behold, He is coming with clouds, and every eye will see Him, even they who pierced Him. And all the tribes of the earth will mourn because of Him. Even so, Amen."** But 1 Corinthians 15:51-52 says, **"Behold, I tell you a mystery: We shall not all sleep, but we shall all be changed—in a moment, in the twinkling of an eye, at the last trumpet. For the trumpet will sound, and the dead will be raised incorruptible, and we shall be changed."** There is no way that **"every eye"** could see something that will take place **"in a moment, in the twinkling of an eye."**

THOUGHTS ABOUT PROPHETIC SUBJECTS

All these are indeed material differences between various unfulfilled prophecies about our Lord's coming But there are two that overshadow all the rest of them. These two differences are both so radical that the two different statements could not even possibly describe events that will take place at the same time. These two radical differences are between the parable of the ten virgins (Matthew 25:1-12) and two other passages of scripture.

First, we read in Matthew 25:10 that **"the bridegroom came, and those who were ready went in with him to the wedding."** Here, we need to notice that this is a specific statement that as **"the bridegroom,"** the Lord will take **"those who were ready" "in" "to" "the wedding."** But in Luke 12:35-36, the Lord said: **"Let your waist be girded and *your* lamps burning; and you yourselves be like men who wait for their master, when he will return from the wedding, that when he comes and knocks they may open to him immediately."** Here, we need to notice that, as opposed to His statement in Matthew 25:10 that He would take **"those who were ready" "in" "to" "the wedding,"** here, in ths scripture, He just as clearly said that, as the **"master,"** He **"will return from the wedding."** Now it is physically impossible to go **"in" "to" "the wedding"** and to **"return from the wedding"** at the same time. [16] So a comparison of these two scriptures makes it absolutely unquestionable that Jesus Himself was clearly saying that He would come more than just one time.

---

16. In each of these cases, the Greek text includes the definite article **"the,"** indicating that it is speaking about a specific wedding, not just about *"a"* wedding. In Matthew 25:10, **"those who were ready went" "with him"** εις τους γαμους, *eis tous gamos* in our alphabet. These three Greek words translate literally as **"into the wedding."** But in Luke 12 36, **"their master" "will return"** εκ των γαμων, *ek ton gamon* in our alphabet. These Greek words translate literally as **"from the wedding."** (The differences in spellings in these two phrases are due to the words **"the wedding"** being different parts of speech in the two sentences.) So both of these two phrases plainly refer to **"the wedding"** which in Revelation 19:7 Is called **"the marriage of the Lamb,"** and is also **"the wedding"** arranged by **"the king"** for **"his Son"** in the parable of Matthew 22:2-13.

And second, we read that **"the bridegroom came, and those who were ready went in with him to the wedding; and the door was shut. Afterward the other virgins came also, saying, 'Lord, Lord, open to us!' But he answered and said, 'Assuredly, I say to you, I do not know you.'"** (Matthew 25:10-12) here we plainly see the righteous taken into the Lord's presence while the wicked are left outside a door that remains closed in spite of their pleading. But that is not all that we see here. The word **"afterward"** in this parable indicates a delay between the time when **"they that were ready went in with him"** and the time when **"other virgins came also."** This is significant because it indicates that the **"other virgins"** were still outside *after* the time when **"they that were ready went in with him."**

But in the parable of the wheat and the tares (Matthew 13:24-30) we read that at the time of harvest the owner of the field will say, **"First gather together the tares and bind them in bundles to burn them, but gather the wheat into my barn."** (Matthew 13:30) The word **"first"** in this command clearly indicates that the wicked are to be gathered *before* the righteous. Now this order of events is exactly the opposite of the order indicated in Matthew 25. (And yes, the words **"afterward"** and **"first"** are in the Greek text of these two parables.) The contrast between these orders of action clearly shows that the two parables are speaking of two different events that take place at different times.

Again, in the explanation of the parable of the wheat and the tares, (Matthew 13:37-43) Jesus said this meant that **"The Son of Man will send out His angels, and they will gather out of His kingdom all things that offend, and those who practice lawlessness, and will cast them into the furnace of fire. There will be wailing and gnashing of teeth. Then the righteous will shine forth as the sun in the kingdom of their Father. "** (Matthew 13:41-43) He then added that **"Again, the kingdom of heaven is like a dragnet that was cast into the** sea and gathered some of every kind, which, when it was full, they drew to shore; and they sat down and gathered the good into vessels, but threw the bad away. So it will be at the end of the age. The angels will come forth, separate the wicked from among the just, and cast them into the furnace of fire. There will be wailing and gnashing of teeth." (Matthew 13:47-50)

This is again radically different from the scene presented in Matthew 25. In Matthew 13, the unrighteous are taken **"from among the just."** In Matthew 25, the just are taken from among the unrighteous. In Matthew 13, the wicked are removed and cast into the fire. In Matthew 25, the wicked are left where they are, but are given no further chance to repent.

This fact that they are given no further chance to repent is stressed in 2 Thessalonians 2:9-12, where we read that **"The coming of the *lawless one* is according to the working of Satan, with all power, signs, and lying wonders, and with all unrighteous deception among those who perish, because they did not receive the love of the truth, that they might be saved. And for this reason God will send them strong delusion, that they should believe the lie, that they all may be condemned who did not believe the truth but had pleasure in unrighteousness."** The reason for this is distinctly stated. God will do this as a punishment **"because they did not receive the love of the truth,"** that is, because they did not *wish* to know the truth. This awful punishment is because, instead of receiving the truth, they **"had pleasure in unrighteousness."**

Nor is this only stated in the New Testament. We also see it in the last chapter of Isaiah, where we read:

"Just as they have chosen their own ways,

And their soul delights in their abominations,

So will I choose their delusions,

And bring their fears on them;

> **Because, when I called, no one answered,**
> **When I spoke they did not hear;**
> **But they did evil before My eyes,**
> **And chose *that* in which I do not delight."**
> (Isaiah 66:3-4)

So the scriptures clearly teach that there is a time coming in which those who had previously rejected the gospel will have no more chance to repent. This is in perfect keeping with the statement of Matthew 25:10 that **"the door was shut"** after **"the bridegroom came, and those who were ready went in with him to the wedding."** It is also in perfect keeping with the statement of Matthew 25:11-12 that **"Afterward the other virgins came also, saying, 'Lord, Lord, open to us!' But he answered and said, 'Assuredly, I say to you, I do not know you.'"** This parable clearly shows that there will be those that seek a relationship with the bridegroom after He has come. But at that time it will be too late. 2 Thessalonians 2:9-12 clearly states that at that time, those that had previously rejected God's word will be turned over to believe **"the lie."** And Isaiah 66:3-4 just as clearly states that at that time God **"will choose their delusions."** The time being spoken of here is plainly the time we call the tribulation. But it takes place after **"the bridegroom came, and those who were ready went in with him to the wedding."**

Again we read in John 14:2-3, **"In my Father's house are many mansions: if *it were* not *so*, I would have told you. I go to prepare a place for you. And if I go and prepare a place for you, I will come again, and receive you unto myself; that where I am, *there* ye may be also."** But we also read in 1 Thessalonians 3:12-13, **"And may the Lord make you increase and abound in love to one another and to all, just as we *do* to you, so that He may establish your hearts blameless in ho-**

liness before our God and Father at the coming of our Lord Jesus Christ with all His saints."

In the first of these, our Lord says **"I will come again, and receive you to myself."** In the second, we read of **"the coming of our Lord Jesus Christ with all His saints."** In the first passage He comes to receive His own to Himself. In the second one He comes with them, for He comes **"with all His saints."** If He is going to come *for* His own and He is also going to come *with* them, He has to come *for* them before He can come *with* them. This is a simple matter of the meaning of words. No other interpretation is possible.

Again, in the order of events in Revelation 19, we see the marriage of the lamb taking place in heaven in verses 7-8, **"'Let us be glad and rejoice and give Him glory, for the marriage of the Lamb has come, and His wife has made herself ready.' And to her it was granted to be arrayed in fine linen, clean and bright, for the fine linen is the righteous acts of the saints."** Then, after that, we see the Lord going forth out of heaven as the mighty conqueror, followed by the armies of heaven in verses 11-16 **"Now I saw heaven opened, and behold, a white horse. And He who sat on him *was* called Faithful and True, and in righteousness He judges and makes war. His eyes *were* like a flame of fire, and on His head *were* many crowns. He had a name written that no one knew except Himself. He *was* clothed with a robe dipped in blood, and His name is called The Word of God. And the armies in heaven, clothed in fine linen, white and clean, followed Him on white horses. Now out of His mouth goes a sharp sword, that with it He should strike the nations. And He Himself will rule them with a rod of iron. He Himself treads the winepress of the fierceness and wrath of Almighty God. And He has on *His* robe and on His thigh a name written: KING OF KINGS AND LORD OF LORDS."** This sequence of events clearly shows the church, the bride of Christ, already in heaven before the Lord comes in power and glory to judge the world. But it does not just show that. It clearly shows the armies proceeding out of heaven with the Lord **"clothed in fine linen, white and clean."** But it had just told us, only six verses earlier, that **"the fine linen is the righteous acts of the saints."** These two things together show that the saints will already be in heaven before the Lord comes to judge the world.

Now many produce various arguments to prove that this conclusion is incorrect. But almost every argument they produce is one that fails to take into account the marked differences between the scriptures about our Lord's coming in blessing to receive His own to Himself and his coming in vengeance to judge the world. Many insist that there is no such distinction. But as we have seen, there are many such distinctions, and that in some cases they are mutually exclusive. That is, that it is physically impossible for them to take place at the same time.

These distinctions allow no logical conclusion except that they indicate that the unfulfilled prophecies about the future coming of Christ follow the precedent established in the Old Testament scriptures, that of showing, even though not stating, that there would be more than one such future coming. And this understanding completely nullifies almost all arguments that can be offered against the doctrine that the church will be raptured before **"the hour of trial which shall come upon the whole world, to test those who dwell on the earth,"** (Revelation 3:10) that is, the seventieth **"week"** of Daniel's prophecy of the **"seventy weeks,"** (Daniel 9:24-27) the time that we call "the tribulation."

A Widely Circulated Error About the Greek Word Apantesis and the Pre-tribulation Rapture

One of the most precious promises in the Bible is 1 Thessalonians 4:16-17, where we read:

"For the Lord himself shall descend from heaven with a shout, with the voice of the archangel, and with the trump of God: and the dead in Christ shall rise first: Then we which are alive *and* remain shall be caught up together with them in the clouds, to meet the Lord in the air: and so shall we ever be with the Lord."

This well known event has come to be commonly called "the rapture."

For about ninety years now, many widely recognized experts have been claiming that the Greek word which is here translated *to meet*, does not simply mean *to meet*, as this phrase is commonly used. That Greek word is απαντησις, *apantesis* in our alphabet, word number 529 in Strong's Greek Dictionary, which occurs in this verse in a future passive form απαντησιν, *apantesin* in our alphabet. These people claim that, in the Greek language, this was a technical word referring specifically to an ancient Greek custom in which a formal reception was given to a visiting dignitary. In this custom, the locals went a short distance out of their city to meet a visiting dignitary and escort him back into the city. From this they reason that this passage does not teach that the Lord will come to get us and to take us back to heaven, but only that the

Lord will pick us up on the way down as He descends in power and glory to judge the wicked.

This idea comes from a paper published in 1930 by a German theologian named Erik Peterson. In that paper he quoted a number of examples from ancient Greek literature in which this word was used in describing formal receptions of a dignitary. The opponents of the doctrine of a rapture before **"the great tribulation"** immediately seized upon this with great elation, concluding that it was positive proof that the rapture would not take place until after **"the great tribulation."** But their elation was premature.

For, as Dispensationalists had rejected this as a wrested interpretation of scripture, in the early 1990s, Michael R. Cosby, of Sioux Falls College, set out to positively prove it was correct. To prove it, he did an exhaustive search of all the uses of any form of the Greek word *apantesis* in a huge data base of ancient Greek literature, which by then had been stored in computers. But to his horror, the proof that he found was exactly the opposite of what he had hoped to find. Being an honest researcher, he published his findings in a paper titled "Hellenistic Formal Receptions and Paul's Use of APANTHSIS in 1 Thessalonians 4:17," which he published in the "Bulletin for Biblical Research" 4 (1994) 15-34. In this paper he reported his distress upon finding that *apantesis* simply means *to meet*. So a systematic study of the usage of this Greek word in a large body of ancient Greek literature proved this claim to be completely incorrect.

But we do not have to rely upon his conclusions. For the "Concordance to the Septuagint," by Hatch and Redpath, lists sixty-eight places where some form of *apantesis* was used in that translation of the Old Testament and Apocrypha into Greek, which is believed to date from about 250 B.C.

In the studies below, we will use a parallel English - Greek version of the Septuagint made in 1851 by Sir Lancelot C. L. Brenton.

THOUGHTS ABOUT PROPHETIC SUBJECTS

This document is easily available online at: https://www.ellopos.net/elpenor/greek-texts/septuagint/. [17]

Of the sixty-eight places where the Septuagint uses some form of *apantesis*, twenty-five of them contain exactly the form of *apantesis* which is translated "**to meet**" in 1 Thessalonians 4:17. Anyone can easily check online and see that, in each of these twenty-five places, this Greek word απαντησιν, that is, *apantesin* in our alphabet, was clearly used.

The study presented below clearly demonstrates that the Greek word *apantesin* most assuredly does not have the technical meaning alleged for it, but simply means "*to meet*," as we commonly use this phrase. For only two of these twenty-five places could even possibly have had the technical meaning which its root form, *apantesis* is alleged to always have.

Of the twenty-five places where this Greek word was used in this online versions of the Septuagint:

1. *Apantesin* was used in the following two places to describe meeting someone, not to honor him, but to heap scorn upon his head:

"And David returned to bless his house. And Melchol the daughter of Saul came out to meet (*apantesin*) David and saluted him, and said, How was the king of Israel glorified to-day, who was to-day uncovered in the eyes of the handmaids of his servants, as one of the dancers wantonly uncovers himself!" (Kings 2 [Samuel 2] 6:20 LXX)

"And, behold, [there is] with thee Semei the son of Gera, a Benjamite of Baurim: and he cursed me with a grievous curse in the day when I went into the camp; and he came down to Jordan to meet (*apantesin*) me, and I swore to him by the Lord, saying, I will not put thee to death with the sword." (Kings 3 [Kings 1] 2:8 LXX)

---

17. This online version has some of the English text modernized from the forms used by Brenton

2. *Apantesin* was used in the following five places to describe a hostile meeting, as in battle:

"And it came to pass in those days that the Philistines gathered themselves together against Israel to war; and Israel went out to meet (*apantesin*) them and encamped at Abenezer, and the Philistines encamped in Aphec." (Kings 1 [Samuel 1] 4:1 LXX)

"And when Saul saw David going out to meet (*apantesin*) the Philistine, he said to Abenner the captain of the host. Whose son is this youth? and Abenner said, As thy soul lives, king, I know not." (Kings 1 [Samuel 1] 17:55 LXX)

"And the Philistines heard that David was anointed king over all Israel: and all the Philistines went up to seek David; and David heard [it], and went out to meet (*apantesin*) them." (Chronicles 1 14:8 LXX)

"It is not for you to fight: understand these things, and see the deliverance of the Lord with you, Juda and Jerusalem: fear not, neither be afraid to go forth to-morrow to meet (*apantesin*) them; and the Lord shall be with you." (Chronicles 2 20:17 LXX)

"And Ismael went out to meet (*apantesin*) them; [and] they went on and wept: and he said to them, Come in to Godolias. And it came to pass, when they had entered into the midst of the city, [that] he slew them [and cast them] into a pit. " (Jeremiah 41 [or 48]:6-7 LXX) - order of chapters different in different Codexes)

3. *Apantesin* was used in the following two places to describe meeting to apologize in order to prevent a battle:

"And David said to Abigaia, Blessed [be] the Lord God of Israel, who sent thee this very day to meet (*apantesin*) me:" (Kings 1 [Samuel 1] 25:32 LXX)

"But surely as the Lord God of Israel lives, who hindered me this day from doing thee harm, if thou hadst not hasted and come to meet (*apantesin*) me, then I said, There shall [surely] not be left

THOUGHTS ABOUT PROPHETIC SUBJECTS

to Nabal till the morning one male." (Kings 1 [Samuel 1] 25:34 LXX)

4. *Apantesin* was used in the following place to describe meeting a fleeing king to bring him supplies:

"And David passed on a little way from Ros; and, behold, Siba the servant of Memphibosthe [came] to meet (*apantesin*) him; and he had a couple of asses laden, and upon them two hundred loaves, and a hundred [bunches of] raisins, and a hundred [cakes of] dates, and bottle of wine." (Kings 2 [Samuel 2] 16:1 LXX)

5. *Apantesin* was used in the following seven places to describe messengers meeting people:

"And Samuel rose early and went to meet (*apantesin*) Israel in the morning, and it was told Saul, saying, Samuel has come to Carmel, and he has raised up help for himself: and he turned his chariot, and came down to Galgala to Saul; and, behold, he was offering up a whole-burnt-offering to the Lord, the chief of the spoils which he brought out of Amalec." (Kings 1 [Samuel 1] 15:12 LXX)

"And they brought David word concerning the men; and he sent to meet (*apantesin*) them, for the men were greatly dishonoured: and the king said, Remain in Jericho till your beards have grown, and [then] ye shall return." (Kings 2 [Samuel 2] 10:5 LXX)

"And there came men to report to David concerning the men: and he sent to meet (*apantesin*) them, for they were greatly disgraced: and the king said, Dwell in Jericho until your beards have grown, and return." (Chronicles 1 19:5 LXX)

"and he went out to meet (*apantesin*) Asa, and all Juda and Benjamin, and said, Hear me, Asa, and all Juda and Benjamin. The Lord [is] with you, while ye are with him; and if ye seek him out, he will be found of you; but if ye forsake him, he will forsake you." (Chronicles 2 15:2 LXX)

"And there went out to meet (*apantesin*) him Jeu the prophet the son of Anani, and said to him, King Josaphat, doest thou help a sinner, or act friendly towards one hated of the Lord? Therefore has wrath come upon thee from the Lord." (Chronicles 2 19:2 LXX)

"And there was there a prophet of the Lord, his name [was] Oded: and he went out to meet (*apantesin*) the host that were coming to Samaria, and said to them, Behold, the wrath of the Lord God of your fathers [is] upon Juda, and he has delivered them into your hands, and ye have slain them in wrath, and it has reached even to heaven." (Chronicles 2 28:9 LXX)

"One shall rush, running to meet (*apantesin*) another runner, and one shall go with tidings to meet another with tidings, to bring tidings to the king of Babylon, that his city is taken." (Jeremiah 51 [or 28]:31 LXX) - order of chapters different in different Codices

6. *Apantesin* was used in the following place to describe a surprise meeting.

"And the men of Baethsamys were reaping the wheat harvest in the valley; and they lifted up their eyes, and saw the ark of the Lord, and rejoiced to meet (*apantesin*) it." (Kings 1 [Samuel 1] 6:13 LXX)

7. *Apantesin* was used in the following five places in the general sense of "*to meet*," as we commonly use this phrase.

"And it came to pass when he had finished offering the whole-burnt-offering, that Samuel arrived, and Saul went out to meet (*apantesin*) him, [and] to bless him." (Kings 1 [Samuel 1] 13:10 LXX)

"And David comes to the two hundred men who were left behind that they should not follow after David, and he had caused them to remain by the brook of Bosor; and they came forth to meet (*apantesin*) David, and to meet (*apantesin*) his people with him: and David drew near to the people, and they asked him how he did." (Kings 1 [Samuel 1] 30:21 LXX)

"And David came as far as Ros, where he worshipped God: and behold, Chusi the chief friend of David came out to meet (*apantesin*) him, having rent his garment, and earth [was] upon his head." (Kings 2 [Samuel 2] 15:32 LXX)

"And Memphibosthe the son of Saul's son went down to meet (*apantesin*) the king, and had not dressed his feet, nor pared his nails, nor shaved himself, neither had he washed his garments, from the day that the king departed, until the day when he arrived in peace." (Kings 2 [Samuel 2] 19:24 LXX)

"And it came to pass when he went into Jerusalem to meet (*apantesin*) the king, that the king said to him, Why didst thou not go with me, Memphibosthe?" (Kings 2 [Samuel 2] 19:25 LXX)

8. And finally, of the twenty-five places where *apantesin* was found in the Canonical books in this online version of the Septuagint, only the following two could realistically be interpreted to have the technical meaning which it is alleged to always have.

"And the king returned, and came as far as Jordan. And the men of Juda came to Galgala on their way to meet (*apantesin*) the king, to cause the king to pass over Jordan." (Kings 2 [Samuel 2] 19:15 LXX)

"And Semei the son of Gera, the Benjamite, of Baurim, hasted and went down with the men of Juda to meet (*apantesin*) king David." (Kings 2 [Samuel 2] 19:16 LXX)

So, in conclusion, although the Greek word *apantesis*, or its form *apantesin*, was indeed sometimes used in regard to formal receptions of a dignitary, that usage is actually found in less than ten percent of the many places where this word occurs in ancient Greek literature. And thus, this argument against the doctrine of a rapture before **"the great tribulation,"** though widely used in many modern seminaries, is completely incorrect.

Eight Scriptural Proofs that the Lord Will Return Twice

1, In Matthew 25:10, the Lord taught that He will come and take **"those who were ready"** **"in"** **"to the wedding."** and in Luke 12:36, He explicitly said that He **"will return from the wedding."** These are plain statements, from the Lord's own mouth, of two different comings at two different times.

2. In Matthew 25:11, after the Lord has taken His own **"in"** **"to the wedding"** in the previous verse, **"Afterward,"** the wicked will come, seeking admittance, and will be denied entrance. But in Matthew 13:24-30, the wicked will be **"First"** gathered and bound **"in bundles to burn them,"** before the righteous will be gathered. This reversal of the order of events would be a flat contradiction if the Lord were only returning one time. And yes, the words **"Afterward"** and **"First"** are distinctly present in the Greek texts of these two passages.

3. In John 14:2-3, the Lord clearly taught that He would **"come again"** and take His own to His **"Father's house."** And in Jeremiah 16:14-18, He explicitly said He would bring **"the children of Israel,"** **"back into their land which I gave to their fathers."** This is two different gatherings, of two different groups of His people, into two different places.

4. In 2 Revelation 3:10 the Lord promises to **"keep"** the faithful **"out of"** the time of "testing," for that is the actual meaning of the Greek word there translated **"trial."** But Isaiah 66:15-20 says that Israel will be gathered after the Lord comes **"with fire,"** **"To render His anger with fury, And His rebuke with flames of fire."** These are distinctly different statements of timing.

5. In 2 Peter 2:4-9, the Holy Spirit uses the examples of Noah and Lot, both of whom were removed from the scene of judgment before it fell, to demonstrate that **"the Lord knows how to deliver the godly out of temptations and to reserve the unjust under punishment for the day of judgment."** But in Jeremiah 16:14-18, when He says that He will bring Israel **"back into their land which I gave to their fathers,"** He adds, **"And first I will repay double for their iniquity and their sin."** So we are clearly taught that one group of the Lord's own will be removed from the scene of judgment before it falls, while the other group of His own will be severely punished before they are gathered.

6. 1 Thessalonians 4:15-18 explicitly says that the Lord's own **"shall be caught up together... in the clouds to meet the Lord in the air."** But Matthew 25:31-32 Explicitly says that **"all the nations will be gathered before"** the Lord when He comes **"and He will separate them one from another."** This would be a flat contradiction if these passages spoke of the same event.

7. 1 Thessalonians 4:15-18 explicitly says that the Lord's own **"shall be caught up together... in the clouds to meet the Lord in the air."** And Matthew 25:46 explicitly says of the wicked, that **"these will go away into everlasting punishment."** This reversal of which group will be removed, and which one will be left behind, would be a flat contradiction if He were only returning one time.

8. Amos 5:18-20 says **"Woe to you who desire the day of the Lord!"** But 2 Timothy 4:8 says that the Lord will give **"the crown of righteousness"** to all who **"have loved His appearing."** One scripture very clearly states God's displeasure with anyone desiring **"the day of the Lord,"** and another scripture just as clearly states his pleasure with those who **"have loved His appearing."** This would be a flat contradiction if these scriptures were speaking of the same event.

JAMES C. MORRIS

The Scriptures Describe Different Gatherings of God's People, Into Different Places, In Different Ways, and at Different Times

The debate about Bible prophecy rages on, with all sides insisting that the scriptures clearly teach whatever view they are espousing. It is clear that some real Christians seriously misunderstand the prophetic scriptures. After having participated in such debates for many years, I have come to the conclusion that most of the misunderstanding does not come from unbelief. Instead, it comes from a failure to notice the fine details of the words actually used by God. Jesus said that **"one jot or one tittle will by no means pass from the law till all is fulfilled."** (Matthew 5:18) In so speaking, He was saying that not only is every word in the Bible important, but even the spelling of each individual word. That is, that every detail of every passage of scripture is important.

Closely related to this important principle is a second one that is often missed. And that is that God intentionally worded many of His statements in a way designed to conceal their meaning from unbelievers. Jesus told His own, **"it has been given to you to know the mysteries of the kingdom of heaven, but to them it has not been given."** (Matthew 13:11)

When these two principles are considered together, we realize that it is a serious error to assume anything about what our God has told us. Not only is it true that He said what He meant, and He meant what He said. But it is also true that He did *not* mean what He did *not* say. So we need to clearly distinguish between what God *actually* said and what we think *that* means. And most of the errors in interpreting the scriptures come from a failure to make this distinction.

There are two concepts that are so solidly fixed in the minds of many real Christians, that they think God said them. One of these is that the Lord is only coming back one time. And the other is that there is only one group of God's people. Many insist that the Bible teaches both of these. But neither of them is actually stated anywhere in the entire Bible. And when we carefully examine the fine details of the prophetic scriptures, we learn that neither of them is even correct.

The point of this article is to demonstrate that our God has clearly told us that He will gather two *different* groups of His people into two *different* places. And that He will gather them in two *different* ways and at two *different* times.

The first of these gatherings is described in the following words:

> "**16 For the Lord Himself will descend from heaven with a shout, with the voice of an archangel, and with the trumpet of God. And the dead in Christ will rise first. 17 Then we who are alive *and* remain shall be caught up together with them in the clouds to meet the Lord in the air. And thus we shall always be with the Lord.**" (1 Thessalonians 4:13-17)

And again:

> "**51 Behold, I tell you a mystery: We shall not all sleep, but we shall all be changed-- 52 in a moment, in the twinkling of an eye, at the last trumpet. For the trumpet will sound, and the dead will be raised incorruptible, and we shall be changed.**" (1 Corinthians 15:51-52)

And the second gathering is described in the following words:

> "¹⁴ 'Therefore behold, the days are coming,' says the LORD, 'that it shall no more be said, "The LORD lives who brought up the children of Israel from the land of Egypt," ¹⁵ but, "The LORD lives who brought up the children of Israel from the land of the north and from all the lands where He had driven them." For I will bring them back into their land which I gave to their fathers.
>
> ¹⁶ 'Behold, I will send for many fishermen,' says the LORD, 'and they shall fish them; and afterward I will send for many hunters, and they shall hunt them from every mountain and every hill, and out of the holes of the rocks.'" (Jeremiah 16:14-16)

And:

> "²⁴ For I will take you from among the nations, gather you out of all countries, and bring you into your own land. ²⁵ Then I will sprinkle clean water on you, and you shall be clean; I will cleanse you from all your filthiness and from all your idols. ²⁶ I will give you a new heart and put a new spirit within you; I will take the heart of stone out of your flesh and give you a heart of flesh. ²⁷ I will put My Spirit within you and cause you to walk in My statutes, and you will keep My judgments and do *them*. ²⁸ Then you shall dwell in the land that I gave to your fathers; you shall be My people, and I will be your God." (Ezekiel 36:24-28)

Even upon the most casual inspection, it should be obvious to anyone that these scriptures describe two entirely different gatherings of two entirely different groups of God's people.

Many real Christians imagine that the promise contained in these last two scriptures was fulfilled in the days of Ezra and

Nehemiah. But the return that took place at that time was a return of only a very small part of Judah, while the Lord had said:

> "**¹² I will surely assemble all of you, O Jacob,**
> **I will surely gather the remnant of Israel;**
> **I will put them together like sheep of the fold,**
> **Like a flock in the midst of their pasture;**
> **They shall make a loud noise because of** *so many* **people."** (Micah 2:12)

And a unique prophecy in Ezekiel 36 is addressed to the **"mountains of Israel,"** along with **"the hills, the rivers, the valleys, the desolate wastes, and the cities that have been forsaken, which became plunder and mockery to the rest of the nations all around–,"** (Ezekiel 36:4) telling them that **"¹⁰ I will multiply men upon you, all the house of Israel, all of it; and the cities shall be inhabited and the ruins rebuilt."** (Ezekiel 36:10) So the return of only very small part of Judah was most certainly not a fulfillment of these promises.

Furthermore, they were explicitly promised that **"²⁵ Then they shall dwell in the land that I have given to Jacob My servant, where your fathers dwelt; and they shall dwell there, they, their children, and their children's children, forever; and My servant David** *shall be* **their prince forever."** (Ezekiel 37:25) We all know that after the return in the days of Ezra and Nehemiah, they were again expelled from the land. So this promise has most certainly not been fulfilled, even to this day.

But now we must ask, where will each of these groups be gathered? This is not left to our imagination. In the case of the second group, we notice that each of these passages explicitly said it would be to **"the land"** that God had given to their **"fathers."** But what about the first group? Where will they be taken when they are gathered?

Jesus said: "**² In My Father's house are many mansions; if** *it were* **not** *so,* **I would have told you. I go to prepare a place for you. ³ And if I go and prepare a place for you, I will come again and receive you to Myself; that where I am,** *there* **you may be also."** (John 14:2-3)

Again, we are plainly told, "**¹ For we know that if our earthly house,** *this* **tent, is destroyed, we have a building from God, a house not made with hands, eternal in the heavens. ² For in this we groan, earnestly desiring to be clothed with our habitation which is from heaven,"** (2 Corinthians 5:1-2)

And:

> "**³ Blessed** *be* **the God and Father of our Lord Jesus Christ, who according to His abundant mercy has begotten us again to a living hope through the resurrection of Jesus Christ from the dead, ⁴ to an inheritance incorruptible and undefiled and that does not fade away, reserved in heaven for you, ⁵ who are kept by the power of God through faith for salvation ready to be revealed in the last time."** (1 Peter 1:3-5)

In the first of these two passages our Lord plainly told us where He was going. It was to **"My Father's house."** And He told us why He was going there. It was **"to prepare a place for you."** So the place He was preparing for us was in **"My Father's house."** And He said **"I will come again and receive you to Myself."** But why will he do this? **"That where I am,** *there* **you may be also."** But where would that be? He clearly said He was going to His **"Father's house."** So His **"Father's house"** is the place where He will take us. And in the second of these passages, we are just as plainly told that **"we have"** **"a house,"** that is **"eternal in the heavens,"** and that **"our habitation"** **"is from heaven."** And in the third of these passages, we are told that our **"inheritance"** is **"reserved in heaven"** for us.

So, while **"Israel"** is promised to be brought **"back into their land which I gave to their fathers,"** we are promised **"a house,"** that is **"eternal in the heavens."** Thus, even as these are obviously different groups, they will also be gathered into places that are obviously different.

But now we need to examine the ways in which these two groups will be gathered. In the case of the first group, we are told that the one to gather them will be **"the Lord Himself,"** and that they will be **"caught up" "in the clouds, to meet the Lord in the air,"** and that it will take place **"in a moment, in the twinkling of an eye."**

But the gathering of the second group will be completely different. In Jeremiah 16:16, the Lord said, **"I will send for many fishermen.. and afterward I will send for many hunters, and they shall hunt them from every mountain and every hill, and out of the holes of the rocks."** And in Matthew 24:31, He said **"He will send His angels with a great sound of a trumpet, and they will gather together His elect from the four winds, from one end of heaven to the other."** These certainly sound like two descriptions of the same process.

But Jeremiah 16 clearly speaks about a gathering of Israel. And Matthew 24 just as clearly says that ones that will be gathered by **"the angels"** will be **"His elect."** Every Christian knows that God repeatedly called the church **"His elect."** But not nearly as many Christians know that He also called Israel, **"My elect."** For the Lord said:

"⁹ I will bring forth descendants from Jacob,

And from Judah an heir of My mountains;

My elect shall inherit it,

And My servants shall dwell there.

¹⁰ Sharon shall be a fold of flocks,

And the Valley of Achor a place for herds to lie down,

For My people who have sought Me." (Isaiah 65:9-10)

We need to notice that in this passage, the Lord called Israel **"My elect"** in specific reference to this end time gathering of Israel that we have been discussing.

But this end time gathering of Israel will not only involve angels. For we also read:

> "**[15] 'For behold, the LORD will come with fire**
> **And with His chariots, like a whirlwind,**
> **To render His anger with fury,**
> **And His rebuke with flames of fire.**
> **[16] For by fire and by His sword**
> **The LORD will judge all flesh;**
> **And the slain of the LORD shall be many.**
> **[17] 'Those who sanctify themselves and purify themselves,**
> ***To go* to the gardens**
> **After an *idol* in the midst,**
> **Eating swine's flesh and the abomination and the mouse,**
> **Shall be consumed together,' says the LORD.**
> **[18] 'For I *know* their works and their thoughts. It shall be that I will gather all nations and tongues; and they shall come and see My glory. [19] I will set a sign among them; and those among them who escape I will send to the nations: *to* Tarshish and Pul and Lud, who draw the bow, and Tubal and Javan, *to* the coastlands afar off who have not heard My fame nor seen My glory. And they shall declare My glory among the Gentiles. [20] Then they shall bring all your brethren for an offering to the LORD out of all nations, on horses and in chariots and in litters, on mules and on camels, to My holy mountain Jerusalem,' says the LORD, 'as the children of Israel bring an offering in a clean vessel into the house of the LORD.'"** (Isaiah 66:15-20)

Here we see that it will not be only angels that will be used in the process of gathering Israel, but mere humans, and even animals, will also be used. **"Then they shall bring all your brethren for an offering to the LORD out of all nations, on horses and in chariots and in litters, on mules and on camels, to My holy mountain Jerusalem."**

But not only will the agencies doing the gathering be different, what the Lord Himself will do at this time will also be different. For we read, **"33 'As I live,' says the Lord GOD, 'surely with a mighty hand, with an outstretched arm, and with fury poured out, I will rule over you. 34 I will bring you out from the peoples and gather you out of the countries where you are scattered, with a mighty hand, with an outstretched arm, and with fury poured out. 35 And I will bring you into the wilderness of the peoples, and there I will plead My case with you face to face. 36 Just as I pleaded My case with your fathers in the wilderness of the land of Egypt, so I will plead My case with you,' says the Lord GOD. 37 'I will make you pass under the rod, and I will bring you into the bond of the covenant; 38 I will purge the rebels from among you, and those who transgress against Me; I will bring them out of the country where they dwell, but they shall not enter the land of Israel. Then you will know that I *am* the LORD.'"** (Ezekiel 20:33-38)

So not only will the agencies used to do the gathering be different. There will also be a difference in the treatment of those gathered. In one case, only the righteous will be gathered. And in the other, all of Israel will be gathered, but only the righteous will be allowed to enter the land.

Finally, in Isaiah 66:15-20, we clearly see when this gathering will take place. It will be after **"the LORD will come with fire,"** **"To render His anger with fury, And His rebuke with flames of fire."** and after He **"will gather all nations and tongues; and they shall come and see"** His **"glory."** **"And those among them who escape,"** from the destruction at that time, He **"will send to the nations."** And **"Then they shall bring all your brethren... to My holy mountain Jerusalem."** The time is again stated in Micah 5, where we read:

> **"Therefore He shall give them up,**
> **Until the time *that* she who is in labor has given birth;**
> **Then the remnant of His brethren**
> **Shall return to the children of Israel."** (Micah 5:3)

So we see that its timing coincides with the timing stated in Matthew 24:29-31, which was **"immediately afer the tribulation of those days."**

But what about the timing of the other gathering? This also is not left to our imagination. We are told the timing of that gathering in several scriptures. The first place we find it is in the parable of the wise and foolish virgins. **"[10] And while they went to buy, the bridegroom came, and those who were ready went in with him to the wedding; and the door was shut. [11] Afterward the other virgins came also, saying, 'Lord, Lord, open to us!' [12] But he answered and said, 'Assuredly, I say to you, I do not know you.'"** (Matthew 25:10-12)

We have already seen, from John 14:2-3, that the place the Lord will take us is to His **"Father's house."** And we have seen from 2 Corinthians 5:1 that we have a **"house," "eternal in the heavens."** So we know that we will be taken to heaven. But where will the wedding be? We read, **"[5] Then a voice came from the throne, saying, 'Praise our God, all you His servants and those who fear Him, both small and great!' [6] And I heard, as it were, the voice of a great multitude, as the sound of many waters and as the sound of mighty thunderings, saying, 'Alleluia! For the Lord God Omnipotent reigns! [7] Let us be glad and rejoice and give Him glory, for the marriage of the Lamb has come, and His wife has made herself ready.' [8] And to her it was grant-**

ed to be arrayed in fine linen, clean and bright, for the fine linen is the righteous acts of the saints. ⁹Then he said to me, 'Write: "Blessed *are* those who are called to the marriage supper of the Lamb!" ' And he said to me, 'These are the true sayings of God.' " (Revelation 19:5-9) So we see that **"the wedding"** will take place in heaven. And this is the very last scene described as taking place in heaven before the Lord goes forth from heaven in power and glory to judge the world in Revelation 19:11-16.

But we also see the timing of this event in the words, **"those who were ready went in with him to the wedding; and the door was shut."** This closed door, which remains closed in spite of the pleading of those that came **"afterwards,"** is clearly described in two other scriptures.

> "⁹ The coming of the *lawless one* is according to the working of Satan, with all power, signs, and lying wonders, ¹⁰ and with all unrighteous deception among those who perish, because they did not receive the love of the truth, that they might be saved. ¹¹ And for this reason God will send them strong delusion, that they should believe the lie, ¹² that they all may be condemned who did not believe the truth but had pleasure in unrighteousness." (2 Thessalonians 2:9-12)

And:

> "³... Just as they have chosen their own ways,
> And their soul delights in their abominations,
> ⁴ So will I choose their delusions,
> And bring their fears on them;
> Because, when I called, no one answered,
> When I spoke they did not hear;
> But they did evil before My eyes,
> And chose *that* in which I do not delight." (Isaiah 66:3-4)

So we are explicitly told that there is a time coming when the Lord will turn people over to be deceived by **"the lie"** of **"the *lawless one*,"** the Antichrist. And this will be because they had made a willful choice to **"not receive the love of the truth, that they might be saved."** And **"have chosen their own ways."** But we remember that **"the door was shut"** after **"the bridegroom came, and those who were ready went in with him to the wedding."**

And we remember that the Lord instructed His listeners to **"³⁵ Let your waist be girded and *your* lamps burning; ³⁶ and you yourselves be like men who wait for their master, when he will return from the wedding, that when he comes and knocks they may open to him immediately."** (Luke 12:35-36) So here, our Lord distinctly said He **"will return from the wedding."**

This series of scriptures distinctly tells us that the Lord will come, and take **"those who were ready"** **"in"** to heaven **"to the wedding,"** after which **"the door"** will be **"shut"** during the time of the AntichrIst, and then the Lord **"will return from the wedding."**

We see the timing of this gathering again in 2 Peter 2:4-9, where we read,

"⁴ For if God did not spare the angels who sinned, but cast *them* down to hell and delivered *them* into chains of darkness, to be reserved for judgment; ⁵ and did not spare the ancient world, but saved Noah, *one of* eight *people*, a preacher of righteousness, bringing in the flood on the world of the ungodly; ⁶ and turning the cities of Sodom and Gomorrah into ashes, condemned *them* to destruction, making *them* an example to those who afterward would live ungodly; ⁷ and delivered righteous Lot, *who was* oppressed by the filthy conduct of the wicked ⁸ (for that righteous man, dwelling among them, tormented *his* righteous soul from day to day by seeing and hearing *their* lawless deeds)-- ⁹ *then* the Lord knows how to deliver the godly out of temptations and to reserve the unjust under punishment for the day of judgment."

THOUGHTS ABOUT PROPHETIC SUBJECTS

Here, the Lord used the examples of **"Noah"** and **"Lot,"** both of whom were physically removed from the scene of judgment before it fell, to illustrate that He **"knows how to deliver the godly out of temptations and to reserve the unjust under punishment for the day of judgment."** And we notice here that the thing the Lord will deliver **"the godly"** from is not persecution, but **"temptations."** this again speaks of the time of deception under the Antichrist.

And this brings us to the third way in which the scriptures reveal the timing of this gathering.

Out Lord told the faithful in the city of Philadelphia, **"10 Because you have kept My command to persevere, I also will keep you from the hour of trial which shall come upon the whole world, to test those who dwell on the earth."** (Revelation 3:10) This **"hour of trial"** spoken of here is that same hour of **"the *lawless one*,"** the Antichrist, to whose **"lie"** all that **"did not receive the love of the truth"** will be turned over.

So we see that the scriptures indeed describe two different end time gatherings of the people of God, into two different places, in two different ways, and at two different times. The first one will be a gathering of the church by **"the Lord himself,"** into the **"Father's house,"** which will take place **"in a moment, in the twinkling of an eye,"** before **"the wedding,"** and before **"the hour of trial,"** which will be the time of the Antichrist, and the second one will be a gathering of **"the children of Israel" "back into their land which"** God **"gave to their fathers,"** which will be done by **"angels"** and by mere humans, after **"the Lord"** comes **"with fire," "to render His anger with fury, and His rebuke with flames of fire," "immediately after the tribulation," "when he will return from the wedding."**

JAMES C. MORRIS

How We Know the Gathering of His Elect By the Angels Is Not the Rapture

Many erroneously think that the following two passages of scripture describe the rapture.

> "[29] Immediately after the tribulation of those days the sun will be darkened, and the moon will not give its light; the stars will fall from heaven, and the powers of the heavens will be shaken. [30] Then the sign of the Son of Man will appear in heaven, and then all the tribes of the earth will mourn, and they will see the Son of Man coming on the clouds of heaven with power and great glory. [31] And He will send His angels with a great sound of a trumpet, and they will gather together His elect from the four winds, from one end of heaven to the other." (Matthew 24:29-31)

And:

> "[24] But in those days, after that tribulation, the sun will be darkened, and the moon will not give its light; [25] the stars of heaven will fall, and the powers in the heavens will be shaken. [26] Then they will see the Son of Man coming in the clouds with great power and glory. [27] And then He will send His angels, and gather together His elect from the four winds, from the farthest part of earth to the farthest part of heaven." (Mark 13:24-27)

But this is error. For the rapture is described completely differently in the following passages:

> "**¹⁶ For the Lord Himself will descend from heaven with a shout, with the voice of an archangel, and with the trumpet of God. And the dead in Christ will rise first. ¹⁷ Then we who are alive *and* remain shall be caught up together with them in the clouds to meet the Lord in the air. And thus we shall always be with the Lord.**" (1 Thessalonians 4:16-17:)

And:

> "**⁵¹ Behold, I tell you a mystery: We shall not all sleep, but we shall all be changed-- ⁵² in a moment, in the twinkling of an eye, at the last trumpet. For the trumpet will sound, and the dead will be raised incorruptible, and we shall be changed. ⁵³ For this corruptible must put on incorruption, and this mortal *must* put on immortality. ⁵⁴ So when this corruptible has put on incorruption, and this mortal has put on immortality, then shall be brought to pass the saying that is written: *'Death is swallowed up in victory.'*** "(1 Corinthians 15:51-54)

The first thing we need to notice, is that in the rapture, it is **"the Lord Himself"** who comes for us. But when He comes **"with power and great glory,"** **"He will send His angels"** to do the gathering. And it is impossible to **"see"** an event that will take place **"in a moment, in the twinkling of an eye."** We also need to notice that the Greek word translated **"caught up"** in 1 Thessalonians 4:17 is a future passive form of the Greek word ἁρπαζω, *harpazo* in our alphabet, word number 726 in Strong's Greek Dictionary, which means to seize, or to catch away. But the Greek word translated **"gather together"** in both Matthew 24:31 and Mark 13:27 is a future active form of ἐπισυναγω, *episunago* in our alphabet, word number 1996 in Strong's Greek Dictionary, which means to gather together into one place. So the meanings of these two Greek words is entirely different. Although these indeed are only differences between these two sets of passages, there are other scriptures which clearly state details which conclusively prove that the gathering at the time He comes **"with power and great glory"** is not the rapture.

The most glaringly obvious of these is a comparison between Luke 12:35-40 and Matthew 25:1-13.

Jesus plainly said:

> **"³⁵ Let your waist be girded and *your* lamps burning; ³⁶ and you yourselves be like men who wait for their master, when he will return from the wedding, that when he comes and knocks they may open to him immediately. ³⁷ Blessed *are* those servants whom the master, when he comes, will find watching. Assuredly, I say to you that he will gird himself and have them sit down *to eat,* and will come and serve them. ³⁸ And if he should come in the second watch, or come in the third watch, and find *them* so, blessed are those servants. ³⁹ But know this, that if the master of the house had known what hour the thief would come, he would have watched and not allowed his house to be broken into. ⁴⁰ Therefore you also be ready, for the Son of Man is coming at an hour you do not expect."** (Luke 12:35-40)

This passage compares His coming to that of a **"thief,"** and clearly says that He will break into **"the house."** This shows that this refers to His coming **"in power"** So we see that it clearly refers to the same coming as the one in Matthew 24:29-31 and Mark 3:24-27. But there is a critical detail that we need to notice. Luke 12:36 explicitly says that this will be **"when he will return from the wedding."** Why is this detail so important to the current question? We see the critical nature of this detail when we compare it with a detail in the parable of the ten virgins:

> "**¹ Then the kingdom of heaven shall be likened to ten virgins who took their lamps and went out to meet the bridegroom. ² Now five of them were wise, and five *were* foolish. ³ Those who *were* foolish took their lamps and took no oil with them, ⁴ but the wise took oil in their vessels with their lamps. ⁵ But while the bridegroom was delayed, they all slumbered and slept. ⁶ And at midnight a cry was *heard:* 'Behold, the bridegroom is coming; go out to meet him!' ⁷ Then all those virgins arose and trimmed their lamps. ⁸ And the foolish said to the wise, 'Give us *some* of your oil, for our lamps are going out.' ⁹ But the wise answered, saying, *'No,* lest there should not be enough for us and you; but go rather to those who sell, and buy for yourselves.' ¹⁰ And while they went to buy, the bridegroom came, and those who were ready went in with him to the wedding; and the door was shut. ¹¹ Afterward the other virgins came also, saying, 'Lord, Lord, open to us!' ¹² But he answered and said, 'Assuredly, I say to you, I do not know you.' ¹³ Watch therefore, for you know neither the day nor the hour in which the Son of Man is coming."** (Matthew 25:1-13)

In this passage, we need to particularly notice verse 10, where it says, **"the bridegroom came, and those who were ready went in with him to the wedding."** This is a clear statement of a coming that is distinctly *before* **"he will return from the wedding."** This is not interpretation. It is what Jesus *actually* said in these two scriptures. For if anyone goes into an event, and returns from that event, he unquestionable goes into it at an earlier time than when he returns from it. So in these two passages, we have two exceedingly clear statements, out of the very mouth of Jesus Himself, that He will come at *two distinctly different times.* The only way to escape this *necessary* conclusion is to pretend that Jesus did not actually mean what He so clearly said.

And His coming as **"the bridegroom,"** which is unquestionably earlier than **"when he will return from the wedding,"** is obviously the rapture. For this is when **"the bridegroom"** comes for His bride and her associates. So here, it is distinctly stated that the rapture will take place before **"He will send His angels, and gather together His elect from the four winds."** But this comparison does not even imply how much time will pass between these two comings. That is revealed in other scriptures. But that question is immaterial to the current discussion.

But if the rapture takes place at an earlier time, what gathering will take place at the time He will come **"with power and great glory"**? Our God has explicitly told us.

"**15 For behold, the LORD will come with fire
And with His chariots, like a whirlwind,
To render His anger with fury,
And His rebuke with flames of fire.
16 For by fire and by His sword
The LORD will judge all flesh;
And the slain of the LORD shall be many.
17 Those who sanctify themselves and purify themselves,
To go to the gardens
After an *idol* in the midst,
Eating swine's flesh and the abomination and the mouse,
Shall be consumed together,' says the LORD.
18 For I *know* their works and their thoughts. It shall be that I will gather all nations and tongues; and they shall come and see My glory. 19 I will set a sign among them; and those among them who escape I will send**

to the nations: *to* Tarshish and Pul and Lud, who draw the bow, and Tubal and Javan, *to* the coastlands afar off who have not heard My fame nor seen My glory. And they shall declare My glory among the Gentiles. ²⁰ Then they shall bring all your brethren for an offering to the LORD out of all nations, on horses and in chariots and in litters, on mules and on camels, to My holy mountain Jerusalem,' says the LORD, 'as the children of Israel bring an offering in a clean vessel into the house of the LORD. ²¹ And I will also take some of them for priests *and* Levites,' says the LORD." (Isaiah 66:15-21)

Here, our Lord's **"coming... with power and great glory"** is clearly described. But immediately after that, it says, **"Then they shall bring all your brethren for an offering to the LORD out of all nations, on horses and in chariots and in litters, on mules and on camels, to My holy mountain Jerusalem."** As this was said to **"Jerusalem,"** (see verses 10-14) the **"brethren"** spoken of here are unquestionably the nation of Israel, as the Holy Spirit inspired Paul to write, **"my brethren, my countrymen according to the flesh."** (Romans 9:3b) And they be gathered **"to My holy mountain Jerusalem."** So there can be no question that this gathering, which will take place when He comes **"with power and great glory,"** is a gathering of **"Israel,"** not of **"the church."** This passage only mentions humans and animals being used in this gathering. But the following scripture shows that angelic forces will also be used.

" ¹⁴ Therefore behold, the days are coming,' says the LORD, 'that it shall no more be said, "The LORD lives who brought up the children of Israel from the land of Egypt," ¹⁵ but, "The LORD lives who brought up the children of Israel from the land of the north and from all the lands where He had driven them." For I will

> bring them back into their land which I gave to their fathers. '¹⁶Behold, I will send for many fishermen,' says the LORD, 'and they shall fish them; and afterward I will send for many hunters, and they shall hunt them from every mountain and every hill, and out of the holes of the rocks.' " (Jeremiah 16:14-16)

As the mission of these **"hunters"** is to **"hunt them from every mountain and every hill, and out of the holes of the rocks,"** it is obvious that this would require angelic powers. For mere human powers could not find **"all"** of them on **"every hill,"** and hiding in **"holes of the rocks."** And the fact that the Lord says, **"I will bring them back into their land which I gave to their fathers,"** is conclusive proof that this is speaking of the physical nation of **"Israel,"** not some imagined "spiritual Israel."

So we have seen, both that the scriptures clearly tell us that the rapture will take place before the time spoken of in Matthew 24:29-31 and Mark 13:24-27, and that it is **"Israel,"** rather than **"the church"** that will be gathered at that time. But there is one more problem we need to address. For many imagine that the words **"His elect"** in Matthew 24:31 and Mark 13:27 necessarily mean the church. But again, that is an error.

"The church" is often referred to as either **"elect"** or **"chosen,"** and is called **"God's elect"** in Romans 8:33 and Titus 1:1. But in the entire Bible, there is not even one place that is unquestionably speaking about **"the church,"** where a pronoun is attached to the Hebrew or Greek word that is alternately translated as **"chosen"** or **"elect."** In the Hebrew, this word is בחיר, *bāhîr* in our alphabet, word number 977 In Strong's Hebrew Dictionary, which means to choose, or to select. Its Greek equivalent is ἐκλεκτος, *eklektos* in our alphabet, word number 1588 in Strong's Greek Dictionary, which has the same meaning. But **"Israel"** is called **"His chosen"** in 1 Chronicles 16:13, Psalm 105:6, and Psalm

105:43, and is called either **"My chosen"** or **"My elect"** in Isaiah 43:20, Isaiah 45:4, Isaiah 65:9, Isaiah 65:15, and Isaiah 65:22. So the fact that both Matthew 24:31 and Mark 13:27 mention the Lord sending **"angels"** to **"gather"** **"His elect"** tends more to indicate a gathering of **"Israel"** than of **"the church."** And, as we have seen, other scriptures indicate both that the rapture will take place at an earlier time, and that it is **"Israel"** that will be gathered at that time.

All of this is how we know that the gathering of **"His elect"** by the **"angels"** is a gathering of **"Israel,"** not of **"the church."** And that is how we know it is not speaking about the rapture.

JAMES C. MORRIS

Ten Greek Words Used For the Lord's Coming

In the New Testament, the coming of the Lord is mentioned by using ten different Greek words. Commentators usually only mention three of these, the Greek word παρουσια, *parousia* in our alphabet, word number 3952 in Strong's Greek Dictionary, which is usually translated as **"coming,"** the Greek word αποκαλυψις, *apocalypsis* in our alphabet, word number 602 in Strong's Greek Dictionary, which is usually translated as **"revealing,"** and the Greek word ἐπιφανεια, *epiphaneia* in our alphabet, word number 2015 in Strong's Greek Dictionary, which is usually translated as **"appearing."** But His coming is also mentioned by using seven other Greek words, the Greek word ὁπτανομαι, *optanomai* in our alphabet, word number 3700 in Strong's Greek Dictionary, which is often translated as **"appear,"** the Greek word φανεροω, *phaneroo* in our alphabet, word number 5319 in Strong's Greek Dictionary, which is also often translated as **"appear,"** the Greek word ἔρχομαι, *erchomai* in our alphabet, word number 2064 in Strong;'s Greek Dictionary, which is usually translated as **"come,"** the Greek word ἥκω, *heko* in our alphabet, word number 2240 in Strong's Greek Dictionary, which again is translated as **"come."** the Greek word ἐφιστημι, *ephistemi* on our alphabet, word number 2186 in Strong's Greek Dictionary, which is also usually translated as **"come,"** the Greek word εἰσέρχομαι, *eiserchomai* in our alphabet, word number 1525 in Strong's Greek Dictionary, which is often translated as **"enter,"** and the Greek word ἀναλυω, *analuo* in our alphabet, word number 360 in Strong's Greek Dictionary, which is translated as **"return"** when it is used of the Lord's coming.

THOUGHTS ABOUT PROPHETIC SUBJECTS

As many imagine that the scriptures teach that the Lord will only return one time, they often insist that the first three of these Greek words are used only in regard to our Lord's **"coming... with power and great glory,"** as is stated in Matthew 24:30 and Luke 21:27, which will be both His **"revealing"** to the world and His **"appearing,"** to the world.

In regard to the Greek word *parousia,* many also claim it has a "technical meaning." But as various claims about this "technical meaning" have been disproved, this allegation has been repeatedly modified to "take care of" proven exceptions. So it is rather difficult to pin these people down as to exactly what this word "technically" means. But the end result is that they insist it refers only to our Lord's **"coming... with power and great glory."**

So we will examine numerous times this Greek word was used in situations that obviously do not meet this alleged "technical meaning." We find it twenty-four times in the New Testament. And Hatch and Redpath's "Concordance to the Septuagint" list five times it was used there. [18] But in one of those five times it is missing from our copy. So sources commonly available to Bible students contain it in a total of twenty-eight places. And these twenty-eight places are enough to clearly see its meaning. As we examine these many uses, it becomes obvious that the most common translation of this word that we find, which is **"coming,"** is unquestionably correct. Strong's Greek Dictionary says it is derived from the Geeek word παρειμι, *pareimi* on our alphabet, word number 3918 in Strong's Greek Dictionary, which in the infinitive means *to be present.* But in the normal usage of this word, its obvious sense is the *beginning* of that presence, that is an *arrival.* This can be easily seen in its many uses.

---

18. In this article, as we did in a previous article, we will use a parallel English - Greek version of the Septuagint made in 1851 by Sir Lancelot C. L. Brenton. This document is easily available online at: https://www.ellopos.net/elpenor/greek-texts/septuagint/. This online version has some of the English text modernized from the forms originally used by Brenton

There are indeed nine places in the New Testament where this word refers, as they imagine it always does, to our Lord's **"coming... with power and great glory."**

"³ Now as He sat on the Mount of Olives, the disciples came to Him privately, saying, 'Tell us, when will these things be? And what *will be* the sign of Your coming, and of the end of the age?'" (Matthew 24:3)

"²⁷ For as the lightning comes from the east and flashes to the west, so also will the coming of the Son of Man be." (Matthew 24:27)

"³⁷ But as the days of Noah *were,* so also will the coming of the Son of Man be." (Matthew 24:37)

"³⁹ and did not know until the flood came and took them all away, so also will the coming of the Son of Man be." (Matthew 24:39)

"¹³ so that He may establish your hearts blameless in holiness before our God and Father at the coming of our Lord Jesus Christ with all His saints." (1 Thessalonians 3:13)

"⁸ And then the lawless one will be revealed, whom the Lord will consume with the breath of His mouth and destroy with the brightness of His coming." (2 Thessalonians 2:8)

"¹⁶ For we did not follow cunningly devised fables when we made known to you the power and coming of our Lord Jesus Christ, but were eyewitnesses of His majesty." (2 Peter 1:16)

"⁴ and saying, 'Where is the promise of His coming? For since the fathers fell asleep, all things continue as *they were* from the beginning of creation.'" (2 Peter 3:4)

"¹² looking for and hastening the coming of the day of God, because of which the heavens will be dissolved, being on fire, and the elements will melt with fervent heat?" (2 Peter 3:12)

THOUGHTS ABOUT PROPHETIC SUBJECTS

But in eight other places it clearly refers to the Lord's coming for His own.

"²³ But each one in his own order: Christ the firstfruits, afterward those *who are* Christ's at His coming." (1 Corinthians 15:23)

"¹⁹ For what *is* our hope, or joy, or crown of rejoicing? *Is it* not even you in the presence of our Lord Jesus Christ at His coming?" (1 Thessalonians 2:19)

"¹⁵ For this we say to you by the word of the Lord, that we who are alive *and* remain until the coming of the Lord will by no means precede those who are asleep." (1 Thessalonians 4:15)

"²³ Now may the God of peace Himself sanctify you completely; and may your whole spirit, soul, and body be preserved blameless at the coming of our Lord Jesus Christ." (1 Thessalonians 5:23)

"¹ Now, brethren, concerning the coming of our Lord Jesus Christ and our gathering together to Him, we ask you," (2 Thessalonians 2:1)

"⁷ Therefore be patient, brethren, until the coming of the Lord. See *how* the farmer waits for the precious fruit of the earth, waiting patiently for it until it receives the early and latter rain." (James 5:7)

"⁸ You also be patient. Establish your hearts, for the coming of the Lord is at hand." (James 5:8)

"²⁸ And now, little children, abide in Him, that when He appears, we may have confidence and not be ashamed before Him at His coming." (1 John 2:28)

And now, concerning the claim that *parousia* refers to our Lord's "coming... with power and great glory," we find that it refers to the coming or presence of the Apostle Paul three times.

"¹⁰ 'For *his* letters,' they say, '*are* weighty and powerful, but *his* bodily presence *is* weak, and *his* speech contemptible.' " (2 Corinthians 10:10)

"²⁶ that your rejoicing for me may be more abundant in Jesus Christ by my coming to you again." (Philippians 1:26)

"¹² Therefore, my beloved, as you have always obeyed, not as in my presence only, but now much more in my absence, work out your own salvation with fear and trembling;" (Philippians 2:12)

And it refers to the coming of Titus twice.

"⁶ Nevertheless God, who comforts the downcast, comforted us by the coming of Titus," (2 Corinthians 7:6)

"⁷ and not only by his coming, but also by the consolation with which he was comforted in you, when he told us of your earnest desire, your mourning, your zeal for me, so that I rejoiced even more."
(2 Corinthians 7:7)

When these have been pointed out, the claim that this word refers only to our Lord's **"coming... with power and great glory,"** has often been modified to a claim that the word *parousia* refers only to the coming of leaders or authorities. But it was also used in reference to the coming of three helpers of the Apostles:

"¹⁷ I am glad about the coming of Stephanas, Fortunatus, and Achaicus, for what was lacking on your part they supplied." (1 Corinthians 16:17)

And it was even used to refer to the coming of the Antichrist:

"⁹ The coming of the *lawless one* is according to the working of Satan, with all power, signs, and lying wonders," (2 Thessalonians 2:9)

THOUGHTS ABOUT PROPHETIC SUBJECTS

But now, turning to the Septuagint, which while not scripture, clearly shows what this word actually meant in the ancient Greek language, we see that in the Apocrypha:

Parousia was used once in regard to the coming of an enemy commander:

> **"12 Now when word was brought unto Judas of Nicanor's coming, and he had imparted unto those that were with him that the army was at hand,"** (2 Maccabees 8:12)

It was used once in regard to the coming of an enemy army:

> **"21 Maccabeus seeing the coming of the multitude, and the divers preparations of armour, and the fierceness of the beasts, stretched out his hands toward heaven, and called upon the Lord that worketh wonders, knowing that victory cometh not by arms, but even as it seemeth good to him, he giveth it to such as are worthy:"** (2 Maccabees 15:21)

And it was used in regard to the Maccabees entering a temple:

> **"17 To outward appearance they received us willingly; but belied that appearance by their deeds. When we were eager to enter (parousia) their temple, and to honour it with the most beautiful and exquisite gifts,"** (3 Maccabees 3:17)

And finally, the great clincher is that this word *parousia* was used in regard to the coming of a widow woman:

> **"18 Then was there a concourse throughout all the camp: for her coming was noised among the tents, and they came about her, as she stood without the tent of Holofernes, till they told him of her."** (Judith 10:18)

We need to realize that this was said in regard to this widow (whose name was Judith) before the time she seduced and killed the commander of the enemy army. So at the time the word *parousia* was used in regard to her, she was only famous for her beauty.

So from all of this, it is beyond debate that the Greek word *parousia* does not have a technical meaning, referring only to the coming of the Lord, nor does it have a technical meaning referring only to the coming of a leader, commander, or person in authority. It simply means **"coming,"** regardless of who comes or why they come.

And so, the claim that the word *parousia* has "a technical meaning" is manifestly incorrect, and thus, this argument against the pre-tribulation rapture is groundless.

And the closely related error about the Greek word αποκαλυψις, *apocalypsis* in our alphabet, word number 602 in Strong's Greek Dictionary, is like the erroneous claim that *parousia* always refers to our Lord's **"coming... with power and great glory."** These same people claim that the Greek word *apocalypsis* always refers to His revealing to the world at the time of His **"coming... with power and great glory."** But a simple examination of the many places this Greek word was used, shows this claim to be completely incorrect.

The Greek word *apocalypses* was used eighteen times in the New Testament, and Hatch and Redpath list four times it was used in the Septuagint. But our copy of the Septuagint omits it in one of those places, so we will limit our examination of its meaning to the twenty-one places it was used that anyone can easily look up.

Apocalypses was indeed used in the alleged meaning in both of the following scriptures:

> "**⁵ But in accordance with your hardness and your impenitent heart you are treasuring up for yourself wrath in the day of wrath and revelation of the righteous judgment of God,**" (Romans 2:5)

THOUGHTS ABOUT PROPHETIC SUBJECTS

> "⁷ and to *give* you who are troubled rest with us when the Lord Jesus is revealed from heaven with His mighty angels," (2 Thessalonians 1:7)

And *apocalypses* was used in a closely related meaning in the following scripture.

> "¹⁹ For the earnest expectation of the creation eagerly waits for the revealing of the sons of God." (Romans 8:19)

But in each of the following four scriptures, *apocalypses* was used in regard to our Lord's revealing of himself to His own. So there is not, as has been falsely alleged, just a single **"revealing."** But rather, there will be a revealing of himself to His own, and a revealing of himself to the world.

> "⁷ so that you come short in no gift, eagerly waiting for the revelation of our Lord Jesus Christ," (1 Corinthians 1:7)

> "⁷ that the genuineness of your faith, *being* much more precious than gold that perishes, though it is tested by fire, may be found to praise, honor, and glory at the revelation of Jesus Christ," (1 Peter 1:7)

> "¹³ Therefore gird up the loins of your mind, be sober, and rest *your* hope fully upon the grace that is to be brought to you at the revelation of Jesus Christ;" (1 Peter 1:13)

> "¹³ but rejoice to the extent that you partake of Christ's sufferings, that when His glory is revealed, you may also be glad with exceeding joy." (1 Peter 4:13)

So the truth is, that *apocalypses* was used twice as often in regard to our Lord's revealing of himself to His own, as to His revealing of himself to the world.

Further, in each of the eleven following scriptures, the Greek word *apocalypses* was used in regard to a revealing, not of God himself, but of truth from God.

"**[32] A light to *bring* revelation to the Gentiles, And the glory of Your people Israel.**" (Luke 2:32)

"**[25] Now to Him who is able to establish you according to my gospel and the preaching of Jesus Christ, according to the revelation of the mystery kept secret since the world began**" (Romans 16:25)

"**[6] But now, brethren, if I come to you speaking with tongues, what shall I profit you unless I speak to you either by revelation, by knowledge, by prophesying, or by teaching?**" (1 Corinthians 14:6)

"**[26] How is it then, brethren? Whenever you come together, each of you has a psalm, has a teaching, has a tongue, has a revelation, has an interpretation. Let all things be done for edification.**" (1 Corinthians 14:26)

"**[1] It is doubtless not profitable for me to boast. I will come to visions and revelations of the Lord:**" (2 Corinthians 12:1)

"**[7] And lest I should be exalted above measure by the abundance of the revelations, a thorn in the flesh was given to me, a messenger of Satan to buffet me, lest I be exalted above measure.**" (2 Corinthians 12:7

"**[12] For I neither received it from man, nor was I taught *it*, but *it came* through the revelation of Jesus Christ.**" (Galatians 1:12)

"**[2] And I went up by revelation, and communicated to them that gospel which I preach among the Gentiles, but privately to those who were of reputation, lest by any means I might run, or had run, in vain.**" (Galatians 2:2)

"**[17] that the God of our Lord Jesus Christ, the Father of glory, may give to you the spirit of wisdom and revelation in the knowledge of Him,**" (Ephesians 1:17)

THOUGHTS ABOUT PROPHETIC SUBJECTS

"**³ how that by revelation He made known to me the mystery (as I have briefly written already,**" (Ephesians 3:3)

"**¹ The Revelation of Jesus Christ, which God gave Him to show His servants--things which must shortly take place. And He sent and signified** *it* **by His angel to His servant John,**" (Revelation 1:1)

And finally, in the Septuagint, we find:

"30 And Saul was exceedingly angry with Jonathan, and said to him, Thou son of traitorous damsels! for do I not know that thou art an accomplice with the son of Jessae to thy shame, and to the shame of thy mother's nakedness?" 1 Kings 1 Samuel 20:30) Here, the translators of the Septuagint rendered the Hebrew word that literally means nakedness as *apocalypses*, that is, as "revealing," in the sense of "exposure."

And in the Apocryphal portion of the Septuagint, we find

"27 The affliction of an hour maketh a man forget pleasure: and in his end his deeds shall be discovered." (Sirach 11:27) Here, they rendered the word "discovered" as *apocalypses*, or "revealed."

"22 If thou hast opened thy mouth against thy friend, fear not; for there may be a reconciliation: except for upbraiding, or pride, or disclosing of secrets, or a treacherous wound: for for these things every friend will depart." (Sirach 22:22) And here, they rendered the word "disclosing" as *apocalypses*, or "revealing."

The end result of this study is that the Greek word *apocalypses* was used in a meaning similar to what has been alleged only once out of every seven times it occurred in places we can easily look up. And it was used in that exact meaning less than ten percent of the times it occurred.

But what about the Greek word *epiphaneia*? This Greek word occurs 6 times in the New Testament, and Hatch and Redpath list 12 times it was used in the Septuagint. We find that it refers to our Lord's **"appearing"** at His **"coming... with power and great glory"** only twice, and one of those times, it is translated as **"brightness"** instead of "appearing."

> "⁸ And then the lawless one will be revealed, whom the Lord will consume with the breath of His mouth and destroy with the brightness of His coming." (2 Thessalonians 2:8)

> "¹ I charge *you* therefore before God and the Lord Jesus Christ, who will judge the living and the dead at His appearing and His kingdom:" (2 Timothy 4:1)

And it refers to our Lords **"appearing"** when He comes for His own three times.

> "¹⁴ that you keep *this* commandment without spot, blameless until our Lord Jesus Christ's appearing," (1 Timothy 6:14)

> "⁸ Finally, there is laid up for me the crown of righteousness, which the Lord, the righteous Judge, will give to me on that Day, and not to me only but also to all who have loved His appearing." (2 Timothy 4:8)

> "¹³ looking for the blessed hope and glorious appearing of our great God and Savior Jesus Christ," (Titus 2:130)

And finally for the New Testament, it is used once, not of His future **"appearing,"** but of His past one.

> "¹⁰ but has now been revealed by the appearing of our Savior Jesus Christ, *who* has abolished death and brought life and immortality to light through the gospel," (2 Timothy 1:10)

But what of its usage in the Septuagint? There we find this Greek word used in both of these senses, that is, of both **"brightness"** and **"appearing."**

THOUGHTS ABOUT PROPHETIC SUBJECTS

"And what other nation in the earth [is] as thy people Israel? whereas God was his guide, to redeem for himself a people to make thee a name, to do mightily and nobly, (*epiphaneia*) so that thou shouldest cast out nations and [their] tabernacles from the presence of thy people, whom thou didst redeem for thyself out of Egypt?" (2 Kings [2 Samuel] 7:23)

"And being splendidly (*epiphaneia*) arrayed, [and] having called upon God the Overseer and Preserver of all things, she took her two maids, and she leaned upon one, as a delicate female, and the other followed bearing her train." (Ester 5:1a)

"Wherefore if ye should bring me your whole-burnt-sacrifices and meat-offerings, I will not accept [them]: neither will I have respect to your grand (*epiphaneia*) peace-offerings." (Amos 5:22)

And in the Apocryphal portion of the Septuagint, we find:

"And the manifest (*epiphaneia*) signs that came from heaven unto those that behaved themselves manfully to their honour for Judaism: so that, being but a few, they overcame the whole country, and chased barbarous multitudes," (2 Maccabees 2:21)

"Now as he was there present himself with his guard about the treasury, the Lord of spirits, and the Prince of all power, caused a great apparition, (*epiphaneia*) so that all that presumed to come in with him were astonished at the power of God, and fainted, and were sore afraid." (2 Maccabees 3:24)

"Wherefore every man prayed that that apparition (*epiphaneia*) might turn to good." (2 Maccabees 5:4)

"But when Judas his first band came in sight, (*epiphaneia*) the enemies, being smitten with fear and terror through the appearing of him who seeth all things, fled amain, one running into this way, another that way, so as that they were often hurt of their own men, and wounded with the points of their own swords" (2 Maccabees 12:22)

Now when the Jews heard of Nicanor's coming, and that the heathen were up against them, they cast earth upon their heads, and made supplication to him that had established his people for ever, and who always helpeth his portion with manifestation (*epiphaneia*) of his presence." (2 Maccabees 14:15)

"So that fighting with their hands, and praying unto God with their hearts, they slew no less than thirty and five thousand men: for through the appearance (*epiphaneia*) of God they were greatly cheered." (2 Maccabees 15:27)

"Thou, O King, when thou createdst the illimitable and measureless earth, didst choose out this city: thou didst make this place sacred to thy name, albeit thou needest nothing: thou didst glorify (*epiphaneia*) it with thine illustrious presence, after constructing it to the glory of thy great and honourable name." (3 Maccabees 2:9)

"to overthrow the evil purpose which was gone out against them, and to deliver them by extraordinary manifestation (*epiphaneia*) from that death which was in store for them." (3 Maccabees 5:8)

"sent up an exceeding great cry entreating the Lord of all power to reveal (*epiphaneia*) himself, and have mercy upon those who now lay at the gates of hades." (3 Maccabees 5:51)

So we see that none the three Greek word *parousia. apocalypses,* or *epiphaneia,* refer *only* to our Lord's **"coming... with power and great glory."** In addition to being used in many other ways, all three of these words are used equally of His **"coming... with power and great glory"** and of His coming as **"the bridegroom"** to take **"those who"** are **"ready" "in" "to the wedding."** (Matthew 25:10) This **"wedding"** is called **"the marriage of the Lamb"** in Revelation 19:5-9, where it is depicted as taking place in heaven in the last vision before the Lord goes forth from heaven as **"KING OF KINGS AND LORD OF LORDS"** in Revelation 19:11-16.

But what of the seven other Greek words used to describe our Lord's coming? As these are less known than the first three, there does not seem to be a claim that any of them only refers to His **"coming... with power and great glory."**

The first of these is the Greek word ὀπτανομαι, *optanomai* in our alphabet, word number 3700 in Strong's Greek Dictionary, which occurs 58 times in the New Testament, of which it is translated "see" 37 times and "appear" 17 times.

It is used of the Lord's **"coming... with power and great glory"** seven times.

> "³⁰ Then the sign of the Son of Man will appear in heaven, and then all the tribes of the earth will mourn, and they will see *(optanomai)* the Son of Man coming on the clouds of heaven with power and great glory." (Matthew 24:30)

> "⁶⁴ Jesus said to him, 'It is as you said. Nevertheless, I say to you, hereafter you will see *(optanomai)* the Son of Man sitting at the right hand of the Power, and coming on the clouds of heaven.'" (Matthew 26:64)

> "²⁶ Then they will see *(optanomai)* the Son of Man coming in the clouds with great power and glory." (Mark 13:26)

> "⁶² Jesus said, 'I am. And you will see *(optanomai)* the Son of Man sitting at the right hand of the Power, and coming with the clouds of heaven.'" (Mark 14:61-62)

> "⁶ *And all flesh shall see (optanomai) **the salvation of God.**"* **(Luke 3:6)**

> "²⁷ Then they will see *(optanomai)* the Son of Man coming in a cloud with power and great glory." (Luke 21:27)

> "⁷ Behold, He is coming with clouds, and every eye will see *(optanomai)* Him, even they who pierced Him. And all the tribes of the earth will mourn because of Him. Even so, Amen." (Revelation 1:7)

And it is used in regard to His coming for His own another seven times.

"¹⁶ A little while, and you will not see Me; and again a little while, and you will see *(optanomai)* Me, because I go to the Father.' ¹⁷ Then *some* of His disciples said among themselves, 'What is this that He says to us, "A little while, and you will not see Me; and again a little while, and you will see *(optanomai)* Me"; and, "because I go to the Father" ?" (John 16:16-17)

"¹⁹ Now Jesus knew that they desired to ask Him, and He said to them, 'Are you inquiring among yourselves about what I said, "A little while, and you will not see Me; and again a little while, and you will see Me" ?" (John 16:19)

We should note that in each of the last three passages, the first occasion of the English word **"see"** is a translation of a different Greek word, θεωρέω, *theoreo* in our alphabet, word number 2334 in Strong's Greek Dictionary. But as this word is never used of His future comings, it is not discussed here.

"²² Therefore you now have sorrow; but I will see *(optanomai)* you again and your heart will rejoice, and your joy no one will take from you." (John 16:22)

"²⁸ so Christ was offered once to bear the sins of many. To those who eagerly wait for Him He will appear *(optanomai)* a second time, apart from sin, for salvation." (Hebrews 9:28)

"² Beloved, now we are children of God; and it has not yet been revealed *(optanomai)* what we shall be, but we know that when He is revealed, *(optanomai)* we shall be like Him, for we shall see Him as He is." (1 John 3:2)

Next, we need to consider the Greek word φανεροω, *phaneroo* in our alphabet, word number 5319 in Strong's Greek Dictionary, which occurs 49 times in the New Testament, of which it is trans-

THOUGHTS ABOUT PROPHETIC SUBJECTS

lated as **"manifest"** or **"manifested"** 16 times, as **"appear"** or **"appeared"** 15 times, and as **"revealed"** twice.

It is used twice in one verse, and one other time, in regard to His **"coming... with power and great glory."**

"⁴ **When Christ** *who is* **our life appears,** *(phaneroo)* **then you also will appear** *(phaneroo)* **with Him in glory."** (Colossians 3:4)

"⁴ **Who shall not fear You,**

O Lord, and glorify Your name?

For *You* **alone** *are* **holy.**

For all nations shall come and worship before You,

For Your judgments have been manifested. *(phaneroo)*" (Revelation 15:4)

It is used four times in regard to His coming for His own.

"⁴ **and when the Chief Shepherd appears,** *(phaneroo)* **you will receive the crown of glory that does not fade away."** (1 Peter 5:4)

"²⁸ **And now, little children, abide in Him, that when He appears,** *(phaneroo)* **we may have confidence and not be ashamed before Him at His coming."** (1 John 2:28)

"² **Beloved, now we are children of God; and it has not yet been revealed** *(phaneroo)* **what we shall be, but we know that when He is revealed,** *(phaneroo)* **we shall be like Him, for we shall see Him as He is."** (1 John 3:2)

It is also used twice concerning the judgment seat of Christ.

"⁵ **Therefore judge nothing before the time, until the Lord comes, who will both bring to light the hidden things of darkness and reveal** *(phaneroo)* **the counsels of the hearts. Then each one's praise will come from God."** (1 Corinthians 4:5)

> "¹⁰ For we must all appear *(phaneroo)* before the judgment seat of Christ, that each one may receive the things *done* in the body, according to what he has done, whether good or bad." (2 Corinthians 5:10)

And now we need to discuss the Greek words translated as some tense of the English word "**come.**" The first of these we will consider is the Greek word ἔρχομαι, *erchomai* in our alphabet, word number 2064 in Strong's Greek Dictionary, occurs 664 times in the New Testament, of which it is translated as "**come**" 363 times, "**came**" 253 times, and "**coming**" 32 times.

It is used in regard to His "**coming... with power and great glory,**" forty-three times.

> "²³ When they persecute you in this city, flee to another. For assuredly, I say to you, you will not have gone through the cities of Israel before the Son of Man comes.*(erchomai)*" (Matthew 10:23)

> "²⁷ For the Son of Man will come *(erchomai)* in the glory of His Father with His angels, and then He will reward each according to his works." (Matthew 16:27)

> "³⁹ for I say to you, you shall see Me no more till you say, *'Blessed is He who comes (erchomai) in the name of the LORD!'*" (Matthew 23:39)

> "³⁰ Then the sign of the Son of Man will appear in heaven, and then all the tribes of the earth will mourn, and they will see the Son of Man coming *(erchomai)* on the clouds of heaven with power and great glory." (Matthew 24:30)

> "³⁹ and did not know until the flood came and took them all away, so also will the coming *(erchomai)* of the Son of Man be." (Matthew 24:39)

> "⁴² Watch therefore, for you do not know what hour your Lord is coming.*(erchomai)*" (Matthew 24:42)

THOUGHTS ABOUT PROPHETIC SUBJECTS

"⁴³ But know this, that if the master of the house had known what hour the thief would come, *(erchomai)* he would have watched and not allowed his house to be broken into." (Matthew 24:43)

"⁴⁴ Therefore you also be ready, for the Son of Man is coming *(erchomai)* at an hour you do not expect." (Matthew 24:44)

"⁴⁶ Blessed *is* that servant whom his master, when he comes, *(erchomai)* will find so doing." (Matthew 24:46)

"⁴⁸ But if that evil servant says in his heart, 'My master is delaying his coming,*(erchomai)*'" (Matthew 24:48)

"¹⁹ After a long time the lord of those servants came *(erchomai)* and settled accounts with them." (Matthew 25:19)

"²⁷ So you ought to have deposited my money with the bankers, and at my coming *(erchomai)* I would have received back my own with interest." (Matthew 25:27)

"³¹ When the Son of Man comes *(erchomai)* in His glory, and all the holy angels with Him, then He will sit on the throne of His glory." (Matthew 25:31)

"⁶⁴ Jesus said to him, '*It is as* you said. Nevertheless, I say to you, hereafter you will see the Son of Man sitting at the right hand of the Power, and coming *(erchomai)* on the clouds of heaven.'" (Matthew 26:64)

"³⁸ For whoever is ashamed of Me and My words in this adulterous and sinful generation, of him the Son of Man also will be ashamed when He comes *(erchomai)* in the glory of His Father with the holy angels." (Mark 8:38)

"²⁶ Then they will see the Son of Man coming *(erchomai)* in the clouds with great power and glory." (Mark 13:26)

"³⁵ Watch therefore, for you do not know when the master of the house is coming *(erchomai)* --in the evening, at midnight, at the crowing of the rooster, or in the morning–" (Mark 13:35)

"³⁶ lest, coming *(erchomai)* suddenly, he find you sleeping." (Mark 13:36)

"⁶² Jesus said, 'I am. And you will see the Son of Man sitting at the right hand of the Power, and coming *(erchomai)* with the clouds of heaven.'" (Mark 14:62)

"²⁶ For whoever is ashamed of Me and My words, of him the Son of Man will be ashamed when He comes *(erchomai)* in His *own* glory, and *in His* Father's, and of the holy angels." (Luke 9:26)

"³⁶ and you yourselves be like men who wait for their master, when he will return from the wedding, that when he comes *(erchomai)* and knocks they may open to him immediately." (Luke 12:36)

"³⁷ Blessed *are* those servants whom the master, when he comes, *(erchomai)* will find watching. Assuredly, I say to you that he will gird himself and have them sit down *to eat,* and will come and serve them." (Luke 12:37)

"³⁸ And if he should come *(erchomai)* in the second watch, or come in the third watch, and find *them* so, blessed are those servants." (Luke 12:38)

"³⁹ But know this, that if the master of the house had known what hour the thief would come, *(erchomai)* he would have watched and not allowed his house to be broken into." (Luke 12:39)

"⁴⁰ Therefore you also be ready, for the Son of Man is coming *(erchomai)* at an hour you do not expect." (Luke 12:39-40)

"⁴⁵ But if that servant says in his heart, 'My master is delaying his coming,' *(erchomai)* and begins to beat the male and female servants, and to eat and drink and be drunk," (Luke 12:45)

THOUGHTS ABOUT PROPHETIC SUBJECTS

"*35* See! Your house is left to you desolate; and assuredly, I say to you, you shall not see Me until *the time comes when you say, 'Blessed is He who comes (erchomai) in the name of the LORD!'*" (Luke 13:35)

Note: the first case of the word "**comes**" in this verse is a translation of the Greek word *heko*, and is treated below.

"*8* I tell you that He will avenge them speedily. Nevertheless, when the Son of Man comes, *(erchomai)* will He really find faith on the earth?" (Luke 18:8)

"*13* So he called ten of his servants, delivered to them ten minas, and said to them, 'Do business till I come. *(erchomai)*'" (Luke 19:13)

"*23* Why then did you not put my money in the bank, that at my coming *(erchomai)* I might have collected it with interest?" (Luke 19:23)

"*27* Then they will see the Son of Man coming *(erchomai)* in a cloud with power and great glory." (Luke 21:27)

"*18* for I say to you, I will not drink of the fruit of the vine until the kingdom of God comes. *(erchomai)*" (Luke 22:18)

"*11* who also said, 'Men of Galilee, why do you stand gazing up into heaven? This *same* Jesus, who was taken up from you into heaven, will so come *(erchomai)* in like manner as you saw Him go into heaven.'" (Acts 1:11)

"*20 The sun shall be turned into darkness, And the moon into blood, Before the coming (erchomai) of the great and awesome day of the LORD.*" (Acts 2:20)

"*19* Repent therefore and be converted, that your sins may be blotted out, so that times of refreshing may come *(erchomai)* from the presence of the Lord," (Acts 3:19)

"² For you yourselves know perfectly that the day of the Lord so comes *(erchomai)* as a thief in the night." (1 Thessalonians 5:2)

"¹⁰ when He comes, *(erchomai)* in that Day, to be glorified in His saints and to be admired among all those who believe, because our testimony among you was believed." (2 Thessalonians 1:10)

"⁸ Because finding fault with them, He says: *'Behold, the days are coming, (erchomai) says the LORD, when I will make a new covenant with the house of Israel and with the house of Judah'*" (Hebrews 8:8)

"¹⁴ Now Enoch, the seventh from Adam, prophesied about these men also, saying, 'Behold, the Lord comes *(erchomai)* with ten thousands of His saints,'" (Jude 1:14)

"⁷ Behold, He is coming *(erchomai)* with clouds, and every eye will see Him, even they who pierced Him. And all the tribes of the earth will mourn because of Him. Even so, Amen." (Revelation 1:7)

"¹⁷ For the great day of His wrath has come, *(erchomai)* and who is able to stand?" (Revelation 6:17)

"¹⁸ The nations were angry, and Your wrath has come, *(erchomai)*

And the time of the dead, that they should be judged,

And that You should reward Your servants the prophets and the saints,

And those who fear Your name, small and great,

And should destroy those who destroy the earth." (Revelation 11:18)

"⁷ saying with a loud voice, 'Fear God and give glory to Him, for the hour of His judgment has come; *(erchomai)* and worship Him who made heaven and earth, the sea and springs of water.'" (Revelation 14:7)

"¹⁵ And another angel came out of the temple, crying with a loud voice to Him who sat on the cloud,

'Thrust in Your sickle and reap, for the time has come *(erchomai)* for You to reap, for the harvest of the earth is ripe.' " (Revelation 14:15)

"¹⁵ Behold, I am coming *(erchomai)* as a thief. Blessed *is* he who watches, and keeps his garments, lest he walk naked and they see his shame." (Revelation 16:15)

And it is used in regard to His coming for His own nineteen times.

"⁶ And at midnight a cry was *heard:* 'Behold, the bridegroom is coming; *(erchomai)* go out to meet him!' " (Matthew 25:6)

"¹⁰ And while they went to buy, the bridegroom came, *(erchomai)* and those who were ready went in with him to the wedding; and the door was shut." (Matthew 25:10)

"¹³ Watch therefore, for you know neither the day nor the hour in which the Son of Man is coming. *(erchomai)*" (Matthew 25:13)

"³⁰ who shall not receive a hundredfold now in this time--houses and brothers and sisters and mothers and children and lands, with persecutions--and in the age to come, *(erchomai)* eternal life." (Mark 10:30)

"³⁰ who shall not receive many times more in this present time, and in the age to come *(erchomai)* eternal life." (Luke 18:30)

"²⁸ Do not marvel at this; for the hour is coming *(erchomai)* in which all who are in the graves will hear His voice" (John 5:28)

"²² Jesus said to him, 'If I will that he remain till I come, *(erchomai)* what *is that* to you? You follow Me.' " (John 21:22)

"⁵ Therefore judge nothing before the time, until the Lord comes, *(erchomai)* who will both bring to light the hidden things of darkness and reveal the counsels of the hearts. Then each one's praise will come from God." (1 Corinthians 4:5)

"²⁶ **For as often as you eat this bread and drink this cup, you proclaim the Lord's death till He comes.** *(erchomai)*" (1 Corinthians 11:26)

"¹⁰ **But when that which is perfect has come,** *(erchomai)* **then that which is in part will be done away.**" (1 Corinthians 13:10)

"³⁵ **But someone will say, 'How are the dead raised up? And with what body do they come** *(erchomai)*?' " (1 Corinthians 15:35)

"¹⁰ **and to wait for His Son from heaven, whom He raised from the dead,** *even* **Jesus who delivers us from the wrath to come.** *(erchomai)*" (1 Thessalonians 1:10)

"³⁷ *For yet a little while, And He who is coming* (erchomai) *will come and will not tarry.*" (Hebrews 10:37)

Note: the words **"will come"** in this verse are a translation of the Greek word *heko*, and is treated below.

"¹⁰ **Because you have kept My command to persevere, I also will keep you from the hour of trial which shall come** *(erchomai)* **upon the whole world, to test those who dwell on the earth.**" (Revelation 3:10)

"¹¹ **Behold, I am coming** *(erchomai)* **quickly! Hold fast what you have, that no one may take your crown.**" (Revelation 3:11)

"⁷ **Behold, I am coming** *(erchomai)* **quickly! Blessed** *is* **he who keeps the words of the prophecy of this book.**" (Revelation 2:7)

"¹⁷ **And the Spirit and the bride say, 'Come!'** *(erchomai)* **And let him who hears say, 'Come!'***(erchomai)* **And let him who thirsts come. Whoever desires, let him take the water of life freely.**" (Revelation 22:17)

Note, the third case of the English word **"come"** in this verse is a translation of the same Greek word. But it is not stressed here because in that case, it does not refer to our Lord's coming, but to our coming to Him.

> "**²⁰ He who testifies to these things says, 'Surely I am coming** *(erchomai)* **quickly.' Amen. Even so, come, Lord Jesus!**" (Revelation 22:20)

And it is used once in regard to the coming of the Antichrist.

> "**¹⁸ Little children, it is the last hour; and as you have heard that the Antichrist is coming,** *(erchomai)* **even now many antichrists have come, by which we know that it is the last hour.**" (1 John 2:18)

The second Greek word that is translated as **"come"** that we need to consider is the Greek word ἥκω, *heko* in our alphabet, word number 2240 in Strong's Greek Dictionary. This Greek word occurs 27 times in the New Testament, where it is always translated as **"come."**

It is used of the Lord's **"coming... with power and great glory"** nine times.

> "**¹⁴ And this gospel of the kingdom will be preached in all the world as a witness to all the nations, and then the end will come.** *(heko)*" (Matthew 24:14)

> "**⁵⁰ the master of that servant will come** *(heko)* **on a day when he is not looking for** *him* **and at an hour that he is not aware of,**" (Matthew 24:50)

> "**⁴⁶ the master of that servant will come** *(heko)* **on a day when he is not looking for** *him,* **and at an hour when he is not aware, and will cut him in two and appoint** *him* **his portion with the unbelievers.**" (Luke 12:46)

> "**³⁵ See! Your house is left to you desolate; and assuredly, I say to you, you shall not see Me until** *the time* **comes**

(heko) **when you say, 'Blessed is He who comes in the name of the LORD!'"** (Luke 13:35)

Note: the second case of the word **"comes"** in this verse is a translation of the Greek word *erchomai,* and is treated above.

"²⁶ And so all Israel will be saved, as it is written:
The Deliverer will come (heko) out of Zion,
And He will turn away ungodliness from Jacob;'" (Romans 11:26)
"³⁷ For yet a little while, And He who is coming will come *(heko)* **and will not tarry."** (Hebrews 10:37)

Note: the word **"coming"** in this verse is a translation of the Greek word *erchomai,* and is treated above.

"¹⁰ But the day of the Lord will come *(heko)* **as a thief in the night, in which the heavens will pass away with a great noise, and the elements will melt with fervent heat; both the earth and the works that are in it will be burned up."** (2 Peter 3:10)

"³ Remember therefore how you have received and heard; hold fast and repent. Therefore if you will not watch, I will come *(heko)* **upon you as a thief, and you will not know what hour I will come** *(heko)* **upon you."** (Revelation 3:3)

And it is used once in regard to His coming for His own.

"²⁵ But hold fast what you have till I come. *(heko)*" (Revelation 2:25)

And the third Greek word that is translated as some form of the English word **"come"** when speaking of the Lord's coming is the Greek word ἐφιστημι, *ephistemi* on our alphabet, word nimber 2186 in Strong's Greek Dictionary, which ocurs 21 times in the New Testament, of which it is ranslated either as **"come on,"** **"come upon,"** or **"come"** ten times.

It is used of the Lord's **"coming... with power and great glory"** two times.

> "**34** **But take heed to yourselves, lest your hearts be weighed down with carousing, drunkenness, and cares of this life, and that Day come** *(ephistemi)* **on you unexpectedly."** (Luke 21:34)

> "**3** **For when they say, 'Peace and safety!' then sudden destruction comes** *(ephistemi)* **upon them, as labor pains upon a pregnant woman. And they shall not escape."** (1 Thessalonians 5:3)

We should note that, of the eight Greek words we have consodred thus far, this is the first one that is not used of both of our Lord's comings. And of the entire ten, there is only one other that is used exclusively of His **"coming... with power ad great glory."**

And finally, we find a contrast between two Greek words, in extremely important details of two passages of scripture. The first of these is the Greek word εἰσέρχομαι, *eiserchomai* in our alphabet, word number 1525 in Strong's Greek Dictionary, which occurs 198 times in the New Testament, of which it is translated as **"enter," "enter in," "come in,"** or **"go in"** 161 times.

It is used of the Lord's **"coming... with powerand great glory"** two times.

> "**29** **Or how can one enter** *(eiserchomai)* **a strong man's house and plunder his goods, unless he first binds the strong man? And then he will plunder his house."** (Matthew 12:29)

> "**27** **No one can enter** *(eiserchomai)* **a strong man's house and plunder his goods, unless he first binds the strong man. And then he will plunder his house."** (Mark 3:27)

But the contrast is found in its use in regard to the Lord's coming for His own. For Jesus plainly said:

> "¹⁰ **And while they went to buy, the bridegroom came, and those who were ready went in** *(eiserchomai)* **with him to the wedding; and the door was shut.**" (Matthew 25:10)

This statement is contrasted to the Greek word ἀναλυω, *analuo* in our alphabet, word number 360 in Strong's Greek Dictionary, which occurs only twice in the entire New Testament, and it is correctly translated as "**return**" in the one place where it is used in regard to His "**coming... with power and great glory.**"

> "³⁶ **and you yourselves be like men who wait for their master, when he will return** *(analuo)* **from the wedding, that when he comes and knocks they may open to him immediately.**" (Luke 12:36)

The significance of the contrast between these two statements could hardly be over exaggerated. For it is physically impossible to "**enter**" an event and to "**return from**" it at the same time. So the contrast between these two Greek words amounts to clear statements, from the very mouth of Jesus Himself, that He will come at two *distinctly different* times. This particluar contrast does not even imply how long the delay between these two comings will be. But it could not be more clear in explicitly stating that they will take place at different times.

THOUGHTS ABOUT PROPHETIC SUBJECTS

The Four Formal Judgments of Scripture

The Holy Scriptures describe four distinct formal judgments that will take place after the Lord comes for us. That is, they describe four different occasions when judgments will take place to determine the rewards or punishments that will be received by those brought before the Lord for evaluation.

Taking these formal judgments in the order in which they will take place, two different scriptures call the first one, "**the judgment seat of Christ.**" The first of these is:

> "But why do you judge your brother? Or why do you show contempt for your brother? For we shall all stand before the judgment seat of Christ. For it is written:
>
> *'As I live, says the LORD,*
>
> *Every knee shall bow to Me,*
>
> *And every tongue shall confess to God.'*
>
> So then each of us shall give account of himself to God." (Romans 14:10-12)

And the second one is:

> "For we know that if our earthly house, *this* tent, is destroyed, we have a building from God, a house not made with hands, eternal in the heavens. For in this we groan, earnestly desiring to be clothed with our habitation which is from heaven, if indeed, having been clothed, we shall not be found naked. For we who are in *this* tent groan, being burdened, not because we want to be unclothed, but further clothed,

that mortality may be swallowed up by life. Now He who has prepared us for this very thing is God, who also has given us the Spirit as a guarantee. So *we are* always confident, knowing that while we are at home in the body we are absent from the Lord. For we walk by faith, not by sight. We are confident, yes, well pleased rather to be absent from the body and to be present with the Lord.

"Therefore we make it our aim, whether present or absent, to be well pleasing to Him. For we must all appear before the judgment seat of Christ, that each one may receive the things *done* in the body, according to what he has done, whether good or bad." (2 Corinthians 5:1-10)

The material surrounding both of these mentions of **"the judgment seat of Christ"** is included so we can clearly see that they are both about a judgment of people that have truly trusted in the Lord Jesus, His own redeemed. These are the ones who will be judged at **"the judgment seat of Christ."**

This can again be clearly seen in its description in another scripture:

"According to the grace of God which was given to me, as a wise master builder I have laid the foundation, and another builds on it. But let each one take heed how he builds on it. For no other foundation can anyone lay than that which is laid, which is Jesus Christ. Now if anyone builds on this foundation *with* gold, silver, precious stones, wood, hay, straw, each one's work will become clear; for the Day will declare it, because it will be revealed by fire; and the fire will test each one's work, of what sort it is. If anyone's work which he has built on *it* endures, he will receive a reward. If anyone's work is burned, he will suffer loss; but he himself will be saved, yet so as through fire." (1 Corinthians 3:10-15)

So it is clear that this is a judgment for rewards, not for punishment. As we read in another place, **"behold, I am coming quickly, and My reward *is* with Me, to give to every one according to his work."** (Revelation 22:12)

But now we must ask, when will this judgment take place? We are told:

> **"But with me it is a very small thing that I should be judged by you or by a human court. In fact, I do not even judge myself. For I know nothing against myself, yet I am not justified by this; but He who judges me is the Lord. Therefore judge nothing before the time, until the Lord comes, who will both bring to light the hidden things of darkness and reveal the counsels of the hearts. Then each one's praise will come from God."** (1 Corinthians 4:3-5)

So this **"judgment seat of Christ,"** in which Christians will be evaluated to see what rewards they will receive, will take place when **"the Lord comes."** And the fact that only real Christians will be involved in this judgment is shown by the fact that it clearly says that **"each one's praise will come from God."** And, "**If anyone's work is burned, he will suffer loss; but he himself will be saved.**" For we remember that salvation is not based on works, but on faith. As we read, **"For by grace you have been saved through faith, and that not of yourselves; *it is* the gift of God, not of works, lest anyone should boast."** (Ephesians 2:8-9)

But we are told more about this than simply that it will take place **"when the Lord comes."** For Jesus told His own that **"In My Father's house are many mansions; if *it were* not *so*, I** would have told you. I go to prepare a place for you. And if I go and prepare a place for you, I will come again and receive you to Myself; that where I am, *there* you may be also." (John 14:2-3) So the place where Jesus went **"to prepare a place"** for us was His **"Father's house,"** that is, heaven. And that is the place from which He will come to **"receive"** us to Himself, that where He is, there we **"may be also."**

And in Revelation 19 we find **"the marriage of the Lamb,"** (verses 7-9) taking place in heaven just before the Lord goes forth out of heaven as the **"KING OF KINGS AND LORD OF LORDS."** (verses 11-21) And it says of **"His wife,"** that **"to her it was granted to be arrayed in fine linen, clean and bright, for the fine linen is the righteous acts of the saints."** (Revelation 19:8) But **"the righteous acts of the saints"** will not be made manifest until this judgment takes place, as Jesus said, **"there is nothing covered that will not be revealed, nor hidden that will not be known."** (Luke 12:2) So we see that this judgment has to take place before the Lord comes in power and glory to judge the wicked.

But a different judgment is described as taking place **"when the Son of Man comes in His glory."**

> **"When the Son of Man comes in His glory, and all the holy angels with Him, then He will sit on the throne of His glory. All the nations will be gathered before Him, and He will separate them one from another, as a shepherd divides *his* sheep from the goats. And He will set the sheep on His right hand, but the goats on the left. Then the King will say to those on His right hand, 'Come, you blessed of My Father, inherit the kingdom prepared for you from the foundation of the world: for I was hungry and you gave Me food; I was thirsty and you gave Me drink; I was a stranger and you took Me in; I *was* naked and you clothed Me; I was sick and you visited Me; I was in prison and you came to Me.'**

> Then the righteous will answer Him, saying, 'Lord, when did we see You hungry and feed You, or thirsty and give *You* drink? When did we see You a stranger and take *You* in, or naked and clothe *You*? Or when did we see You sick, or in prison, and come to You?' And the King will answer and say to them, 'Assuredly, I say to you, inasmuch as you did it to one of the least of these My brethren, you did *it* to Me.' Then He will also say to those on the left hand, 'Depart from Me, you cursed, into the everlasting fire prepared for the devil and his angels: for I was hungry and you gave Me no food; I was thirsty and you gave Me no drink; I was a stranger and you did not take Me in, naked and you did not clothe Me, sick and in prison and you did not visit Me.' Then they also will answer Him, saying, 'Lord, when did we see You hungry or thirsty or a stranger or naked or sick or in prison, and did not minister to You?' Then He will answer them, saying, 'Assuredly, I say to you, inasmuch as you did not do *it* to one of the least of these, you did not do *it* to Me.' And these will go away into everlasting punishment, but the righteous into eternal life." (Matthew 25:31-46)

Here we see a completely different judgment. For while in the first judgment **"each one's praise will come from God."** And, **"If anyone's work is burned, he will suffer loss; but he himself will be saved."** In this judgment, some **"will go away into everlasting punishment, but the righteous into eternal life."**

But there is an even bigger difference between these judgments than that. For **"the judgment seat of Christ,"** being a judgment of the redeemed after the Lord comes, is a judgment of saints that will take place after **"we shall all be changed-- in a moment, in the twinkling of an eye, at the last trumpet. For the trumpet will sound, and the dead will be raised incorruptible, and we shall be changed."** (1 Corinthians 15:51-52)

But in this judgment "**all the nations will be gathered before Him.**" That is, this is a judgment of people that are still in their natural bodies. "**The judgment seat of Christ**" is a judgment to determine the degree of reward to be received in heaven. But this is a judgment to determine whether people who are still in their natural bodies will be condemned to "**the everlasting fire**" or allowed to "**inherit the kingdom,**" that is, to live on into the millennium. "**For the Son of Man will come in the glory of His Father with His angels, and then He will reward each according to his works.**" (Matthew 16:27)

And at about the same time as this judgment, there will be another one that is less well known. This is most certainly a different judgment from the last one. For the second judgment we discussed was a judgment of "**all the nations,**" that is, of "gentiles." But this will be a judgment of Israelites as they will be in the act of returning to the land after Messiah comes. That return, as well as when it will take place, is found in the last chapter of Isaiah.

> " 'For I *know* their works and their thoughts. It shall be that I will gather all nations and tongues; and they shall come and see My glory. I will set a sign among them; and those among them who escape I will send to the nations: to Tarshish and Pul and Lud, who draw the bow, and Tubal and Javan, to the coastlands afar off who have not heard My fame nor seen My glory. And they shall declare My glory among the Gentiles. Then they shall bring all your brethren for an offering to the LORD out of all nations, on horses and in chariots and in litters, on mules and on camels, to My holy mountain Jerusalem,' says the LORD, 'as the children of Israel bring an offering in a clean vessel into the house of the LORD.' " (Isaiah 66:18-20)

This passage describes the great battle of Armageddon, without naming it, and then says that the Lord will send the survivors from that battle out to tell all the world about Himself. And **"Then they shall bring all your brethren... to My holy mountain Jerusalem."** The fact that this return will take place after Armageddon would seem to indicate that it will take place after the judgment we just discussed. This also seems to be indicated by the fact that, in the parable of the wheat and the tares, (Matthew 13:24-30) the Lord said, **"at the time of harvest I will say to the reapers, "First gather together the tares and bind them in bundles to burn them, but gather the wheat into my barn."** (Matthew 13:30) As **"the tares"** will be gathered **"to burn them,"** before **"the wheat"** is gathered into the **"barn,"** it seems that the previous judgment will take place before Israel is brought back to the land. And this next judgment will take place while Israel is in the act of returning to the land, as is clearly stated in the following scripture:

> " 'As I live,' says the Lord GOD, 'surely with a mighty hand, with an outstretched arm, and with fury poured out, I will rule over you. I will bring you out from the peoples and gather you out of the countries where you are scattered, with a mighty hand, with an outstretched arm, and with fury poured out. And I will bring you into the wilderness of the peoples, and there I will plead My case with you face to face. Just as I pleaded My case with your fathers in the wilderness of the land of Egypt, so I will plead My case with you,' says the Lord GOD. 'I will make you pass under the rod, and I will bring you into the bond of the covenant; I will purge the rebels from among you, and those who transgress against Me; I will bring them out of the country where they dwell, but they shall not enter the land of Israel. Then you will know that I am the LORD.' " (Ezekiel 20:33-38)

As this judgment will take place while these people are returning to the land, and as the Lord will deal with them **"face to face"** when He makes this judgment, we see that it will take place at the time of the return described in Isaiah 66. So, while the last judgment was of the gentiles, to determine which of them would be allowed to live on into the millennium, this will be a similar judgment of the Israelites, for the same purpose. For it says, **"I will purge the rebels from among you, and those who transgress against Me; I will bring them out of the country where they dwell, but they shall not enter the land of Israel."**

This scripture does not state what will happen to the rebels that will be purged **"from among"** Israel. But other scriptures show us what will happen to them. For Ezekiel 36:1-11 says that **"all the house of Israel, all of it"** will again inhabit the **"mountains of Israel,"** along with **"the hills, the rivers, the valleys, the desolate wastes, and the cities that have been forsaken, which became plunder and mockery to the rest of the nations all around."** This would be a flat contradiction of the words **"they shall not enter the land of Israel."** if **"the rebels"** who had been so purged had been allowed to live. So we see that the fate of the sinners among the nation of Israel will be the same as that of the sinners among the gentile nations. That is, that **"these will go away into everlasting punishment."**

We see this again in two other scriptures. For in Isaiah 4 we read:

> **"In that day the Branch of the LORD shall be beautiful and glorious;**
>
> **And the fruit of the earth** *shall be* **excellent and appealing For those of Israel who have escaped.**
>
> **And it shall come to pass that** *he who is* **left in Zion and remains in Jerusalem will be called holy--everyone who is recorded among the living in Jerusalem. When the Lord has washed away the filth of the daughters of Zion, and purged the blood of Jerusalem from her**

midst, by the spirit of judgment and by the spirit of burning." (Isaiah 4:2-4)

Then again, we read in Zachariah 12:

"And I will pour on the house of David and on the inhabitants of Jerusalem the Spirit of grace and supplication; then they will look on Me whom they pierced. Yes, they will mourn for Him as one mourns for *his* **only** *son,* **and grieve for Him as one grieves for a firstborn. In that day there shall be a great mourning in Jerusalem, like the mourning at Hadad Rimmon in the plain of Megiddo. And the land shall mourn, every family by itself: the family of the house of David by itself, and their wives by themselves; the family of the house of Nathan by itself, and their wives by themselves; the family of the house of Levi by itself, and their wives by themselves; the family of Shimei by itself, and their wives by themselves; all the families that remain, every family by itself, and their wives by themselves."** (Zechariah 12:10-14)

These two scriptures speak explicitly of these blessings coming upon **"those of Israel who have escaped," "everyone who is recorded among the living,"** and **"all the families that remain."** So we see that those of Israel who will not be allowed to partake of these blessings will no longer be living.

Finally, the last of the four formal judgments will be delayed until after the millennium. We realize the reason for this when we realize that this last formal judgment will be a judgment of the wicked dead. During the millennium, there will still be sinners in the earth, and after it ends, there will be a final rebellion. So there will still be more wicked dead to deal with until that final rebellion has been put down. We find this final judgment in Revelation 20:

> "Then I saw a great white throne and Him who sat on it, from whose face the earth and the heaven fled away. And there was found no place for them. And I saw the dead, small and great, standing before God, and books were opened. And another book was opened, which is *the Book* of Life. And the dead were judged according to their works, by the things which were written in the books. The sea gave up the dead who were in it, and Death and Hades delivered up the dead who were in them. And they were judged, each one according to his works. Then Death and Hades were cast into the lake of fire. This is the second death. And anyone not found written in the Book of Life was cast into the lake of fire." (Revelation 20:11-15)

We need to notice that at this judgment, **"the dead... were judged, each one according to his works."** But the deciding factor will not be their works, but rather, **"anyone not found written in the Book of Life was cast into the lake of fire."**

What is this **"Book of Life"**? We find it mentioned several other times in scripture. The first place we find it is Philippians 4:3, where we read, **"I urge you also, true companion, help these women who labored with me in the gospel, with Clement also, and the rest of my fellow workers, whose names *are* in the Book of Life."** That is the only place in the entire Bible where ths term is found outside of its six occurrences in the Revelation. The most significant of these, for our present purpose, is Revelation 21:27, which says of **"the holy city, New Jerusalem,"** (verse 2) that **"there shall by no means enter it anything that defiles, or causes an abomination or a lie, but only those who are written in the Lamb's Book of Life."** And we also note that those who are written in this book, have been there **"from the foundation of the world."** (Revelation 17:8) The NKJV, which we are using, as well as the KJV, also has this

THOUGHTS ABOUT PROPHETIC SUBJECTS

term in Revelation 22:19. But almost all other translations render that phrase as "the tree of life," instead of **"the Book of Life."** [19]

It is critical to notice that at this judgment, there is no mention of anyone being exonerated, that is, of anyone being found "not guilty." Why is this? because the righteous dead will have been resurrected and gone to their rewards a thousand years earlier, as we read earlier in the same chapter:

> **"And I saw thrones, and they sat on them, and judgment was committed to them. Then I *saw* the souls of those who had been beheaded for their witness to Jesus and for the word of God, who had not worshiped the beast or his image, and had not received *his* mark on their foreheads or on their hands. And they lived and reigned with Christ for a thousand years. But the rest of the dead did not live again until the thousand years were finished. This *is* the first resurrection. Blessed and holy *is* he who has part in the first resurrection. Over such the second death has no power, but they shall be priests of God and of Christ, and shall reign with Him a thousand years. But the rest of the dead did not live again until the thousand years were finished. This is the first resurrection. Blessed and holy is he who has part in the first resurrection. Over such the second death has no power, but they shall be priests of God and of Christ, and shall reign with Him a thousand years."** (Revelation 20:4-6)

---

19. In both the NKJV and the KJV, the New Testament is based on the "textus receptus," which is a Greek text produced in 1550 by Stephanus, along with an almost identical Greek text produced in 1598 by Beza. So this Greek version of the New Testament is often called "the received text of Stephanus and Beza." But the majority text, which is a text determined by using whatever reading is found in the largest number of Byzantine manuscripts, agrees with the texts of Tischendorf and the Greek Orthodox Church, as well as the Nestle text and that of Wescott and Horst, in rendering this as "the tree of life," rather than **"the Book of Life."**

So it is plain that the judgment at the **"great white throne,"** is a judgment of the wicked dead. No one judged at that time will be found in **"the Book of Life,"** so they will all be **"cast into the lake of fire."**

We have seen four distinctly different formal judgments described in the word of God, the Bible. Two of these, the first one and the last one, are of those who are either dead or transformed. The first one is of the righteous dead or transformed and the last one is of the wicked dead. The other two formal judgments are of those living at the time the Lord returns. One is of the nations (gentiles.) And the other is of Israel, as it is being brought back to the land. The grand point we need to keep in mind is that these four formal judgments, and the differences between them, are not mere interpretations of scriptures that are less than completely clear. Each one of them is explicitly described, in plain, clear, words. So all four of these formal judgments will certainly take place, exactly as God has told us.

And each one of us needs to prayerfully consider whether or not we are ready to face whichever of these four formal judgments we will have to face. If we have truly trusted in the Lord Jesus Christ, we will most assuredly be in the first one. But even at that, will we receive the rewards that we imagine we will receive? Or will our efforts be wasted, be burned up? Only what is done out of love for Christ, and in accordance with His word, will be rewarded. But on the other hand, everyone who never trusts in the Lord Jesus will most assuredly face one of the other three formal judgments, and at that judgment will most assuredly be condemned to eternal punishment. Any and all "good deeds" that such a person may have committed will be wasted. For the only thing that will count is whether or not their names are **"written in the Lamb's Book of Life."**

A Note On the Meaning of the Word All

Like English, both Greek and Hebrew have different terms for "all" in a general sense, and "absolutely all." We often use the word "all" in a general sense, without even intending the thought of "absolutely all." For instance, when we say, "all over the place." We do not mean every possible spot, but many spots in many places.

Greek and Hebrew are the same. The Greek word πας, *pas* in our alphabet, word number 3956 in Strong's Greek Dictionary, and the Hebrew word כל, *kol* in our alphabet, word number 3605 in Strong's Hebrew Dictionary, are both direct equivalents of the English word "all." But like the English word "all," they do not *necessarily* mean "absolutely all." In all three languages, this word is sometimes used in the sense of "absolutely all." But in none of these three languages does it *necessarily* have that meaning.

In English, to make the word "all" absolute, we add a word, saying "absolutely all."

In Greek, this is done by adding a syllable, rather than an entire word, changing the word πας, *pas* in our alphabet, to απας, *hapas* in our alphabet, word number 537 in Strong's Greek Dictionary. To understand how this works in the New Testament, we notice that *pas* is the Greek word used in Matthew 27:1, where we read that **"all the chief priests and elders of the people plotted against Jesus to put Him to death."** But Luke 23:50-51 says that Joseph of Arimathea was a member of the council and **"had not consented to their decision and deed."** Also, Nicodemus opposed the council in John 7:50-51 and came with Joseph to bury Jesus in John 19:39. But *hapas* is the Greek word used in Luke 17:27, where we read that **"Noah entered the ark, and the flood came and**

destroyed them all." But we also need to realize that, even as in English, we sometimes use the word "all" in the absolute sense, even without the word "absolutely," *pas* is sometimes used by itself in the absolute sense. We see this in Acts 13:39, where we read, **"³⁹ and by Him everyone who believes is justified from all things from which you could not be justified by the law of Moses."** In this verse, both the word **"everyone"** and the word **"all"** are English renditions of the Greek word *pas*.

In Hebrew, the word "*kol*" is made absolute by doubling it, saying "kol kol," which translates literally as "all all." We see how this works by first examining the general use of the Hebrew word *kol* in 2 Samuel 6:5. **"⁵ Then David and all the house of Israel played *music* before the LORD on "all kinds of" *instruments of* fir wood, on harps, on stringed instruments, on tambourines, on sistrums, and on cymbals."** The Hebrew word here translated **"all kinds of"** is *kol*. Now it should be evident to even the most casual reader that David and his people could not have been using every musical instrument in the entire world (or even in the entire city, for that matter). So from the context it is obvious that the correct translation is, as our translators rendered it here, "**all kinds of**", not *all*. But in Ezekiel 36:7-10, we read: **"⁸ But you, O mountains of Israel, you shall shoot forth your branches and yield your fruit to My people Israel, for they are about to come. ⁹ For indeed I *am* for you, and I will turn to you, and you shall be tilled and sown. ¹⁰ I will multiply men upon you, all the house of Israel, all of it; and the cities shall be inhabited and the ruins rebuilt."** Here, the English words **"all... all of it"** are a literal translation of the Hebrew phrase "*kol kol.*"

But, like the Greek word *pas* and the English word *all*, the Hebrew word *kol* is sometimes used in an absolute sense. We see this use in Deuteronomy 4:23, where we read, **"²³ Take heed to yourselves, lest you forget the covenant of the LORD your God which He made with you, and make for yourselves** a carved image in the form of anything which the LORD your God has forbidden you." Here, the Hebrew word translated "**anything**" is *kol*.

So in all three languages, the word that literally means *"all"* can mean "absolutely all." But it does not *necessarily* have that meaning.

But now we come to the question, why is this important? What is its significance in regard to Bible prophecy? Many people stress the words *all*, or *every* when they find them in Bible prophecy, incorrectly imagining that these words are used in the absolute sense. But whenever we find these words in our English Bibles, we need to check the original text, to see if the Holy Spirit stated either of these words in absolute terms.

The most common occurrence of this error is in the imagination that the scriptures each that the Roman "**beast**" will become the official ruler of the entire world. This would *seem* to be what we see in Revelation 13:7, where we read that he was given "**authority over every tribe, tongue, and nation.**" as well as Revelation 13: 3, where we read that "**all the world marveled and followed the beast**" and Revelation 13: 8, where we read that "**All who dwell on the earth will worship him...**" But this conclusion collapses when we realize that the Greek word used in each of these cases was only *pas*, not *hapas*. So these scriptures do not actually *say* that "**the beast**" will become the official ruler of the entire world. And other scriptures clearly tell us otherwise.

We see this in Revelation 16, where, as "**the beast**" is gathering his last great army, we read of "**the kings of the East**" in verse 12 and "**the kings of the earth and of the whole world.**" in verse 14. These references are only general, but scripture specifically speaks of two great powers that will continue to exist during that time.

The first of these is "**the Assyrian.**" Isaiah 10:12 says that this evil invader will be punished "**when the Lord has performed** all His work on mount Zion and on Jerusalem." Verse 20 of the same chapter says "**And it shall come to pass in that day *That* the remnant of Israel, And such as have escaped of the house of Jacob, Will never again depend on him who defeated them, But will depend on the Lord, the Holy One of Israel, in truth.**" It should be clear to even the most casual student of prophecy that the Lord's "**work on mount Zion and on Jerusalem**" will not be completed until He returns in power, nor will Israel learn to "**depend on the Lord, the Holy One of Israel, in truth**" until that time.

The second of these powers is Gog. Ezekiel 39:7 says that after Gog is destroyed the Lord "**will not *let them* profane**" His holy name "**anymore.**" Again, Ezekiel 39:22 says that "**the house of Israel shall know that I *am* the LORD their God from that day forward**"

Neither of these could possibly apply until after the time when they allow "**the man of sin**" to sit "**as God in the temple of God, showing himself that he is God.**" (2 Thessalonians 2:3-4)

So we see that, not only do the scriptures not *say* that "**the beast**" will become the official ruler of the entire world, they also *show* that he will not.

This same problem occasionally causes other misunderstandings in interpreting Bible prophecy. But this is the most common one.

THOUGHTS ABOUT PROPHETIC SUBJECTS

Who Are the Seed of Abraham?

Many make very bad usage of the following scripture:

> "**Brethren, I speak in the manner of men: Though it is only a man's covenant, yet *if it is* confirmed, no one annuls or adds to it. Now to Abraham and his Seed were the promises made. He does not say, 'And to seeds,' as of many, but as of one, *'And to your Seed,'* who is Christ. And this I say, *that* the law, which was four hundred and thirty years later, cannot annul the covenant that was confirmed before by God in Christ, that it should make the promise of no effect. For if the inheritance is of the law, *it is* no longer of promise; but God gave *it* to Abraham by promise."** (Galatians 3:15-18)

Because of this passage, these people imagine that all the promises made to Abraham were only made to "**Christ,**" and not to any of Abraham's other physical "**descendants.**" And as "**the church**" is in "**Christ,**" they reason that the scriptural term "**the seed of Abraham**" means "**the church.**" But when we examine the scriptures carefully, we see that this cannot be correct. For God unquestionably referred to Abraham's "**seed**" in other senses than the one referred to here. This can be seen in the following:

> "**And Sarah saw the son of Hagar the Egyptian, whom she had borne to Abraham, scoffing. Therefore she said to Abraham, 'Cast out this bondwoman and her son; for the son of this bondwoman shall not be heir with my son, *namely* with Isaac.' And the matter was very displeasing in Abraham's sight because of his son. But God said to Abraham, "Do not let it be displeas-**

ing in your sight because of the lad or because of your bondwoman. Whatever Sarah has said to you, listen to her voice; for in Isaac your seed shall be called. Yet I will also make a nation of the son of the bondwoman, because he *is* your seed.'" (Genesis 21:9-13)

Here, the Hebrew word זֶרַע, *zera'* in our alphabet, word number 2233 in Strong's Hebrew Dictionary, which translates literally as **"seed,"** was specifically used of two different physical descendants of Abraham, one of whom, **"Isaac"** was the one through whom Abraham's **"seed"** would **"be called."** But the other, **"Ishmael"** was also Abraham's **"seed."** This Hebrew word, or some form of it, is the one used in every Old Testament promise about Abraham's **"seed,"** or his **"descendants,"** as the translation we are using (the NKJV) often (correctly) renders it.

The Greek equivalent of this Hebrew word is found in the first passage we examined. For the Greek word translated **"seed"** two times in Galatians 3:16 is σπέρματι, *spermati* in our alphabet, This is the dative singular neuter form of the Greek word σπέρμα, *sperma* in our alphabet, word number 4690 in Strong's Greek Dictionary, whose English derivative is obvious. Likewise, the Greek word translated **"seeds"** in that same verse is σπέρμασιη, *spermatisin* in our alphabet. which is the dative plural neuter form of that same Greek word.

The fact is, that although Galatians 3:16 speaks of one of the promises made to **"Abraham,"** the scriptures themselves distinctly differentiate between various promises made to him. For we read in Romans 4:13 that **"the promise that he would be the heir of the world was not to Abraham or to his seed through the law, but through the righteousness of faith."** Here, the Greek word translated **"or"** is the single letter ἤ, *e* in our alphabet, word number 2228 in Strong's Greek Dictionary. Strong defines this word as "a primary particle of distinction between two con-

THOUGHTS ABOUT PROPHETIC SUBJECTS

nected terms." This word is distinctly different from the Greek word translated **"and"** in Galatians 3:16. There, the Greek word is καί, *kai* in our alphabet, word number 2532 in Strong's Greek Dictionary. This Greek word literally means **"and."** So in one place the New Testament combines the two words **"Abraham"** and **"seed"** with the word **"and,"** meaning both of them, and in another place, it combines them with the word **"or,"** meaning either of them. That is, there was a promise made to both **"Abraham"** and his **"Seed,"** which the scriptures distinctly tell us speaks of **"Christ."** And there was also a promise made individually to both **"Abraham"** and to his **"seed."** And the promise made individually to each of them was **"the promise that he would be the heir of the world."**

Again the New Testament quotes two different promises made to Abraham. The first of these is:

"I will bless those who bless you, And I will curse him who curses you; And in you all the families of the earth shall be blessed." (Genesis 12:3) This is the promise referred to in Genesis 18:17-18, where we read. **"And the LORD said, 'Shall I hide from Abraham what I am doing, since Abraham shall surely become a great and mighty nation, and all the nations of the earth shall be blessed in him?'"** This is quoted in Acts 3:25, where we read, **"You are sons of the prophets, and of the covenant which God made with our fathers, saying to Abraham, *'And in your seed all the families of the earth shall be blessed.'*"**

But a highly similar promise was made to Abraham a number of years later The words used the second time were almost, but not exactly, identical, saying **"In your seed all the nations of the earth shall be blessed, because you have obeyed My voice."** (Genesis 22:18)

The first time the blessing was stated to be **"in"** **"Abraham,"** and about **"all the families of the earth."** But the second time it was stated to be **"in"** Abrahams **"seed,"** and the word **"fami-**

lies" was changed to "**nations,**" saying, "**And I will make your descendants multiply as the stars of heaven; I will give to your descendants all these lands; and in your seed all the nations of the earth shall be blessed.**" (Genesis 26:4) This is the one quoted in Galatians 3:8, which says, "**And the Scripture, foreseeing that God would justify the Gentiles by faith, preached the gospel to Abraham beforehand,** *saying, 'In you all the nations shall be blessed.'* "

So we have seen that the New Testament clearly differentiates between various promises made to Abraham, and specifically quoted different ones of these promises in different places.

And, as we have seen, we know that the promise made to Abraham in Genesis 12:3 was about the gospel, And the promise made to him in Genesis 22:18 was about Christ. We know these because in both cases we are explicitly told so in the New Testament. But does this mean that all the promises made to Abraham's "**seed**" were references to Christ? Most absolutely not. For there are two other senses of this expression plainly set forth in scripture.

Those who think that "**the church**" is "**Israel**" also make much of the following passage, imagining that it re-defines the term, "**the seed of Abraham.**" But such is not the case.

> "**Therefore know that** *only* **those who are of faith are sons of Abraham. And the Scripture, foreseeing that God would justify the Gentiles by faith, preached the gospel to Abraham beforehand, saying,** *'In you all the nations shall be blessed.'* **So then those who are of faith are blessed with believing Abraham**" (Galatians 3:7-9)

This is speaking of becoming children by faith, in the same sense as Paul wrote to the Corinthians, "**I do not write these things to shame you, but as my beloved children I warn you. For though you might have ten thousand instructors** in Christ, yet *you do* not *have* many fathers; for in Christ Jesus I have begotten you through the gospel." (1 Corinthians 4:14-15) And as He also wrote "Unto Timothy, my own son in the faith." (1 Timothy 1:2 KJV) and "To Timothy, my dearly beloved son." (2 Timothy 1:2 KJV)

But another, and far more common, sense for this term is found in numerous other scriptures. In each of the following passages, the Hebrew word correctly translated **"descendants"** is the same Hebrew word זרע, that is, *zera'* that we have noticed before, which literally translates as "seed." But in Each of these cases, it was most certainly correctly translated as **"descendants,"** rather than "seed," even though "seed" would have been a more literal translation, and was used in other translations. For in each of them, the meaning was plainly the physical **"descendants"** of **"Abraham"**, being considered together as a group.

> **"And the LORD said to Abram, after Lot had separated from him: 'Lift your eyes now and look from the place where you are--northward, southward, eastward, and westward; for all the land which you see I give to you and your descendants forever. And I will make your descendants as the dust of the earth; so that if a man could number the dust of the earth, *then* your descendants also could be numbered.'"** (Genesis 13:14-16)

> **"Then Abram said, 'Look, You have given me no offspring; indeed one born in my house is my heir!' And behold, the word of the LORD *came* to him, saying, 'This one shall not be your heir, but one who will come from your own body shall be your heir.' Then He brought him outside and said, 'Look now toward heaven, and count the stars if you are able to number them.' And He said to him, 'So shall your descendants be.'"** (Genesis 15:3-5)

> **"He said to Abram: 'Know certainly that your descendants will be strangers in a land *that* is not theirs, and**

> will serve them, and they will afflict them four hundred years. And also the nation whom they serve I will judge; afterward they shall come out with great possessions.'" (Genesis 15:13-14)
>
> "By Myself I have sworn, says the LORD, because you have done this thing, and have not withheld your son, your only son - blessing I will bless you, and multiplying I will multiply your descendants as the stars of the heaven and as the sand which is on the seashore; and your descendants shall possess the gate of their enemies." (Genesis 22:16-17)

In the first of these four passages, "**Abraham**" was told that his "**descendants**," that is, his "seed," would be "**as the dust of the earth**," in that they would beyond counting. In the second and fourth, he was told the same thing, except the comparison was to the uncountable number of "**stars**." And in the fourth, he was also told that they would be "**as the sand which is on the seashore**." But in the third, he was also told that they would be enslaved "**in a land *that* is not theirs**" for "**four hundred years**."

These promises did not refer to all of the physical "**descendants**" of "**Abraham**." For in each case, it was speaking only of the physical "**descendants**" of "**Abraham**" through one of his sons, "**Isaac**" and only through one of Isaac's sons, "**Jacob**," whose name had been changed by God to "**Israel**." For God has clearly told us that they are not "**all children because they are the seed of Abraham; but, *In Isaac your seed shall be called.*' That is, those who are the children of the flesh, these are not the children of God; but the children of the promise are counted as the seed.**" (Romans 9:6-8)

But now we come to a promise which speaks of **Abraham's** "**descendants**" in a different way. In this promise, "**Abraham**" was told that his "**descendants**" would become "**many nations.**"

but one particular group of his **"descendants"** was singled out, God promising to give them **"the land"** wherein Abraham had lived as **"a stranger,"** **"as an everlasting possession."**

> **"When Abram was ninety-nine years old, the LORD appeared to Abram and said to him, 'I *am* Almighty God; walk before Me and be blameless. And I will make My covenant between Me and you, and will multiply you exceedingly.' Then Abram fell on his face, and God talked with him, saying: 'As for Me, behold, My covenant is with you, and you shall be a father of many nations. No longer shall your name be called Abram, but your name shall be Abraham; for I have made you a father of many nations. I will make you exceedingly fruitful; and I will make nations of you, and kings shall come from you. And I will establish My covenant between Me and you and your descendants after you in their generations, for an everlasting covenant, to be God to you and your descendants after you. Also I give to you and your descendants after you the land in which you are a stranger, all the land of Canaan, as an everlasting possession; and I will be their God.'"**
> (Genesis 17:1-8)

We find other examples of referring to Abraham's **"descendants,"** that is, his "seed," as the nation of **"Israel,"** in the following passages:

> **"But you, Israel, *are* My servant,**
> **Jacob whom I have chosen,**
> **The descendants of Abraham My friend.**
> ***You* whom I have taken from the ends of the earth,**
> **And called from its farthest regions,**
> **And said to you,**
> **'You *are* My servant,**

I have chosen you and have not cast you away:
Fear not, for I *am* with you;
Be not dismayed, for I *am* your God.
I will strengthen you,
Yes, I will help you,
I will uphold you with My righteous right hand.'
"Behold, all those who were incensed against you
Shall be ashamed and disgraced;
They shall be as nothing,
And those who strive with you shall perish.
You shall seek them and not find them--
Those who contended with you.
Those who war against you
Shall be as nothing,
As a nonexistent thing.
For I, the LORD your God, will hold your right hand,
Saying to you, 'Fear not, I will help you.'
"Fear not, you worm Jacob,
You men of Israel!
I will help you,' says the LORD
And your Redeemer, the Holy One of Israel." (Isaiah 41:8-14)

And:
"Thus says the LORD,
Who gives the sun for a light by day,
The ordinances of the moon and the stars for a light by night,
Who disturbs the sea,
And its waves roar
(The LORD of hosts is His name):

> 'If those ordinances depart
> From before Me, says the LORD,
> *Then* the seed of Israel shall also cease
> From being a nation before Me forever.'
> Thus says the LORD:
> 'If heaven above can be measured,
> And the foundations of the earth searched out beneath,
> I will also cast off all the seed of Israel
> For all that they have done, says the LORD." (Jeremiah 31:35-37)

These last two promises are indeed the key to this entire question. For both of them clearly refer to the nation of **"Israel,"** even calling them **"Jacob."** And the first one calls that nation **"The descendants of Abraham My friend."** But the second one explicitly calls **"Israel"** a **"nation,"** And then promises that **"nation"** that God would never cast them off. And here again, the Hebrew word translated **"descendants"** is the same Hebrew word זרע, *zera'* in our alphabet, that translates literally as "seed."

We need to particularly notice that there were no conditions attached to any of these promises. Nor is this just a human idea. For in the New Testament, the same God that made these promises stressed the absolutely unconditional nature of His sworn promise to Abraham, by saying:

> **"For when God made a promise to Abraham, because He could swear by no one greater, He swore by Himself, saying,** *'Surely blessing I will bless you, and multiplying I will multiply you.'* **And so, after he had patiently endured, he obtained the promise. For men indeed swear by the greater, and an oath for confirmation is for them an end of all dispute. Thus God, determining to show more abundantly to the heirs of promise the**

immutability of His counsel, confirmed *it* by an oath, that by two immutable things, in which it is impossible for God to lie, we might have strong consolation, who have fled for refuge to lay hold of the hope set before us. This *hope* we have as an anchor of the soul, both sure and steadfast." (Hebrews 6:13-19)

This passage clearly shows, not only the absolutely unconditional nature of the promises made to Abraham, but also the fact that this unconditional nature of the promises of God is fundamental to the Christian faith. For the fact that God **"confirmed it"** to **"Abraham" "by an oath"** is pointed out to have the purpose of showing **"more abundantly to the heirs of promise the immutability of His counsel."** And then this immutability of the promises of God is made a basis for our own faith. This is why this doctrine is so very important. For if God could legitimately tell **"Abraham"** that he did not literally mean his physical **"descendants,"** but that instead, He meant a different people that would come in a future day, He could just as legitimately tell us the same thing concerning the promises He made to us. That is, if the promises made to **"Abraham"** were not absolutely sacrosanct, then neither would be the promises our God has made to us.

Thus we see that the doctrine that **"the seed of Abraham"** means **"the church,"** and thus that the promises that God made to **"the seed of Abraham"** do not apply to his physical **"descendants,"** is destructive of the very foundations of the Christian faith. For that would mean that the promises that God made to the ancient **"nation"** of **"Israel"** will not actually be kept. But God himself twice stated, that if He were not going to actually keep these promises, He would have been lying when he made them. We find this first in a prophecy made to **"Baalak"** through the prophet **"Baalam."**

"**God is not a man, that He should lie,**
Nor a son of man, that He should repent.

> Has He said, and will He not do?
> Or has He spoken, and will He not make it good?"
> (Numbers 23:19)

And again, He said of David:
> "My mercy I will keep for him forever,
> And My covenant shall stand firm with him.
> His seed also I will make to *endure* forever,
> And his throne as the days of heaven.
> If his sons forsake My law
> And do not walk in My judgments,
> If they break My statutes
> And do not keep My commandments,
> Then I will punish their transgression with the rod,
> And their iniquity with stripes.
> Nevertheless My lovingkindness
> I will not utterly take from him,
> Nor allow My faithfulness to fail.
> My covenant I will not break,
> Nor alter the word that has gone out of My lips.
> Once I have sworn by My holiness;
> I will not lie to David:" (Psalm 89:28-35)

So this doctrine, though widely held, even by many godly Christians, is a deception from the enemy. For if the promises of God were not absolutely reliable, we would have nothing to base our faith upon. And thus, we would have no basis for being certain of either the fact that our sins have been forgiven, or the fact that we will be in heaven. Our entire faith is based on the absolute reliability of every promise that God ever made, as He said in Romans 11:29, **"For the gifts and the calling of God are irrevocable."**

JAMES C. MORRIS

The Ancient Promises

In very ancient times, God made a long series of promises, beginning with the famous promises to **"Abraham"** and his **"seed,"** which were repeated to **"Isaac"** and **"Jacob,"** and later to the ancient **"nation"** of **"Israel."** Long after that, God made additional promises to each of the sub-nations of **"Ephraim"** and **"Judah,"** to each of **"the twelve tribes of Israel"** by name, and even to the physical land occupied in ancient times by the **"nation"** of **"Israel,"** going so far as to define the future **"borders"** of that *plot of real estate*. Along the way, He also made promises to the descendants of **"Phinehas," "David," "Jonadab," "Zadok," "Nathan," "Levi,"** and **"Shimei,"** as well as to **"Zion"** and to **"Jerusalem."** All of these promises were explicitly stated in plain, clear words. And most of them were unconditional.

Much later, but still in ancient times, the same God made *much better* promises, not to a specific nation, but to whoever would believe. Today, some people imagine that these *better* promises canceled the promises God had made so much earlier. But no scripture says, or even implies, such an idea. In fact, the scriptures explicitly say the very opposite. For, long after the Jews had rejected their Messiah at Calvary, the Holy Spirit, in speaking through the Apostle Paul, said of these hardened rebels, **"Concerning the gospel *they are* enemies for your sake, but concerning the election *they are* beloved for the sake of the fathers. For the gifts and the calling of God *are* irrevocable."** (Romans 11:28-29)

And much earlier than this, God had clearly said that His promises were so absolute that even sin could not cancel them. For He said of His promise to David:

> "If his sons forsake My law
> And do not walk in My judgments,
> If they break My statutes
> And do not keep My commandments,
> *Then* I will punish their transgression with the rod,
> And their iniquity with stripes.
> Nevertheless My lovingkindness
> I will not utterly take from him,
> Nor allow My faithfulness to fail.
> My covenant I will not break,
> Nor alter the word that has gone out of My lips."
> (Psalm 89:30-34)

We need to notice that these words, **"My covenant I will not break, Nor alter the word that has gone out of My lips,"** were declared in explicit reference to His previous words **"If his sons forsake My law And do not walk in My judgments, If they break My statutes And do not keep My commandments."** So God was here plainly declaring that even sin could not cause Him to alter the word that had gone out of His lips. For *that* would be breaking His covenant. Sin, if it came, would be dealt with. But the punishment would *not* be a cancellation of the promises, for they were **"irrevocable,"** as Romans 11:29 puts it.

And even earlier than the time of David, God had said that:

> "God is not a man, that He should lie,
> Nor a son of man, that He should repent.
> Has He said, and will He not do?
> Or has He spoken, and will He not make it good?"
> (Numbers 23:19)

This last two pronouncements show us the reason this subject is so important. For in each of them, God himself basically said that, if He were not going to actually keep these promises, He would have been lying when He made them. The people who say that these promises have been cancelled do not realize what a serious sin they are committing. For they are making God out to be a liar.

These people reason that the promises were conditional, and that Israel, having failed to meet the conditions, lost them. But as was mentioned previously, and as we will see as we examine these promises, most of them were *not* conditional. And God had already foretold that Israel would reject their Messiah before He made most of these unconditional promises. For Psalm 22 was written during the days of David, long before God made most of the promises we will examine. And that psalm graphically describes our Lord's suffering on the tree, even giving His exact words, **"My God, My God, why have You forsaken Me?"** So if Israel's failure were going to cancel the promises, God knew His *unconditional* promises would not be kept at the time He made them. So it is undeniable that if the promises were going to be retracted if Israel failed, then God would have been lying when He made these promises without attaching *any* conditions to them.

Other people, not going so far as to say that God "retracted" these promises, claim instead that He was only using symbolic language when He made them, that the name **"Israel"** in the prophecies simply meant God's people, in a general sense, as it were. So, they argue, these prophecies actually apply to **"the church"** instead of to the ancient **"nation"** of **"Israel."**

But this argument will not stand up to a careful examination of the wording of the prophecies themselves. For God said concerning the **"nation"** of **"Israel:"**

"Thus says the LORD,

Who gives the sun for a light by day,

> **The ordinances of the moon and the stars for a light by night,**
> **Who disturbs the sea,**
> **And its waves roar**
> **(The LORD of hosts is His name):**
> **'If those ordinances depart**
> **From before Me,' says the LORD,**
> ***Then*** **the seed of Israel shall also cease**
> **From being a nation before Me forever.'**
> **Thus says the LORD:**
> **'If heaven above can be measured,**
> **And the foundations of the earth searched out beneath,**
> **I will also cast off all the seed of Israel**
> **For all that they have done,' says the LORD."**
> (Jeremiah 31:35-37)

We need to notice that here God clearly said that **"Israel"** would never cease to be a **"nation,"** and that would He would never cast them off. So this promise was made to a particular **"nation,"** the **"nation"** of **"Israel,"** not just to the people of God generally. But, not only was it made to the **"nation"** of **"Israel,"** it was made in specific reference to their sins. For the promise ends by clearly saying the He would never **"cast off all the seed of Israel For all that they have done."**

But in addition to this, as we noticed earlier, there were unconditional promises made, not only to the **"nation"** of **"Israel,"** but to each of the sub-nations of **"Ephraim"** and **"Judah,"** to each of the **"twelve tribes of Israel"** by name, and not only to the descendants of **"Abraham," "Isaac,"** and **"Jacob,"** but also to the descendants of **"Phinehas," "David," "Jonadab," "Zadok," "Nathan," "Levi,"** and **"Shimei."** And there is absolutely no passage, anywhere in the entire Bible, that even hints at an idea that *any* of these *other* names means "**the church.**"

There are indeed a few scriptures that some people interpret to mean that the name "**Israel**" represents "**the church.**" None of these scriptures actually *say* that, but many people think they *mean* it. So we will examine some of these scriptures, and see what they actually say.

The one scripture they quote more often that any other is, "**But it is not that the word of God has taken no effect. For they *are* not all Israel who *are* of Israel.**" (Romans 9:6) They imagine that the words "**they *are* not all Israel who *are* of Israel,**" mean that the *true* "**Israel**" is a completely different group than "**they... who are of Israel.**" This, of course, is pure interpretation. This conclusion is nothing but human reasoning about the meaning of what God said. But it is not only merely human reasoning. It is directly contrary to God's own explanation of what He was saying. For the next few verses read:

> "**Nor *are they* all children because they are the seed of Abraham; but, *'In Isaac your seed shall be called.'* That is, those who *are* the children of the flesh, these *are* not the children of God; but the children of the promise *are* counted as the seed. For this is the word of promise: *'At this time I will come and Sarah shall have a son.'* And not only *this*, but when Rebecca also had conceived by one man, even by our father Isaac (for the children not yet being born, nor having done any good or evil, that the purpose of God according to election might stand, not of works but of Him who calls), it was said to her, *The older shall serve the younger.'* "**(Romans 9:7-12)

Here, God explained, three times over, what He meant by this statement. First, He said that not "**all**" of "**the seed of Abraham**" were his "**children.**" And then He added the words, "**that is.**" This is a clear statement that what is about to follow is an explanation of what He had just said. And that explanation was that it was not just **"the children of the flesh"** who were **"the seed"** but those who were also **"the children of promise."** Now here, I added the words "just," and "also," but those words were indeed implied in the words **"nor"** and **"all"** in the clause **"nor *are they* all children."** This was also demonstrated in the two examples given in the following verses. For both of these examples were cases of some, but all of Abraham's **"children of the flesh"** being **"the children of promise."** The two examples given were **"Isaac"** being chosen over **"Ishmael"** and Abraham's other physical offspring, and **"Jacob"** being chosen over **"Esau."** But nothing in this passage even suggests a notion that anyone who was not one of **"the children of the flesh"** could even possibly be one of the **"children of promise."**

Further, this notion contradicts the context of the statement. For just before saying this, the Apostle, writing under the inspiration of the Holy Spirit, had said:

> **"I tell the truth in Christ, I am not lying, my conscience also bearing me witness in the Holy Spirit, that I have great sorrow and continual grief in my heart. For I could wish that I myself were accursed from Christ for my brethren, my countrymen according to the flesh, who are Israelites, to whom *pertain* the adoption, the glory, the covenants, the giving of the law, the service *of God*, and the promises; of whom *are* the fathers and from whom, according to the flesh, Christ *came*, who is over all, *the* eternally blessed God. Amen."** (Romans 9:1-5)

This statement could not have been more clear in saying who the Apostle was speaking about. It was Paul's **"countrymen according to the flesh, who are Israelites."** This leaves zero "wiggle room" for even trying to pretend that he was speaking of anyone other than the physical **"nation"** of **"Israel,"** and most definitely *not* "**the church.**" But what did the Holy Spirit inspire him to say about this physical nation of Israel? "**To whom *pertain* the adoption, the glory, the covenants, the giving of the law, the service *of God*, and the promises.**"

This was said by the Holy Spirit long after "**they all cried out at once, saying, 'Away with this *Man*, and release to us Barabbas.'**" (Luke 23:18) and long after, through the stoning of Stephen, (Acts 7:57-60) they had "**sent a delegation after him, saying, 'We will not have this *man* to reign over us.'**" (Luke 19:14) But even after this flat rejection of their Messiah, the Holy Spirit *still* said of Paul's "**countrymen according to the flesh, who are Israelites,**" that all these things pertained to them. And what were these things that *still* pertained to *them*?

"**the adoption,**

the glory,

the covenants,

the giving of the law,

the service *of God*,

and the promises."

All of these things are important. But the item that concerns our present subject is the last one in the list. This passage explicitly says that "**the promises**" still "***pertain***" - to whom? To Paul's "**countrymen according to the flesh, who are Israelites!**" This, indeed, is the death knell to all their cavils. For here, in the New Testament, God explicitly said that "**the promises**" *still* pertain to Paul's "**countrymen according to the flesh, who are Israelites.**"

Again, these people make much of a scripture that says, "**For in Christ Jesus neither circumcision nor uncircumcision avails anything, but a new creation. And as many as walk according to this rule, peace and mercy *be* upon them, and upon the Israel of God.**" (Galatians 6:15-16) They imagine that this scripture defines **"the Israel of God"** as the group that **"walk according to this rule,"** that is, **"the church."** For the **"rule"** mentioned here was **"in Christ Jesus neither circumcision nor uncircumcision avails anything, but a new creation."**

As in the case above, this is pure human reasoning. The Bible simply does not say that **"as many as walk according to ths rule"** are **"the Israel of God."** But further, this mere human reasoning goes counter to what the Holy Ghost actually said. For this passage explicitly differentiates between two groups of people. One of these groups is **"as many as walk according to this rule."** that is, **"the church."** and the other group is **"the Israel of God."** These two groups are differentiated by the word **"and."**

"And" does not mean, *that is.* it means *also.* That is, this word does not indicate that the two groups mentioned are the *same*, but that they are *different.* Nor is this word simply one that the translators added, to make up the sense as they understood it. This word is distinctly present in the Greek text of this statement, as the Greek word καί, *kai* in our alphabet, word number 2532 in Strong's Geek Dictionary, which translates literally as **"and."**

Further, these two groups are not only differentiated by the word **"and,"** but also by a distinct repetition of the word **"upon."** This word, which in the Greek text is ἐπί, *epi* in our alphabet, word number 1909 in Strong's Greek Dictionary, is distinctly used in regard to *each* of these two groups. That is, the Holy Spirit said, **"peace UPON"** **"as many as walk according to this rule"** **"and UPON"** **"the Israel of God."** So God clearly referred to **"as many as walk according to this rule"** and **"the Israel of God,"** as two *distinct* groups.

Again, these people love to quote, **"Now to Abraham and his Seed were the promises made. He does not say, 'And to seeds,' as of many, but as of one, 'And to your Seed,' who is Christ."** (Galatians 3:16) We first need to notice the context of this statement. Immediately before saying this, the Holy Spirit, in speaking through the Apostle Paul, had said, "**Brethren, I speak in the manner of men: Though it is only a man's covenant, yet if it is confirmed, no one annuls or adds to it.**" (Galatians 3:15) And immediately after it, He said, "**And this I say, *that* the law, which was four hundred and thirty years later, cannot annul the covenant that was confirmed before by God in Christ, that it should make the promise of no effect. For if the inheritance *is* of the law, *it is* no longer of promise; but God gave *it* to Abraham by promise.**" (Galatians 3:17-18) So the context of this statement, of which they make such bad use, is the absolutely unchangeable nature of the "**covenant**" that God made with "**Abraham.**" Now the people who make such bad use of this verse, which, as we have seen, they take out of its context, say that, since the promises were made to "**Christ,**" then we, that is, "**the church,**" being "**in Christ,**" are the true heirs of the promises, instead of the "**nation**" of "**Israel.**"

Again, this sounds reasonable, but it is erroneous. There were many promises made to Abraham. So which one of these many promises was Galatians 3:16 speaking of? In its context, this passage speaks of God making a "**covenant**" with "**Abraham,**" and quoted from that "**covenant,**" "***And to your Seed.***" The only place in the Old Testament which mentions a "**covenant**" with "**Abraham,**" and includes the words "**And to your seed,**" is Genesis 17:1-8, "**When Abram was ninety-nine years old, the LORD appeared to Abram and said to him, 'I *am* Almighty God; walk before Me and be blameless. And I will make My covenant between Me and you, and will multiply you exceedingly.' Then Abram fell on his face, and God talked with him, saying: 'As for Me, behold, My covenant is with you, and you shall be a father of many nations. No longer shall your name be called Abram, but your name shall be Abraham; for I have made you a father of many nations. I will make you exceedingly fruitful; and I will make nations of you, and kings shall come from you. And I will** establish My covenant between Me and you and your descendants after you in their generations, for an everlasting covenant, to be God to you and your descendants after you. Also I give to you and your descendants after you the land in which you are a stranger, all the land of Canaan, as an everlasting possession; and I will be their God.'"** As this is the only Old Testament passage that matches Galatians 3:15-18, this has to be the one that the Holy Spirit was speaking of.

But we need to notice that the Hebrew word here translated **"descendants"** in the NKJV, which we are using, is rendered "seed" in the KJV. And in the phrase "and to your seed," this Hebrew word is indeed singular in the Hebrew text, [20] even as Galatians 3:16 says. Yet, even before getting to the end of that same promise, God himself changed the sense of this same word to the plural when He said, **"I will establish My covenant between Me and you and your descendants after you in their generations."** (Genesis 17:7) So we see that, although what Galatians 3:16 says is absolutely true and correct, in regard to the promises it was referring to, this statement did not apply to all the promises God made to Abraham.

We again see this, and very plainly, in Genesis 15:13-16, **"Then He said to Abram: 'Know certainly that your descendants will be strangers in a land that is not theirs, and will serve them, and they will afflict them four hundred years. And also the nation whom they serve I will judge; afterward they shall come out with great possessions. Now as for you, you shall go to your fathers in peace; you shall be buried at a good old age. But in the fourth generation they shall return here, for the iniquity of the Amorites is not yet complete.'"** There can

---

20. We should note that the Hebrew word translated "descendants" in the NKJV, which we are using, (but which is translated "seed" in the KJV) is זרע, zeraʻ in our alphabet, (word number 2233 in Strong's Hebrew Dictionary.) This is the Hebrew equivalent of the Greek word σπέρμα, sperma in our alphabet, (word number 4690 in Strong's Greek Dictionary,) which is translated "seed" in Galatians 3;16.

be absolutely no question whatsoever that our Lord Jesus was not the subject of this pronouncement. For, although Jesus was taken to Egypt as an infant, He was not there for **"four hundred years,"** and He was not **"afflicted"** there. Further, the Hebrew word forms translated **"theirs,"** **"them,"** and **"they,"** (the last one being used three times) are all in the plural in the Hebrew text. So in this case, the **"seed,"** that is, the **"descendants"** of Abraham, clearly meant the physical descendants of Abraham. Here, it was most certainly not referring to our Lord Jesus.

So if the word **"seed"** can, in at least some cases, be properly translated **"descendants"** (of **"Abraham,"**) as we see that, in this case, this translation was obviously correct, what did God actually promise to the physical **"descendants"** of **"Abraham"**? In addition to the promises we have already examined, the promise of a specific **"land"** was made again and again. We find this in each of the following promises:

> **"Then the LORD appeared to Abram and said, 'To your descendants I will give this land.' And there he built an altar to the LORD, who had appeared to him."** (Genesis 12:7)

> **"And the LORD said to Abram, after Lot had separated from him: 'Lift your eyes now and look from the place where you are--northward, southward, eastward, and westward; for all the land which you see I give to you and your descendants forever. And I will make your descendants as the dust of the earth; so that if a man could number the dust of the earth, *then* your descendants also could be numbered. Arise, walk in the land through its length and its width, for I give it to you.'"** (Genesis 13:14-17)

> **"Then He said to him, 'I *am* the LORD, who brought you out of Ur of the Chaldeans, to give you this land to inherit it.'"** (Genesis 15:7)

THOUGHTS ABOUT PROPHETIC SUBJECTS

> "On the same day the LORD made a covenant with Abram, saying: 'To your descendants I have given this land, from the river of Egypt to the great river, the River Euphrates-- the Kenites, the Kenezzites, the Kadmonites, the Hittites, the Perizzites, the Rephaim, the Amorites, the Canaanites, the Girgashites, and the Jebusites.'" (Genesis 15:18-21)

We need to realize that in each these places, God explicitly made an unconditional promise to give that **"land"** to the **"descendants"** of **"Abraham."** And He explicitly promised that this would be **"forever."** (Genesis 13:16) But this unconditional promise was not only made to Abraham.

God repeated this unconditional promise to Isaac, saying, **"Dwell in this land, and I will be with you and bless you; for to you and your descendants I give all these lands, and I will perform the oath which I swore to Abraham your father. And I will make your descendants multiply as the stars of heaven; I will give to your descendants all these lands; and in your seed all the nations of the earth shall be blessed; because Abraham obeyed My voice and kept My charge, My commandments, My statutes, and My laws."** (Genesis 26:3-5)

And He again repeated it unconditionally to Abraham's grandson Jacob, saying, **"I *am* the LORD God of Abraham your father and the God of Isaac; the land on which you lie I will give to you and your descendants. Also your descendants shall be as the dust of the earth; you shall spread abroad to the west and the east, to the north and the south; and in you and in your seed all the families of the earth shall be blessed. Behold, I *am* with you and will keep you wherever you go, and will bring you back to this land; for I will not leave you until I have done what I have spoken to you."** (Genesis 28:13-15)

We should notice that each of these promises contained two distinct parts. One part was the promise, repeated from that to Abraham, that **"in your seed all the nations of the earth shall be blessed"** (to Isaac) and **"in your seed all the families of the earth shall be blessed"** (to Jacob.) And the other part was the land promise, also repeated from the promise made to Abraham. As He had promised Abraham, He promised Isaac that **"to you and your descendants I give all these lands,"** and He promised Jacob that **"the land on which you lie I will give to you and your descendants."**

Now the promise that in them **"all the nations** (or **families) of the earth"** would **"be blessed,"** was obviously a promise about the coming of our blessed Lord, Jesus the Christ. And that was, unquestionably, the most important part of the promises. But that does not do away with the other part of these promises, which as we saw in the case of Abraham, was the promise of a specific **"land."**

God repeated this promise of a specific **"land"** to **"the children of Israel,"** saying, **"I will bring you into the land which I swore to give to Abraham, Isaac, and Jacob; and I will give it to you as a heritage: I *am* the LORD."** (Exodus 6:8)

And we know that this promise of that specific **"land"** was literally fulfilled, exactly as God had promised it. **"So the LORD gave to Israel all the land of which He had sworn to give to their fathers, and they took possession of it and dwelt in it. The LORD gave them rest all around, according to all that He had sworn to their fathers. And not a man of all their enemies stood against them; the LORD delivered all their enemies into their hand. Not a word failed of any good thing which the LORD had spoken to the house of Israel. All came to pass."** (Joshua 21:43-45)

But even as they were ready to enter the land, the Lord warned them that, if they did not obey His law, **"the LORD will scatter** you among the peoples, and you will be left few in number among the nations where the LORD will drive you. And there you will serve gods, the work of men's hands, wood and stone, which neither see nor hear nor eat nor smell." (Deuteronomy 4:27-28) And we are all aware of the sad fact that this threat was carried out, and this guilty nation was indeed **"scattered" "among the peoples,"** and **"left few in number among the nations."**

Yet, even as He gave them this warning, their God added a promise, saying, **"But from there you will seek the LORD your God, and you will find Him if you seek *Him* with all your heart and with all your soul. When you are in distress, and all these things come upon you in the latter days, when you turn to the LORD your God and obey His voice (for the LORD your God *is* a merciful God), He will not forsake you nor destroy you, nor forget the covenant of your fathers which He swore to them."** (Deuteronomy 4:29-31)

As this promise was conditional, many people imagine that ALL of God's promises of an eventual restoration of this ancient nation were conditional. But that is not the case. For their merciful God unconditionally promised them that this condition would be met, that He would eventually bring them to repentance. For, even while He was declaring their final expulsion from the land because of their wickedness, God said, **"Now therefore, thus says the LORD, the God of Israel, 'concerning this city of which you say, "It shall be delivered into the hand of the king of Babylon by the sword, by the famine, and by the pestilence:" Behold, I will gather them out of all countries where I have driven them in My anger, in My fury, and in great wrath; I will bring them back to this place, and I will cause them to dwell safely. They shall be My people, and I will be their God; then I will give them one heart and one way, that they may fear Me forever, for the good of them** and their children after them. And I will make an everlasting covenant with them, that I will not turn away from doing them good; but I will put My fear in their hearts so that they will not depart from Me. Yes, I will rejoice over them to do them good, and I will assuredly plant them in this land, with all My heart and with all My soul.'

> "For thus says the LORD: 'Just as I have brought all this great calamity on this people, so I will bring on them all the good that I have promised them.' " (Jeremiah 32:36-42)

God did not just promise this a time or two, but again and again, as we see below:

> "Then I will give them a heart to know Me, that I *am* the LORD; and they shall be My people, and I will be their God, for they shall return to Me with their whole heart." (Jeremiah 24:7)

> " 'Behold, the days are coming,' says the LORD, 'when I will make a new covenant with the house of Israel and with the house of Judah-- not according to the covenant that I made with their fathers in the day *that* I took them by the hand to lead them out of the land of Egypt, My covenant which they broke, though I was a husband to them,' says the LORD. 'But this *is* the covenant that I will make with the house of Israel after those days,' says the LORD: 'I will put My law in their minds, and write it on their hearts; and I will be their God, and they shall be My people. No more shall every man teach his neighbor, and every man his brother, saying, "Know the LORD," for they all shall know Me, from the least of them to the greatest of them,' says the LORD. 'For I will forgive their iniquity, and their sin I will remember no more.' " (Jeremiah 31:31-34)

> " 'And it shall be, in that day,'

THOUGHTS ABOUT PROPHETIC SUBJECTS

Says the LORD,
'That you will call Me "My Husband,"
And no longer call Me "My Master,"
For I will take from her mouth the names of the Baals,
And they shall be remembered by their name no more.
In that day I will make a covenant for them
With the beasts of the field,
With the birds of the air,
And *with* the creeping things of the ground.
Bow and sword of battle I will shatter from the earth,
To make them lie down safely.
" 'I will betroth you to Me forever;
Yes, I will betroth you to Me
In righteousness and justice,
In lovingkindness and mercy;
I will betroth you to Me in faithfulness,
And you shall know the LORD.
" 'It shall come to pass in that day
That I will answer,' says the LORD;
'I will answer the heavens,
And they shall answer the earth.
The earth shall answer
With grain,
With new wine,
And with oil;
They shall answer Jezreel.
Then I will sow her for Myself in the earth,
And I will have mercy on *her who had* not obtained mercy;
Then I will say to *those who were* not My people,

"You *are* My people!"
And they shall say,
"*You are* my God!" ' " (Hosea 2:16-23)

"For the children of Israel shall abide many days without king or prince, without sacrifice or sacred pillar, without ephod or teraphim. Afterward the children of Israel shall return and seek the LORD their God and David their king. They shall fear the LORD and His goodness in the latter days." (Hosea 3:4-5)

"In that day you shall not be shamed for any of your deeds In which you transgress against Me; For then I will take away from your midst Those who rejoice in your pride, And you shall no longer be haughty In My holy mountain. I will leave in your midst A meek and humble people, And they shall trust in the name of the LORD. The remnant of Israel shall do no unrighteousness And speak no lies, Nor shall a deceitful tongue be found in their mouth; For they shall feed *their* flocks and lie down, And no one shall make *them* afraid." (Zephaniah 3:11-13)

So we see that, even though the promise of their eventual restoration was, in some places, made conditional upon their repentance, yet that repentance was unconditionally promised. So the end result is that *all* the promises of their restoration become unconditional, even though the condition of repentance was placed upon *some* of the promises.

When Israel finally sees their long awaited Messiah, "*one* shall say unto him, What *are* these wounds in thine hands? Then he shall answer, *Those* with which I was wounded *in* the house of my friends." (Zechariah 13:6 KJV) I have used the KJV rendering here because I think it more accurately represents the true meaning of the question than the NKJV rendering, which says, **"What are these wounds between your arms?"**

THOUGHTS ABOUT PROPHETIC SUBJECTS

The result of this revelation will be that **"In that day there shall be a great mourning in Jerusalem, like the mourning at Hadad Rimmon in the plain of Megiddo. And the land shall mourn, every family by itself: the family of the house of David by itself, and their wives by themselves; the family of the house of Nathan by itself, and their wives by themselves; the family of the house of Levi by itself, and their wives by themselves; the family of Shimei by itself, and their wives by themselves; all the families that remain, every family by itself, and their wives by themselves."** (Zechariah 12:11-14) The promised result of this is, **"And it shall come to pass that *he who* is left in Zion and remains in Jerusalem will be called holy--everyone who is recorded among the living in Jerusalem. When the Lord has washed away the filth of the daughters of Zion, and purged the blood of Jerusalem from her midst, by the spirit of judgment and by the spirit of burning."** (Isaiah 4:3-4)

This unconditional promise of a restoration of the ancient nation of Israel to their God, was closely intertwined with a matching unconditional promise of a restoration of that ancient nation to its ancient homeland in prophecies such as this one:

> "For I will take you from among the nations, gather you out of all countries, and bring you into your own land. Then I will sprinkle clean water on you, and you shall be clean; I will cleanse you from all your filthiness and from all your idols. I will give you a new heart and put a new spirit within you; I will take the heart of stone out of your flesh and give you a heart of flesh. I will put My Spirit within you and cause you to walk in My statutes, and you will keep My judgments and do *them*. Then you shall dwell in the land that I gave to your fathers; you shall be My people, and I will be your God. I will deliver you from all your un-

> cleannesses. I will call for the grain and multiply it, and bring no famine upon you." (Ezekiel 36:24-29)

Once again, this was not just implied a time or two, but was repeatedly and unconditionally promised, in plain, clear words, as we see in the following passages.

> " 'I will gather the remnant of My flock out of all countries where I have driven them, and bring them back to their folds; and they shall be fruitful and increase. I will set up shepherds over them who will feed them; and they shall fear no more, nor be dismayed, nor shall they be lacking,' says the LORD. 'Behold, *the* days are coming,' says the LORD, 'That I will raise to David a Branch of righteousness; A King shall reign and prosper, And execute judgment and righteousness in the earth. In His days Judah will be saved, And Israel will dwell safely; Now this *is* His name by which He will be called: THE LORD OUR RIGHTEOUSNESS.
>
> " 'Therefore, behold, *the* days are coming,' says the LORD, 'that they shall no longer say, "As the LORD lives who brought up the children of Israel from the land of Egypt," but, "As the LORD lives who brought up and led the descendants of the house of Israel from the north country and from all the countries where I had driven them." And they shall dwell in their own land.' " (Jeremiah 23:3-8)
>
> " 'I will cause the captives of Judah and the captives of Israel to return, and will rebuild those places as at the first. I will cleanse them from all their iniquity by which they have sinned against Me, and I will pardon all their iniquities by which they have sinned and by which they have transgressed against Me. Then it shall be to Me a name of joy, a praise, and an honor before all nations of the earth, who shall hear all the good that I do to them; they shall fear and tremble for

all the goodness and all the prosperity that I provide for it.'

"Thus says the LORD: 'Again there shall be heard in this place – of which you say, "It *is* desolate, without man and without beast" – in the cities of Judah, in the streets of Jerusalem that are desolate, without man and without inhabitant and without beast, the voice of joy and the voice of gladness, the voice of the bridegroom and the voice of the bride, the voice of those who will say: "Praise the LORD of hosts, For the LORD *is* good, For His mercy *endures* forever" -- *and* of those *who will* bring the sacrifice of praise into the house of the LORD. For I will cause the captives of the land to return as at the first,' says the LORD.

"Thus says the LORD of hosts: 'In this place which is desolate, without man and without beast, and in all its cities, there shall again be a dwelling place of shepherds causing *their* flocks to lie down. In the cities of the mountains, in the cities of the lowland, in the cities of the South, in the land of Benjamin, in the places around Jerusalem, and in the cities of Judah, the flocks shall again pass under the hands of him who counts them,' says the LORD." (Jeremiah 33:7-13)

"But I will bring back Israel to his home, And he shall feed on Carmel and Bashan; His soul shall be satisfied on Mount Ephraim and Gilead. In those days and in that time," says the LORD, "The iniquity of Israel shall be sought, but *there shall be* none; And the sins of Judah, but they shall not be found; For I will pardon those whom I preserve." (Jeremiah 50:19-20)

"Indeed, what have you to do with Me, O Tyre and Sidon, and all the coasts of Philistia? Will you retaliate against Me? But if you retaliate against Me, Swiftly and speedily I will return your retaliation upon your own head; Because you have taken My silver and My gold, And have carried into your temples My prized possessions. Also the people of Judah and the people of Jerusalem You have sold to the Greeks, That you may remove them far from their borders.

"Behold, I will raise them Out of the place to which you have sold them, And will return your retaliation upon your own head." (Joel 3:4-7)

" 'I will bring back the captives of My people Israel; They shall build the waste cities and inhabit *them*; They shall plant vineyards and drink wine from them; They shall also make gardens and eat fruit from them. I will plant them in their land, And no longer shall they be pulled up From the land I have given them,' Says the LORD your God." (Amos 9:14-15)

Many imagine that this promise of a restoration of Israel to her ancient homeland was fulfilled in the return from "**Babylon.**" But *that* return did not include the ancient sub-kingdom of "**Ephraim,**" which, even to this day, has never returned. The return from Babylon was only the ancient sub-kingdom of Judah, and only a very small part of that. For "**Altogether the whole assembly *was* forty-two thousand three hundred and sixty, besides their male and female servants, of whom *there were* seven thousand three hundred and thirty-seven; and they had two hundred and forty-five men and women singers.**" (Nehemiah 7:66-67) That is a total of only forty-nine thousand nine hundred and ninety two persons. By comparison, 2 Chronicles 17:12-19 informs us that, in the days of Jehoshaphat, the army of Judah was one million, one hundred and sixty thousand men, to say nothing of those that were not in the army. Compare this very small return with the return that God had promised:

"And you, son of man, prophesy to the mountains of Israel, and say, 'O mountains of Israel, hear the word of the LORD! Thus says the Lord GOD: "Because the

THOUGHTS ABOUT PROPHETIC SUBJECTS

enemy has said of you, 'Aha! The ancient heights have become our possession,"' therefore prophesy, and say, 'Thus says the Lord GOD: "Because they made *you* desolate and swallowed you up on every side, so that you became the possession of the rest of the nations, and you are taken up by the lips of talkers and slandered by the people"--therefore, O mountains of Israel, hear the word of the Lord GOD! Thus says the Lord GOD to the mountains, the hills, the rivers, the valleys, the desolate wastes, and the cities that have been forsaken, which became plunder and mockery to the rest of the nations all around--therefore thus says the Lord GOD: 'Surely I have spoken in My burning jealousy against the rest of the nations and against all Edom, who gave My land to themselves as a possession, with whole-hearted joy *and* spiteful minds, in order to plunder its open country.'" Therefore prophesy concerning the land of Israel, and say to the mountains, the hills, the rivers, and the valleys, "Thus says the Lord GOD: 'Behold, I have spoken in My jealousy and My fury, because you have borne the shame of the nations.' Therefore thus says the Lord GOD: 'I have raised My hand in an oath that surely the nations that *are* around you shall bear their own shame.

"But you, O mountains of Israel, you shall shoot forth your branches and yield your fruit to My people Israel, for they are about to come. For indeed I *am* for you, and I will turn to you, and you shall be tilled and sown. I will multiply men upon you, all the house of Israel, all of it; and the cities shall be inhabited and the ruins rebuilt. I will multiply upon you man and beast; and they shall increase and bear young; I will make you inhabited as in former times, and do better *for you* than at your beginnings. Then you shall know that I *am* the LORD." (Ezekiel 36:1-11)

Here, we need to notice the words, "**all the house of Israel, all of it.**" In the Hebrew text here, the word כל, *kol* in our alphabet, is doubled, stressing that the meaning is *absolutely* all of "**the house of Israel.**" Yet the return from Babylon was only a very small part of "**the house of Judah.**"

We also need to notice that the promised return was to "**the mountains of Israel,**" along with "**the hills, the rivers, the valleys, the desolate wastes, and the cities that have been forsaken, which became plunder and mockery to the rest of the nations all around.**" (Ezekiel 36:4) And eleven chapters later, God went so far as to define the future borders of that land.

> "**Thus says the Lord GOD: 'These *are* the borders by which you shall divide the land as an inheritance among the twelve tribes of Israel. Joseph *shall have two* portions. You shall inherit it equally with one another; for I raised My hand in an oath to give it to your fathers, and this land shall fall to you as your inheritance. This *shall be* the border of the land on the north: from the Great Sea, *by* the road to Hethlon, as one goes to Zedad, Hamath, Berothah, Sibraim (which is between the border of Damascus and the border of Hamath), to Hazar Hatticon (which *is* on the border of Hauran). Thus the boundary shall be from the Sea to Hazar Enan, the border of Damascus; and as for the north, northward, it is the border of Hamath. *This is* the north side. On the east side you shall mark out the border from between Hauran and Damascus, and between Gilead and the land of Israel, along the Jordan, and along the eastern side of the sea. *This is* the east side. The south side, toward the South, *shall be* from Tamar to the waters of Meribah by Kadesh, along the brook to the Great Sea. *This is* the south side, toward the South. The west side *shall be* the Great Sea, from the *southern* boundary until one comes to a point opposite Hamath. This *is* the west side.'** " (Ezekiel 47:13-20)

THOUGHTS ABOUT PROPHETIC SUBJECTS

This is nothing less than the definition of a specific *plot of real estate*, first by description (chapter 36) and then by precisely specifying its borders. (chapter 47) Some people demand why we are so interested in a mere *plot of real estate* on the other side of the world. And the answer, of course, is, because God is so interested in it. We can hardly overstress the fact that God has explicitly promised this specific *plot of real estate* to a *particular* "**nation.**" And that promise was unconditional.

But in spite of all these explicitly stated scriptures, there are many who imagine that this is only symbolic language. That when the prophetic scriptures say "**Israel,**" they mean "**the church,**" and when they speak of "**the land,**" they mean "**heaven.**" Major sources of this erroneous notion that we have not yet examined are the scripture that says "**Therefore know that *only* those who are of faith are sons of Abraham. And the Scripture, foreseeing that God would justify the Gentiles by faith, preached the gospel to Abraham beforehand, saying, *'In you all the nations shall be blessed.'* So then those who are of faith are blessed with believing Abraham.**" (Galatians 3:7-9) And another that says, "**For the promise that he would be the heir of the world *was* not to Abraham or to his seed through the law, but through the righteousness of faith. For if those who are of the law *are* heirs, faith is made void and the promise made of no effect, because the law brings about wrath; for where there is no law *there is* no transgression. Therefore *it is* of faith that *it might be* according to grace, so that the promise might be sure to all the seed, not only to those who are of the law, but also to those who are of the faith of Abraham, who is the father of us all.**" (Romans 4:13-16)

Many reason that, since these scriptures plainly call those who share "**the faith of Abraham,**" his "**sons,**" then, when the prophetic scriptures say "**Israel,**" they mean "**the church.**" But the Bible does not say that being a child of Abraham by faith makes a person an Israelite. The concept of being "an Israelite by faith" is not taught anywhere in the Bible. This indeed, *seems* like a reasonable conclusion. But all such reasoning about the scriptures is dangerous. And this notion, which is nothing but mere human reasoning, leads to a seriously false conclusion, that "**the church**" is "spiritual Israel," (a term found nowhere in the entire Bible) and thus, that the promises made to the ancient "**nation**" of "**Israel**" actually belong to "**the church.**" This, as we have seen, is seriously wrong, because it makes God out to be a liar. God did not make these promises to His people generally, but to a *specific* ancient "**nation.**" And He promised to give *that* ancient "**nation**" a specific *plot of real estate.*

But this notion is not only wrong because the Bible never says that "**Israel**" means "**the church.**" It is also wrong because the ancient promises were not only made to the "**nation**" of "**Israel.**" (And remember, we have seen that God explicitly used the word "**nation**" in making these promises.) But there were numerous unconditional promises also made to each of the two sub-nations of "**Ephraim**" and "**Judah,**" and to each of "**the twelve tribes of Israel**" by name, as well as to the descendants of seven specific Israelites. And no scripture even hints at an idea that any of these other names means "**the church.**"

So let us examine some of the unconditional promises made to "**Ephraim**" and "**Judah.**"

> "**It shall come to pass in that day**
> *That* **the LORD shall set His hand again the second time**
> **To recover the remnant of His people who are left,**
> **From Assyria and Egypt,**
> **From Pathros and Cush,**
> **From Elam and Shinar,**
> **From Hamath and the islands of the sea.**
> **He will set up a banner for the nations,**

> And will assemble the outcasts of Israel,
> And gather together the dispersed of Judah
> From the four corners of the earth.
> Also the envy of Ephraim shall depart,
> And the adversaries of Judah shall be cut off;
> Ephraim shall not envy Judah,
> And Judah shall not harass Ephraim.
> But they shall fly down upon the shoulder of the Philistines toward the west;
> Together they shall plunder the people of the East;
> They shall lay their hand on Edom and Moab;
> And the people of Ammon shall obey them."

(Isaiah 11:11-14)

"Again the word of the LORD came to me, saying, 'As for you, son of man, take a stick for yourself and write on it: "For Judah and for the children of Israel, his companions." Then take another stick and write on it, "For Joseph, the stick of Ephraim, and *for* all the house of Israel, his companions." Then join them one to another for yourself into one stick, and they will become one in your hand.

" 'And when the children of your people speak to you, saying, "Will you not show us what you *mean* by these?"-- say to them, "Thus says the Lord GOD: 'Surely I will take the stick of Joseph, which *is* in the hand of Ephraim, and the tribes of Israel, his companions; and I will join them with it, with the stick of Judah, and make them one stick, and they will be one in My hand.' " And the sticks on which you write will be in your hand before their eyes. Then say to them, "Thus says the Lord GOD: 'Surely I will take the children of Israel from among the nations, wherever they have gone, and will gather them from every side and bring

> them into their own land; and I will make them one nation in the land, on the mountains of Israel; and one king shall be king over them all; they shall no longer be two nations, nor shall they ever be divided into two kingdoms again. They shall not defile themselves anymore with their idols, nor with their detestable things, nor with any of their transgressions; but I will deliver them from all their dwelling places in which they have sinned, and will cleanse them. Then they shall be My people, and I will be their God." ' " (Ezekiel 37:15-23)

> "Return to the stronghold,
> You prisoners of hope.
> Even today I declare
> *That* I will restore double to you.
> For I have bent Judah, My *bow,*
> Fitted the bow with Ephraim,
> And raised up your sons, O Zion,
> Against your sons, O Greece,
> And made you like the sword of a mighty man."
> (Zechariah 9:12-13)

All three of these passages explicitly make unconditional promises to both **"Ephraim"** and **"Judah."** And in addition to that, the following two passages from Ezekiel 48, together extend the unconditional promises to each of **"the twelve tribes of Israel"** by name.

> "Now these *are* the names of the tribes: From the northern border along the road to Hethlon at the entrance of Hamath, to Hazar Enan, the border of Damascus northward, in the direction of Hamath, *there shall be* one *section for* Dan from its east to its west side; by the border of Dan, from the east side to the west, one *section for* Asher;

by the border of Asher, from the east side to the west, one *section for* **Naphtali**; by the border of Naphtali, from the east side to the west, one *section for* **Manasseh**; by the border of Manasseh, from the east side to the west, one *section for* **Ephraim**; by the border of Ephraim, from the east side to the west, one *section for* **Reuben**; by the border of Reuben, from the east side to the west, one *section for* **Judah**." (Ezekiel 48:1-7)

" 'As for the rest of the tribes, from the east side to the west, **Benjamin** *shall have* one *section;* by the border of Benjamin, from the east side to the west, **Simeon** *shall have* one *section;* by the border of Simeon, from the east side to the west, **Issachar** *shall have* one *section;* by the border of Issachar, from the east side to the west, **Zebulun** *shall have* one *section;* by the border of Zebulun, from the east side to the west, **Gad** *shall have* one *section;* by the border of Gad, on the south side, toward the South, the border shall be from Tamar *to* the waters of Meribah *by* Kadesh, along the brook to the Great Sea. This *is* the land which you shall divide by lot as an inheritance among the tribes of Israel, and these *are* their portions,' says the Lord GOD." (Ezekiel 48:23-29)

The usage of the area between these sections is defined in Ezekiel 48:8-22.

But now we need to look at *when* the Lord says He will bring them back to the land.

The main places we find this are:

" 'For behold, the LORD will come with fire And with His chariots, like a whirlwind, To render His anger with fury, And His rebuke with flames of fire. For by fire and by His sword The LORD will judge all flesh; And the slain of the LORD shall be many.

" 'Those who sanctify themselves and purify themselves, *To go* to the gardens After an *idol* in the midst, Eating swine's flesh and the abomination and the mouse, Shall be consumed together,' says the LORD.

" 'For I *know* their works and their thoughts. It shall be that I will gather all nations and tongues; and they shall come and see My glory. I will set a sign among them; and those among them who escape I will send to the nations: *to* Tarshish and Pul and Lud, who draw the bow, and Tubal and Javan, *to* the coastlands afar off who have not heard My fame nor seen My glory. And they shall declare My glory among the Gentiles. Then they shall bring all your brethren for an offering to the LORD out of all nations, on horses and in chariots and in litters, on mules and on camels, to My holy mountain Jerusalem,' says the LORD, 'as the children of Israel bring an offering in a clean vessel into the house of the LORD.' " (Isaiah 66:15-20)

Here the Lord describes the great battle of **"Armageddon"** without naming it, and then says that He **"will send" "those among them who escape" "to the nations,"** and that the nations will respond by sending **"all your brethren"** back **"to My holy mountain Jerusalem."** So this prophecy clearly shows that the promised return of all Israel will be *after* the Lord comes in power and glory to judge the world, not *before* He returns. The time of this return is again stated in Micah 5, where we read:

"Therefore He shall give them up,
Until the time *that* she who is in labor has given birth;
Then the remnant of His brethren
Shall return to the children of Israel." (Micah 5:3)

The words, "**Until the time *that* she who is in labor has given birth**" clearly indicate until the end of "**the great tribulation**," (Revelation 7:14) the time which is also called "**the time of Jacob's trouble.**" (Jeremiah 30:7)

But we are told more than that. We are also told:

" 'For thus says the Lord GOD: 'Indeed I Myself will search for My sheep and seek them out. As a shepherd seeks out his flock on the day he is among his scattered sheep, so will I seek out My sheep and deliver them from all the places where they were scattered on a cloudy and dark day. And I will bring them out from the peoples and gather them from the countries, and will bring them to their own land; I will feed them on the mountains of Israel, in the valleys and in all the inhabited places of the country. I will feed them in good pasture, and their fold shall be on the high mountains of Israel. There they shall lie down in a good fold and feed in rich pasture on the mountains of Israel. I will feed My flock, and I will make them lie down,' says the Lord GOD. 'I will seek what was lost and bring back what was driven away, bind up the broken and strengthen what was sick; but I will destroy the fat and the strong, and feed them in judgment.' " (Ezekiel 34:11-16)

" 'Therefore behold, the days are coming,' says the LORD, 'that it shall no more be said, "The "LORD lives who brought up the children of Israel from the land of Egypt," but, "The LORD lives who brought up the children of Israel from the land of the north and from all the lands where He had driven them." For I will bring them back into their land which I gave to their fathers.

" 'Behold, I will send for many fishermen,' says the LORD, 'and they shall fish them; and afterward I will send for many hunters, and they shall hunt them from every mountain and every hill, and out of the holes of the rocks. For My eyes *are* on all their ways; they are not hidden from My face, nor is their iniquity hidden from My eyes. And first I will repay double for their iniquity and their sin, because they have defiled My land; they have filled My inheritance with the carcasses of their detestable and abominable idols.' " (Jeremiah 16:14-18)

So the Lord will not only bring them back generally, but He will **"search for My sheep and seek them out," "seek out My sheep and deliver them from all the places where they were scattered,"** and send **"fishermen"** and **"hunters"** to seek out the residue of them from wherever they might be hidden. Another scripture tells us that these are angelic seekers, for we also read that **"Immediately after the tribulation of those days the sun will be darkened, and the moon will not give its light; the stars will fall from heaven, and the powers of the heavens will be shaken. Then the sign of the Son of Man will appear in heaven, and then all the tribes of the earth will mourn, and they will see the Son of Man coming on the clouds of heaven with power and great glory. And He will send His angels with a great sound of a trumpet, and they will gather together His elect from the four winds, from one end of heaven to the other."** (Matthew 24:29-31)

But many of the children of Israel are rebels. These will be purged **"from among"** those returning to the land at this time. We notice the timing of the following prophecy in the fact that God pleads with them **"face to face,"** just as He did with their **"fathers" "in the wilderness of the land of Egypt."** He could not **"plead"** with them **"face to face"** unless He was *physically* present on the earth. So this detail shows that this purging will take place *after* the Lord returns, not *before*. Yet it takes place *as* they are returning. So this prophecy again shows the timing of their return.

> " '*As* I live,' says the Lord GOD, 'surely with a mighty hand, with an outstretched arm, and with fury poured out, I will rule over you. I will bring you out from the peoples and gather you out of the countries where you are scattered, with a mighty hand, with an outstretched arm, and with fury poured out. And I will bring you into the wilderness of the peoples, and there I will plead My case with you face to face. Just as I pleaded My case with your fathers in the wilderness of the land of Egypt, so I will plead My case with you,' says the Lord GOD.
>
> " 'I will make you pass under the rod, and I will bring you into the bond of the covenant; I will purge the rebels from among you, and those who transgress against Me; I will bring them out of the country where they dwell, but they shall not enter the land of Israel. Then you will know that I *am* the LORD.' " (Ezekiel 20:33-38)

We are not told what fraction of the people will be removed in this purge. But those that will be left are called a remnant, saying, "**I will surely assemble all of you, O Jacob, I will surely gather the remnant of Israel; I will put them together like sheep of the fold, Like a flock in the midst of their pasture; They shall make a loud noise because of *so many* people.**" (Micah 2:12)

We also know that this purging will be by death, for the Lord says "**I will pour on the house of David and on the inhabitants of Jerusalem the Spirit of grace and supplication; then they will look on Me whom they pierced. Yes, they will mourn for Him as one mourns for *his* only *son*, and grieve for Him as one grieves for a firstborn. In that day there shall be a great mourning in Jerusalem, like the mourning at Hadad Rimmon in the plain of Megiddo. And the land shall mourn, every family by itself: the family of the house of David by itself, and their wives by themselves; the family of the house of Nathan by itself, and their wives by themselves; the family of the house of Levi by itself, and their wives by themselves; the family of Shimei by itself, and their wives by themselves; all the families that remain, every family by itself, and their wives by themselves." (Zechariah 12:10-14)

Again, we read, "... **For those of Israel who have escaped. And it shall come to pass that *he who* is left in Zion and remains in Jerusalem will be called holy--everyone who is recorded among the living in Jerusalem. When the Lord has washed away the filth of the daughters of Zion, and purged the blood of Jerusalem from her midst, by the spirit of judgment and by the spirit of burning."** (Isaiah 4:2b-4)

The following clauses from these two prophecies show that they are speaking of those who have survived to this time:

"**all the families that remain**"

"**For those of Israel who have escaped.**"

"***He who* is left in Zion and remains in Jerusalem**"

"**everyone who is recorded among the living in Jerusalem**"

And this purging (by death) is not *only* for those returning at this time. For we are told, concerning **"the time of Jacob's trouble:"** (Jeremiah 30:7)

" 'And it shall come to pass in all the land,'
Says the LORD,
'That two-thirds in it shall be cut off *and* die,
But *one*-third shall be left in it:
I will bring the *one*-third through the fire,
Will refine them as silver is refined,
And test them as gold is tested.

> **They will call on My name,**
> **And I will answer them.**
> **I will say, 'This *is* My people';**
> **And each one will say, 'The LORD *is* my God.'"**
> (Zechariah 13:8-9)

This purging by death is what shows that there is no contradiction between the scriptures that so explicitly say, for instance, that **"all the house of Israel, all of it,"** will again inhabit the **"mountains of Israel,"** along with **"the hills, the rivers, the valleys, the desolate wastes, and the cities that have been forsaken,"** as we saw in Ezekiel 36:1-11, with the other scriptures that say things like:

> **"For though your people,**
> **O Israel, be as the sand of the sea,**
> **A remnant of them will return."** (Isaiah 10:22)

So, although only a **"remnant"** of **"Israel"** will survive these judgmental purges, we are plainly told that absolutely all of them that do survive will not only be settled in their ancient homeland, but also restored to a true and living faith in their God.

But now we need to turn our attention to promises made to specific individuals. We have already noticed the promises in Zechariah 12:12-13 that the families of the houses of **"Nathan,"** **"Levi,"** and **"Shimei"** would repent with bitter weeping. But what about the other individuals to whom promises were made?

We read that the Lord said, " **'Phinehas the son of Eleazar, the son of Aaron the priest, has turned back My wrath from the children of Israel, because he was zealous with My zeal among them, so that I did not consume the children of Israel in My zeal.' Therefore say, 'Behold, I give to him My covenant of peace; and it shall be to him and his descen-**

dants after him a covenant of an everlasting priesthood, because he was zealous for his God, and made atonement for the children of Israel.'" (Numbers 25:11-13)

And the Lord gave a similar reason for saying, " '**the priests, the Levites, the sons of Zadok, who kept charge of My sanctuary when the children of Israel went astray from Me, they shall come near Me to minister to Me; and they shall stand before Me to offer to Me the fat and the blood,'** says the Lord GOD. **'They shall enter My sanctuary, and they shall come near My table to minister to Me, and they shall keep My charge.'"** (Ezekiel 44:15-16)

And it was for a somewhat similar reason that "**Jeremiah said to the house of the Rechabites, 'Thus says the LORD of hosts, the God of Israel: "Because you have obeyed the commandment of Jonadab your father, and kept all his precepts and done according to all that he commanded you, therefore thus says the LORD of hosts, the God of Israel: 'Jonadab the son of Rechab shall not lack a man to stand before Me forever.'"'"** (Jeremiah 35:18-19)

We have already noticed the promise to David which was stated in Psalm 89. As it was originally made, it was worded, **"I took you from the sheepfold, from following the sheep, to be ruler over My people, over Israel. And I have been with you wherever you have gone, and have cut off all your enemies from before you, and have made you a great name, like the name of the great men who** *are* **on the earth. Moreover I will appoint a place for My people Israel, and will plant them, that they may dwell in a place of their own and move no more; nor shall the sons of wickedness oppress them anymore, as previously, since the time that I commanded judges** *to be* **over My people Israel, and have caused you to rest from all your enemies. Also the LORD tells you that He will make you a house.**

THOUGHTS ABOUT PROPHETIC SUBJECTS

"**When your day'-s are fulfilled and you rest with your fathers, I will set up your seed after you, who will come from your body, and I will establish his kingdom. He shall build a house for My name, and I will establish the throne of his kingdom forever. I will be his Father, and he shall be My son. If he commits iniquity, I will chasten him with the rod of men and with the blows of the sons of men. But My mercy shall not depart from him, as I took** *it* **from Saul, whom I removed from before you. And your house and your kingdom shall be established forever before you. Your throne shall be established forever.**" (2 Samuel 7:8-16)

We need to notice several details in this promise. First, the Lord said, "**I will appoint a place for My people Israel, and will plant them, that they may dwell in a place of their own and move no more; nor shall the sons of wickedness oppress them anymore, as previously.**" As they were expelled from the land after their return from Babylon, we know that this promise was not fulfilled at that time.

Next, we need to notice the words, "**If he commits iniquity, I will chasten him with the rod of men and with the blows of the sons of men. But My mercy shall not depart from him, as I took** *it* **from Saul, whom I removed from before you.**" The previous words, "**I will set up your seed after you**" and "**I will establish the throne of his kingdom forever,**" *seem* to be references to Christ. But it would be blasphemous to even suggest that Christ even *might* sin. So this promise is unquestionably speaking of the physical descendants of David, even though it obviously included the Lord Jesus as one of those physical descendants.

We have seen that the unconditional promises include, not only the "**nation**" of "**Israel,**" but also the two ancient sub-nations of "**Ephraim**" and "**Judah,**" each of "**the twelve tribes of Israel**" by name, seven specifically named Israelites, and the physical **"land of Israel."** but now we need to examine the unconditional promises to **"Zion"** and **"Jerusalem,"** which are often intermixed in the same prophecies.

We have already noticed the scripture that says, **"And it shall come to pass that *he who* is left in Zion and remains in Jerusalem will be called holy--everyone who is recorded among the living in Jerusalem. When the Lord has washed away the filth of the daughters of Zion, and purged the blood of Jerusalem from her midst, by the spirit of judgment and by the spirit of burning,"** (Isaiah 4:3-4) But this unconditional promise continues with the words, **"then the LORD will create above every dwelling place of Mount Zion, and above her assemblies, a cloud and smoke by day and the shining of a flaming fire by night. For over all the glory there will be a covering."** (Isaiah 4:5) There can be no question that this has never happened.

Again, we read:

"And the ransomed of the LORD shall return,
And come to Zion with singing,
With everlasting joy on their heads.
They shall obtain joy and gladness,
And sorrow and sighing shall flee away."
(Isaiah 35:10)
"And the LORD will comfort Zion,
He will comfort all her waste places;
He will make her wilderness like Eden,
And her desert like the garden of the LORD;
Joy and gladness will be found in it,
Thanksgiving and the voice of melody."
(Isaiah 51:3)

THOUGHTS ABOUT PROPHETIC SUBJECTS

And:
> "The LORD also will roar from Zion,
> And utter His voice from Jerusalem;
> The heavens and earth will shake;
> But the LORD will be a shelter for His people,
> And the strength of the children of Israel.
> So you shall know that I am the LORD your God,
> Dwelling in Zion My holy mountain.
> Then Jerusalem shall be holy,
> And no aliens shall ever pass through her again."
> (Joel 3:16-17)

Again, as aliens still pass through Jerusalem, this promise has still, even to this day, not been fulfilled.

And we read:
> "Thus says the LORD of hosts:
> 'I am zealous for Zion with great zeal;
> With great fervor I am zealous for her.'
> "Thus says the LORD:
> 'I will return to Zion,
> And dwell in the midst of Jerusalem.
> Jerusalem shall be called the City of Truth,
> The Mountain of the LORD of hosts,
> The Holy Mountain.'" (Zechariah 8:2-3)

And again:
> "Thus says the LORD of hosts:
> 'Old men and old women shall again sit
> In the streets of Jerusalem,
> Each one with his staff in his hand

> Because of great age.
> The streets of the city Shall be full of boys and girls
> Playing in its streets.'"
(Zechariah 8:4-5)

And yet again:
> "Thus says the LORD of hosts:
> 'Behold, I will save My people from the land of the east
> And from the land of the west;
> I will bring them *back*,
> And they shall dwell in the midst of Jerusalem.
> They shall be My people
> And I will be their God,
> In truth and righteousness.'"
(Zechariah 8:7-8)

And again:
> "For thus says the LORD of hosts:
> 'Just as I determined to punish you
> When your fathers provoked Me to wrath,'
> Says the LORD of hosts,
> 'And I would not relent,
> So again in these days I am determined to do good
> To Jerusalem and to the house of Judah.
> Do not fear.'"
(Zechariah 8:14-15)

And this promise was repeated again and again:
> "In those days Judah will be saved,
> And Jerusalem will dwell safely.

And this is *the name* by which she will be called: THE LORD OUR RIGHTEOUSNESS."
(Jeremiah 33:16)

"And the LORD will take possession of Judah as His inheritance in the Holy Land, and will again choose Jerusalem." (Zechariah 2:12)

"Egypt shall be a desolation,
And Edom a desolate wilderness,
Because of violence *against* the people of Judah,
For they have shed innocent blood in their land.
But Judah shall abide forever,
And Jerusalem from generation to generation."
(Joel 3:19-20)

"The LORD will save the tents of Judah first, so that the glory of the house of David and the glory of the inhabitants of Jerusalem shall not become greater than that of Judah. In that day the LORD will defend the inhabitants of Jerusalem; the one who is feeble among them in that day shall be like David, and the house of David *shall be* like God, like the Angel of the LORD before them. It shall be in that day *that* I will seek to destroy all the nations that come against Jerusalem."
(Zechariah 12:7-9)

"And in that day it shall be
***That* living waters shall flow from Jerusalem,**
Half of them toward the eastern sea
And half of them toward the western sea;
In both summer and winter it shall occur.
And the LORD shall be King over all the earth.
In that day it shall be--
'The LORD is one,'
And His name one.

> "All the land shall be turned into a plain from Geba to Rimmon south of Jerusalem. *Jerusalem* shall be raised up and inhabited in her place from Benjamin's Gate to the place of the First Gate and the Corner Gate, and from the Tower of Hananeel to the king's winepresses. *The people* shall dwell in it; And no longer shall there be utter destruction, But Jerusalem shall be safely inhabited." (Zechariah 14:8-11)

But unconditional promises were not *only* made to "**Israel**," and to its parts, land, and cities. They were also made to other nations as well. Some nations will joyfully attack "**Judah**" because of their hatred. These will be destroyed, although that is not the subject of this article. But less guilty nations, though also punished, will afterward be blessed along with "**Israel**." "**Egypt**" and "**Assyria**" are the first nations to be promised this restoration.

> "And the LORD will strike Egypt, He will strike and heal *it*; they will return to the LORD, and He will be entreated by them and heal them. In that day there will be a highway from Egypt to Assyria, and the Assyrian will come into Egypt and the Egyptian into Assyria, and the Egyptians will serve with the Assyrians. In that day Israel will be one of three with Egypt and Assyria; a blessing in the midst of the land." (Isaiah 19:22-24)

Then, "**Moab**," "**Ammon**," and "**Elam**" are promised restoration in highly similar passages.

> "'Yet I will bring back the captives of Moab In the latter days,' says the Lord." (Jeremiah 48:47)

> "'But afterward I will bring back The captives of the people of Ammon,' says the Lord." (Jeremiah 49:6)

And "'But it shall come to pass in the latter days: I will bring back the captives of Elam,' says the Lord." (Jeremiah 49:39)

And in a very long prophecy beginning with the words, **"Thus says the Lord GOD to Jerusalem,"** (Ezekiel 16:3) the Lord said, **"When I bring back their captives, the captives of Sodom and her daughters, and the captives of Samaria and her daughters, then** *I will also bring back* **the captives of your captivity among them, that you may bear your own shame and be disgraced by all that you did when you comforted them. When your sisters, Sodom and her daughters, return to their former state, and Samaria and her daughters return to their former state, then you and your daughters will return to your former state."** (Ezekiel 16:53-55)

And finally, the Lord unconditionally promised that the blessing of this wonderful future age, though centered in Jerusalem, will flow out to the whole world. He promised of this day that,

> **"They shall beat their swords into plowshares,**
> **And their spears into pruning hooks;**
> **Nation shall not lift up sword against nation,**
> **Neither shall they learn war anymore."** (Isaiah 2:4)

This is so important it is repeated in Micah 4:3.

We are told concerning **"Israel"** that **"if their being cast away** *is* **the reconciling of the world, what** *will* **their acceptance** *be* **but life from the dead?"** (Romans 11:15) And we read of this day that **"there shall be no more curse."** (Revelation 22:3) This refers to Genesis 3:17, where the Lord told Adam, **"Because you have heeded the voice of your wife, and have eaten from the tree of which I commanded you, saying, 'You shall not eat of it': Cursed** *is* **the ground for your sake; In toil you shall eat** *of* **it All the days of your life."** We see this again in Romans 8:19, where we read that **"the earnest expectation of the creation eagerly waits for the revealing of the sons of God."**

The blessings of this wonderful day are described in glowing terms, like:

> "The wolf also shall dwell with the lamb,
> The leopard shall lie down with the young goat,
> The calf and the young lion and the fatling together;
> And a little child shall lead them.
> The cow and the bear shall graze;
> Their young ones shall lie down together;
> And the lion shall eat straw like the ox.
> The nursing child shall play by the cobra's hole,
> And the weaned child shall put his hand in the viper's den.
> They shall not hurt nor destroy in all My holy mountain,
> For the earth shall be full of the knowledge of the LORD
> As the waters cover the sea." (Isaiah 11:6-9)

And:

> "'No more shall an infant from there *live but a few* days,
> Nor an old man who has not fulfilled his days;
> For the child shall die one hundred years old,
> But the sinner *being* one hundred years old shall be accursed.
> They shall build houses and inhabit them;
> They shall plant vineyards and eat their fruit.
> They shall not build and another inhabit;
> They shall not plant and another eat;

THOUGHTS ABOUT PROPHETIC SUBJECTS

> **For as the days of a tree, *so shall be* the days of My people,**
> **And My elect shall long enjoy the work of their hands.**
> **They shall not labor in vain,**
> **Nor bring forth children for trouble;**
> **For they *shall be* the descendants of the blessed of the LORD,**
> **And their offspring with them.**
> **It shall come to pass**
> **That before they call,**
> **I will answer;**
> **And while they are still speaking,**
> **I will hear.**
> **The wolf and the lamb shall feed together,**
> **The lion shall eat straw like the ox,**
> **And dust *shall be* the serpent's food.**
> **They shall not hurt nor destroy in all My holy mountain,'**
> **Says the LORD."** (Isaiah 65:20-25)

Now many want to deny that this wonderful age of blessing to Israel will actually take place. But, as we have seen, this blessing will flow out, first to the neighboring nations, and them to the whole world. Those who deny this, insist that these scriptures refer to the resurrected state in the **"new heavens and new earth"** described in other scriptures. But the error of this claim becomes obvious when we contrast this last promise with what God said of the new creation:

> "Then I, John, saw the holy city, New Jerusalem, coming down out of heaven from God, prepared as a bride adorned for her husband. And I heard a loud voice from heaven saying, 'Behold, the tabernacle of

God is with men, and He will dwell with them, and they shall be His people. God Himself will be with them *and be* their God. And God will wipe away every tear from their eyes; there shall be no more death, nor sorrow, nor crying. There shall be no more pain, for the former things have passed away.' Then He who sat on the throne said, 'Behold, I make all things new.' " (Revelation 21:2-5)

We notice that in the age described in Isaiah 65:20-25, there will be both death and sin, while in the age described in Revelation 21:2-5, **"there shall be no more death, nor sorrow, nor crying. There shall be no more pain, for the former things have passed away."** Further, in the age described in Isaiah 65:20-25, there will be **"offspring,"** plainly showing that the inhabitants of the earth will be both marrying and bearing children. But Jesus said, **"when they rise from the dead, they neither marry nor are given in marriage, but are like angels in heaven."** (Mark 12:25)

So we plainly see that these *many* promises, which are *unconditional*, describe a state of blessing in this *present* earth that will take place *before* **"the new heavens and new earth."** And thus we see that, although Revelation 20:1-8 is the only scripture that tells how long this blessed state will last, it is *unconditionally* promised in *many* scriptures. And the thousand year span of ths period is stated six times over in this one short passage.

"Then I saw an angel coming down from heaven, having the key to the bottomless pit and a great chain in his hand. He laid hold of the dragon, that serpent of old, who is *the* Devil and Satan, and bound him for a thousand years; and he cast him into the bottomless pit, and shut him up, and set a seal on him, so that he should deceive the nations no more till the thousand years were finished. But after these things he must be released for a little while.

THOUGHTS ABOUT PROPHETIC SUBJECTS

> "And I saw thrones, and they sat on them, and judgment was committed to them. Then *I saw* the souls of those who had been beheaded for their witness to Jesus and for the word of God, who had not worshiped the beast or his image, and had not received his mark on their foreheads or on their hands. And they lived and reigned with Christ for a thousand years. But the rest of the dead did not live again until the thousand years were finished. This is the first resurrection. Blessed and holy *is* he who has part in the first resurrection. Over such the second death has no power, but they shall be priests of God and of Christ, and shall reign with Him a thousand years.
>
> "Now when the thousand years have expired, Satan will be released from his prison and will go out to deceive the nations which are in the four corners of the earth, Gog and Magog, to gather them together to battle, whose number is as the sand of the sea." (Revelation 20:1-8)

Now those that want to deny that this will actually happen, correctly point out that, in every other place where the term **"a thousand years"** is used in the Bible, it is always being used metaphorically to mean "a very long time." But, while this is correct, these people neglect the fact that while this passage indeed says **"a thousand years"** three times, three more times it says **"the thousand years."** That is, in three of these references to the length of this period, The Greek text distinctly contains the word **"the,"** τα in the Greek, which is *ta* in our alphabet. This is a form of the Greek word ὁ, *ho* in our alphabet, word number 3588 in Strong's Greek Dictionary, which translates literally as **"the."**

Why is this significant? Because, in both Greek and Hebrew, the definite article is understood, even when it is not stated. So when it *is* stated, it is stressing that the reference is to a *particular* thing, as opposed to just something in general. And as no other passage in the Bible uses the term **"the thousand years,"** the entire rest of the Bible *never*, even once, uses the term **"the thousand years,"** metaphorically to represent "a very long time." But further, the last time this term is used, it explicitly says, **"when the thousand years have expired."** It would be difficult to make a more definite statement of the passage of a *specific* period of time. So the arguments these people make against interpreting this passage literally are clearly erroneous. For the period referred to in Revelation 20:1-8 is explicitly and repeatedly described in the very many promises we have examined in this article.

In summary, even if these people were correct about God having transferred the promises made to **"Israel"** to **"the church,"** (which is not the case.) Or alternately, that Bible prophecy symbolically uses the word **"Israel"** to mean **"the church,"** (which is also not the case) this would still have no effect on the many other explicitly stated promises that God made.

But no discussion of the restoration of Israel would be complete without a discussion of the golden age that will follow that restoration, the time we call "the Millennium." But as this, by itself, is a very large subject, It is treated in the articles titled **"The Millennium"** and **"The Worship During the Millennium."** But before we examine that subject, we will see what the New Testament adds to these many promises made in the Old Testament.

New Testament Prophecies of the Restoration of Israel

In the last article, titled **"The Ancient Promises,"** we saw that the prophecies found in the Old Testament are literally filled with explicitly stated promises to both the land and the people of Israel. But many people point out such scriptures as **"In that He says, 'A new covenant,' He has made the first obsolete. Now what is becoming obsolete and growing old is ready to vanish away."** (Hebrews 8:13) These people argue that, since the "old covenant" **"is becoming obsolete and growing old,"** and is thus **"ready to vanish away,"** then, the promises made under that "old covenant" have become **"obsolete."** But in the last article, we saw that God Himself said that He would have been lying when He made these promises if He were not going to actually keep them.

But aside from that, these people are neglecting the fact that these prophecies are not limited to the Old Testament. For there are a significant number of New Testament prophecies about the end times that very specifically and explicitly mention both the land and the people of Israel. The first of these we will notice is the discourse of our Lord which is recorded in Matthew 24 and Mark 13. The parts of these two chapters that are particularly important in regard to the land are:

> **"'Therefore when you see the** *"abomination of desolation,"* **spoken of by Daniel the prophet, standing in the holy place' (whoever reads, let him understand), 'then let those who are in Judea flee to the mountains. Let him who is on the housetop not go down to take anything out of his house. And let him who is in the field not go back to get his clothes. But woe to those who are**

pregnant and to those who are nursing babies in those days! And pray that your flight may not be in winter or on the Sabbath. For then there will be great tribulation, such as has not been since the beginning of the world until this time, no, nor ever shall be.'" (Matthew 24:15-21)

And:

"'So when you see the *"abomination of desolation,"* spoken of by Daniel the prophet, standing where it ought not' (let the reader understand), 'then let those who are in Judea flee to the mountains. Let him who is on the housetop not go down into the house, nor enter to take anything out of his house. And let him who is in the field not go back to get his clothes. But woe to those who are pregnant and to those who are nursing babies in those days! And pray that your flight may not be in winter. For in those days there will be tribulation, such as has not been since the beginning of the creation which God created until this time, nor ever shall be.'" (Mark 13:14-19)

Many mistakenly take this as a warning to all Christians to flee to the mountains, and some have even made extensive preparations to hide out in the wilderness for seven years. But, as our Lord stated it, this warning was specifically addressed to those who were in a particular place. Both accounts contain the words **"let those who are in Judea flee to the mountains."** This is a specific and explicit mention of a particular place, the land of **"Judea,"** which is now called "Israel."

And our Lord not only instructed them to flee at this time. He also told them of this need concerning a different time, saying, **"But woe to those who are pregnant and to those who are nursing babies in those days! For there will be great distress** in the land and wrath upon this people. And they will fall by the edge of the sword, and be led away captive into all nations. And Jerusalem will be trampled by Gentiles until the times of the Gentiles are fulfilled." (Luke 21:23-24)

The Greek word translated "**until**," in this passage is αχρι, *achri* in our alphabet. (Word number 891 in Strong's Greek Dictionary) This Greek word literally translates as "**until**," but with the sense that the condition being described will come to an end at the time specified. For it is derived from the Greek word ακρον, *achon*, in our alphabet, word number 206 in Strong's Greek Dictionary, which indicates a *terminus*, that is, an end to something. So here our Lord himself was clearly indicating that there will be a time when Jerusalem will no longer be trampled by Gentiles.

So in these statements our Lord clearly set forth a prophetic program for both the land of "**Judea**" and the city of "**Jerusalem**."

Other New Testament prophecies explicitly mention the nation of "**Israel**." The first of these that we will take notice of is:

> "So they said to him, 'In Bethlehem of Judea, for thus it is written by the prophet: *'But you, Bethlehem, in the land of Judah, Are not the least among the rulers of Judah; For out of you shall come a Ruler Who will shepherd My people Israel.'*" (Matthew 2:5-6)

We know from the New Testament itself that at that time, "**Israel**" rejected the shepherding that was offered to them. So in actual fact, this has not happened. But here we find, in the New Testament, specific reference to the fact that it will happen. As it has not happened, we know it has to happen in the future, or the prophecy would not be true.

Again, we see this in the very words of our Savior himself, when He said:

> "So Jesus said to them, 'Assuredly I say to you, that in the regeneration, when the Son of Man sits on the throne of His glory, you who have followed Me will also sit on twelve thrones, judging the twelve tribes of Israel.'" (Matthew 19:28)
>
> "And I bestow upon you a kingdom, just as My Father bestowed one upon Me, that you may eat and drink at My table in My kingdom, and sit on thrones judging the twelve tribes of Israel." (Luke 22:29-30)

This statement of our Lord, which is recorded in the two passages above, clearly indicates a time when the twelve apostles will be established as judges over the twelve tribes of Israel. But He did not just say *that* this would happen, He just as clearly said *when* it would happen. And that is **"in the regeneration, when the Son of Man sits on the throne of His glory."**

We see a prophetic program for Israel again, and repeatedly, in the inspired writings of the apostles.

> "For I could wish that I myself were accursed from Christ for my brethren, my countrymen according to the flesh, who are Israelites, to whom pertain the adoption, the glory, the covenants, the giving of the law, the service of God, and the promises; of whom are the fathers and from whom, according to the flesh, Christ came, who is over all, the eternally blessed God. Amen." (Romans 9:3-5)

Here, long after our Lord had been rejected and crucified, **"the promises"** still **"*pertained*"** to Paul's **"brethren,"** his **"countrymen according to the flesh."** The words **"according to the flesh"** make it absolutely clear that he was speaking of a fleshly relationship, not a spiritual one. This leaves no logical way to avoid

THOUGHTS ABOUT PROPHETIC SUBJECTS

the fact that **"the promises"** *still* pertained to the fleshly nation of Israel. That is, to the physical descendants of that ancient nation.

Many imagine that the fact that Israel has been rejected means that this rejection is permanent. But, even in the New Testament, God specifically and explicitly said the very opposite:

> *"And it shall come to pass in the place where it was said to them, 'You are not My people,' There they shall be called sons of the living God."* (Romans 9:26)

The reason for this is clearly stated:

> **"Concerning the gospel they are enemies for your sake, but concerning the election they are beloved for the sake of the fathers. For the gifts and the calling of God are irrevocable."** (Romans 11:28-29)

God has made a choice, and that choice is not dependant on any act of man. His **"election"** stands inviolate. **"For the gifts and calling of God are irrevocable."** This is the subject of the following four other New Testament passages.

> **"For the promise that he would be the heir of the world was not to Abraham or to his seed through the law, but through the righteousness of faith. For if those who are of the law are heirs, faith is made void and the promise made of no effect."** (Romans 4:13-14)

> **"And not only *this*, but when Rebecca also had conceived by one man, *even* by our father Isaac (for *the children* not yet being born, nor having done any good or evil, that the purpose of God according to election might stand, not of works but of Him who calls), it was said to her, *The older shall serve the younger.'"* (Romans 9:10-12)

> **"For when God made a promise to Abraham, because He could swear by no one greater, He swore by**

Himself, saying, 'Surely blessing I will bless you, and multiplying I will multiply you.'" (Hebrews 6:13-14)

"And this I say, that the law, which was four hundred and thirty years later, cannot annul the covenant that was confirmed before by God in Christ, that it should make the promise of no effect. For if the inheritance is of the law, it is no longer of promise; but God gave it to Abraham by promise." (Galatians 3:17-18)

This last statement was made specifically about the promise of Christ. But it shows the principle we are discussing, that once God has made a promise, that promise is **"irrevocable."** Nothing can change it. Not even rebellion. This is fully developed in the following passage, which, although it is from the Old Testament, clearly states the principle being applied in the previous four passages from the New Testament.

"If his sons forsake My law
And do not walk in My judgments,
If they break My statutes
And do not keep My commandments,
Then I will punish their transgression with the rod,
And their iniquity with stripes.
Nevertheless My lovingkindness
I will not utterly take from him,
Nor allow My faithfulness to fail.
My covenant I will not break,
Nor alter the word that has gone out of My lips."
(Psalm 89:30-34)

We need to notice that this passage clearly states that even sin could not cause God to **"alter the word that has gone out of"**

THOUGHTS ABOUT PROPHETIC SUBJECTS

His lips, Further, we are explicitly told that God has *not* cast away his people.

> **"I say then, has God cast away His people? Certainly not! For I also am an Israelite, of the seed of Abraham, of the tribe of Benjamin. God has not cast away His people whom He foreknew."** (Romans 11:1-2)

And God's purpose in allowing their fall is just as clearly stated, saying, **"I say then, have they stumbled that they should fall? Certainly not! But through their fall, to provoke them to jealousy, salvation has come to the Gentiles. Now if their fall is riches for the world, and their failure riches for the Gentiles, how much more their fullness! For I speak to you Gentiles; inasmuch as I am an apostle to the Gentiles, I magnify my ministry, if by any means I may provoke to jealousy those who are my flesh and save some of them. For if their being cast away is the reconciling of the world, what will their acceptance be but life from the dead?"** (Romans 11:11-15)

This future restoration of Israel is again stated in the following passage:

> **"And they also, if they do not continue in unbelief, will be grafted in, for God is able to graft them in again. For if you were cut out of the olive tree which is wild by nature, and were grafted contrary to nature into a cultivated olive tree, how much more will these, who are natural branches, be grafted into their own olive tree? For I do not desire, brethren, that you should be ignorant of this mystery, lest you should be wise in your own opinion, that blindness in part has happened to Israel until the fullness of the Gentiles has come in. And so all Israel will be saved, as it is written:** *The Deliverer will come out of Zion, And He will turn away ungodliness from Jacob.'* **"** (Romans 11:23-26)

This passage begins with a condition, but ends with a statement that this condition will indeed be met. The blindness imposed on Israel because of their willful unbelief will indeed come to an end. For in verse 25 we again find that word **"until,"** *"achris"* in the Greek. So here we are being told that there will be a time when the judicial blindness will be removed, and Israel will again have spiritual vision. And at that time, **"He will turn away ungodliness from Jacob." "And so all Israel will be saved."**

This is more completely developed in the epistle to the Hebrews:

> **"For if that first *covenant* had been faultless, then no place would have been sought for a second. Because finding fault with them, He says:** *Behold, the days are coming, says the LORD, when I will make a new covenant with the house of Israel and with the house of Judah-- not according to the covenant that I made with their fathers in the day when I took them by the hand to lead them out of the land of Egypt; because they did not continue in My covenant, and I disregarded them, says the LORD. For this is the covenant that I will make with the house of Israel after those days, says the LORD: I will put My laws in their mind and write them on their hearts; and I will be their God, and they shall be My people. None of them shall teach his neighbor, and none his brother, saying, "Know the LORD," for all shall know Me, from the least of them to the greatest of them. For I will be merciful to their unrighteousness, and their sins and their lawless deeds I will remember no more.'* **In that He says, 'A new covenant,' He has made the first obsolete. Now what is becoming obsolete and growing old is ready to vanish away."** (Hebrews 8:7-13)

Finally, we find the twelve tribes of Israel explicitly mentioned twice in the book of Revelation. First, that twelve thousand will be sealed by God from each of the twelve tribes of Israel:

> **"And I saw another angel ascending from the east, having the seal of the living God: and he cried with a loud**

> voice to the four angels, to whom it was given to hurt the earth and the sea, Saying, Hurt not the earth, neither the sea, nor the trees, till we have sealed the servants of our God in their foreheads. And I heard the number of them which were sealed: and there were sealed an hundred and forty and four thousand of all the tribes of the children of Israel. Of the tribe of Juda were sealed twelve thousand. Of the tribe of Reuben were sealed twelve thousand. Of the tribe of Gad were sealed twelve thousand. Of the tribe of Aser were sealed twelve thousand. Of the tribe of Nepthalim were sealed twelve thousand. Of the tribe of Manasses were sealed twelve thousand. Of the tribe of Simeon were sealed twelve thousand. Of the tribe of Levi were sealed twelve thousand. Of the tribe of Issachar were sealed twelve thousand. Of the tribe of Zabulon were sealed twelve thousand. Of the tribe of Joseph were sealed twelve thousand. Of the tribe of Benjamin were sealed twelve thousand." (Revelation 7:2-8)

And the names of the twelve tribes will be inscribed on the gates of the city.

> "Also she had a great and high wall with twelve gates, and twelve angels at the gates, and names written on them, which are the names of the twelve tribes of the children of Israel:" (Revelation 21:12)

So, in conclusion, we see that a future restoration of the nation of Israel is clearly taught, not only in the Old Testament, but also in the New Testament.

The Promises to the Church

In the last two articles we saw that, in both the Old Testament and the New Testament the ancient nation of Israel is promised a future inheritance in this earth. But the promises made to us are very much better.

For instance, our Lord told His own:

> "[11] **Blessed are you when they revile and persecute you, and say all kinds of evil against you falsely for My sake. [12] Rejoice and be exceedingly glad, for great is your reward in heaven, for so they persecuted the prophets who were before you.**" (Matthew 5:11-12)

And:

> "[23] **Blessed are you when men hate you,**
> **And when they exclude you,**
> **And revile you, and cast out your name as evil,**
> **For the Son of Man's sake.**
> [24] **Rejoice in that day and leap for joy!**
> **For indeed your reward is great in heaven,**
> **For in like manner their fathers did to the prophets.**"
> (Luke 6:22-23)

In both of these passages, the promised reward is explicitly stated to be "**in heaven.**"

Again, He told them:

> "[19] **Do not lay up for yourselves treasures on earth, where moth and rust destroy and where thieves break in and steal; [20] but lay up for yourselves trea-**

sures in heaven, where neither moth nor rust destroys and where thieves do not break in and steal. ²¹ For where your treasure is, there your heart will be also." (Matthew 6:19-21)

And:

"**³² Do not fear, little flock, for it is your Father's good pleasure to give you the kingdom. ³³ Sell what you have and give alms; provide yourselves money bags which do not grow old, a treasure in the heavens that does not fail, where no thief approaches nor moth destroys. ³⁴ For where your treasure is, there your heart will be also.**" (Luke 12:32-34)

In both of these places the Lord tells the **"little flock"** to provide for themselves **"a treasure in the heavens,"** commenting that this was a place safe from moths (decay) and thieves. These are very similar to Matthew 19:21, where "**²¹ Jesus said to him, 'If you want to be perfect, go, sell what you have and give to the poor, and you will have treasure in heaven; and come, follow Me.'** " This is repeated in Mark 10:21, where Jesus said, **"One thing you lack: Go your way, sell whatever you have and give to the poor, and you will have treasure in heaven; and come, take up the cross, and follow Me."** And we find it a third time in Luke 18:22, where the wording is, **"You still lack one thing. Sell all that you have and distribute to the poor, and you will have treasure in heaven; and come, follow Me."**

Jesus further told them:

"**² In My Father's house are many mansions;** *if it were* **not so, I would have told you. I go to prepare a place for you. ² And if I go and prepare a place for you, I will come again and receive you to Myself; that where I am,** *there* **you may be also.**" (John 14:2-3)

Here we see our Lord explicitly referring to the many mansions **"in my Father's house."** This is not "in the earth," but **"in my Father's house."** Then He just as explicitly said **"I go to prepare a place for you."** Here it was obvious that He was going to His **"Father's house."** And we know from other scriptures that the place where He went was not a different place on earth, but His **"Father's house"** in heaven. This was the place where He was going, **"to prepare a place for you."** The meaning was plainly that He was preparing a place for us **"in my Father's house."**

And we are told:

> **"¹ For we know that if our earthly house, this tent, is destroyed, we have a building from God, a house not made with hands, eternal in the heavens. ² For in this we groan, earnestly desiring to be clothed with our habitation which is from heaven,"** (2 Corinthians 5:1-2)

Here we see that the "building from God" that **"we have"** is explicitly said to be **"eternal in the heavens,"** and that our habitation is **"from heaven."**

And:

> **"⁵ because of the hope which is laid up for you in heaven, of which you heard before in the word of the truth of the gospel,"** (Colossians 1:5)

Here our hope is explicitly said to be **"in heaven."**

Furthermore, we are told:

> **"¹⁸ And the Lord will deliver me from every evil work and preserve me for His heavenly kingdom. To Him be glory forever and ever. Amen!"** (2 Timothy 4:18)

Here Paul explicitly says that he will be preserved for the Lord's **"Heavenly kingdom."**

THOUGHTS ABOUT PROPHETIC SUBJECTS

And we are told:

"**²² But you have come to Mount Zion and to the city of the living God, the heavenly Jerusalem, to an innumerable company of angels, ²³ to the general assembly and church of the firstborn *who are* registered in heaven, to God the Judge of all, to the spirits of just men made perfect,**" (Hebrews 12:22-23)

Here we see ourselves having come to "**the heavenly Jerusalem.**"

And:

"**³ Blessed *be* the God and Father of our Lord Jesus Christ, who according to His abundant mercy has begotten us again to a living hope through the resurrection of Jesus Christ from the dead, ⁴ to an inheritance incorruptible and undefiled and that does not fade away, reserved in heaven for you, ⁵ who are kept by the power of God through faith for salvation ready to be revealed in the last time.**" (1 Peter 1:3-5)

Here our "**inheritance**" is explicitly said to be "**reserved in heaven**" for us.

All of these promises are explicitly said to be "**in heaven,**" as opposed to the many promises made to Israel, which are only about blessing on this earth. How much better is a blessing "**in heaven**" than a blessing on earth! So it is indeed sad to see those that have received such wonderful promises as we have been given, trying to deny the much less wonderful promises made to the ancient nation of Israel. For, even though their promises are meager when compared to ours, they are still stupendously wonderful. A land and a blessing from the very God of heaven! And He has promised to make them His children. But He has promised to make us His bride. How much closer is a man to His bride, than to his son or daughter! So our promises are far more blessed than the promises made to Israel. But that does not in any either belittle or do way with the many promises made to them, every one of which will most certainly be kept.

THOUGHTS ABOUT PROPHETIC SUBJECTS

The Church Is Not Israel

There are many that claim that there is only one "people of God." They claim that this one group has been God's people throughout the entire history of the human race. It does not seem to bother them that no scripture, anywhere in the entire Bible, says any such thing. They are so certain that this is correct that they imagine that the scriptures teach it.

The scriptures indeed, and very plainly, teach that in Christ, Jews and Gentiles are united together as one. We see this in scriptures such as "**²⁶ For you are all sons of God through faith in Christ Jesus. ²⁷ For as many of you as were baptized into Christ have put on Christ. ²⁸ There is neither Jew nor Greek, there is neither slave nor free, there is neither male nor female; for you are all one in Christ Jesus. ²⁹ And if you** *are* **Christ's, then you are Abraham's seed, and heirs according to the promise.**" (Galatians 3:26-29)

But, even though in Christ we are indeed united as one, this does not negate the differences inherent in nature. We see this, for instance, in the fact that, even though this scripture explicitly says that **"in Christ Jesus"** **"there is neither slave nor free,"** yet in 1 Timothy 6:1-2 we are just as explicitly told, "**¹ Let as many bondservants as are under the yoke count their own masters worthy of all honor, so that the name of God and** *His* **doctrine may not be blasphemed. ² And those who have believing masters, let them not despise** *them* **because they are brethren, but rather serve** *them* **because those who are benefited are believers and beloved.**" We see it again in the fact that even though we are explicitly told that **"in Christ Jesus"** **"there is neither male nor female,"** yet in 1 Corinthians 14:34

we are just as explicitly told, "**³⁴ Let your women keep silent in the churches, for they are not permitted to speak.**" So we see that our unity in Christ does not negate our inherent differences.

And even as our unity in Christ does not negate the differences inherent in nature, the unity in Christ between Jews and gentiles does not even imply that the nation of Israel has ceased to exist before God. Indeed. The scriptures explicitly say the very opposite. For they clearly say:

"**³⁵ Thus says the LORD,**
Who gives the sun for a light by day,
The ordinances of the moon and the stars for a light by night,
Who disturbs the sea,
And its waves roar
(The LORD of hosts *is* **His name):**
³⁶ 'If those ordinances depart
From before Me, says the LORD,
Then **the seed of Israel shall also cease**
From being a nation before Me forever.' " (Jeremiah 31:35-36)

Here, we are clearly told that **"the seed of Israel,"** that is, the physical descendants of the ancient nation of Israel, shall not **"cease" "From being a nation before Me forever."** For how long? **"Forever."** And what shall they not **"cease from being"**? **"A nation."** So this scripture could not be more clear explicitly stating that **"Israel"** will never cease from being **"a nation" "before"** the Lord.

We are clearly told that this unity in Christ between Jew and gentile is a mystery that was never revealed in the Old Testament.

"**¹ For this reason I, Paul, the prisoner of Christ Jesus for you Gentiles -** **² if indeed you have heard of the dis-**

THOUGHTS ABOUT PROPHETIC SUBJECTS

pensation of the grace of God which was given to me for you, ³ how that by revelation He made known to me the mystery (as I have briefly written already, ⁴ by which, when you read, you may understand my knowledge in the mystery of Christ), ⁵ which in other ages was not made known to the sons of men, as it has now been revealed by the Spirit to His holy apostles and prophets: ⁶ that the Gentiles should be fellow heirs, of the same body, and partakers of His promise in Christ through the gospel." (Ephesians 3:1-6)

But we are also told that, although it had been kept secret, this had been integral to God's overall plan from the very beginning. For Paul wrote, "⁸ **To me, who am less than the least of all the saints, this grace was given, that I should preach among the Gentiles the unsearchable riches of Christ,** ⁹ **and to make all see what *is* the fellowship of the mystery, which from the beginning of the ages has been hidden in God who created all things through Jesus Christ;** ¹⁰ **to the intent that now the manifold wisdom of God might be made known by the church to the principalities and powers in the heavenly *places*,** ¹¹ **according to the eternal purpose which He accomplished in Christ Jesus our Lord."** (Ephesians 3:8-11)

But that is not all this scripture reveals. It also reveals that "now," the church is being used to demonstrate **"the manifold wisdom of God."** This word **"now,"** whch is in the text as the Greek word νυν, *nun* in our alphabet, word number 3569 in Strong's Greek Dictionary, indicates something new, something different from past ages. Jesus told Peter **"¹⁸ And I also say to you that you are Peter, and on this rock I will build My church, and the gates of Hades shall not prevail against it."** (Matthew 16:18) He did not say, "I am building," nor "I have built," but **"I will build My church."** That is, at the time Jesus was still here on this earth, the church was something that did not yet exist. It was something that He was going to **"build"** in the future.

Again, the Holy Spirit, in speaking through the Apostle Paul, told us that the church was something new, something that had not existed in previous ages, saying, **"¹⁴ For He Himself is our peace, who has made both one, and has broken down the middle wall of separation, ¹⁵ having abolished in His flesh the enmity,** *that is,* **the law of commandments** *contained* **in ordinances, so as to create in Himself one new man** *from* **the two,** *thus* **making peace, ¹⁶ and that He might reconcile them both to God in one body through the cross, thereby putting to death the enmity. ¹⁷ And He came and preached peace to you who were afar off and to those who were near. ¹⁸ For through Him we both have access by one Spirit to the Father."** (Ephesians 2:14-18)

But we are not only told that the church is something new, something that did not exist before Calvary. We also see **"Jews"** and **"the church of God"** distinguished as different groups in the instruction that we are to **"³² Give no offense, either to the Jews or to the Greeks or to the church of God,"** (1 Corinthians 10:32) and in the scripture **"¹⁶ And as many as walk according to this rule, peace and mercy** *be* **upon them, and upon the Israel of God."** (Galatians 6:16) In his passage the **"rule"** referred to was what has just been stated, **"¹⁵ For in Christ Jesus neither circumcision nor uncircumcision avails anything, but a new creation."** (Galatians 6:15) So **"as many as walk according to this rule"** plainly means the church. But **"the Israel of God"** is clearly distinguished from this group by the details of this statement. They are distinguished by the word **"and,"** which is clearly in the Greek text as the word καὶ, *kai* in our alphabet, word number 2532 in Strong's Greek Dictionary, which translates literally as **"and." "And"** indeed can, in some cases, tie a description to an item, as in **"our God and Father."** (1 Thessalonians 3:13) But in this passage, the possibility of such an interpretation is eliminated by the repeating of the word **"upon,"** which is clearly in the Geek text twice as the Greek word επι, *epi* in our alphabet, word number 1909 in Strong's Greek Dictionary, which translates literally as "on" or **"upon."** In this passage, this Greek word *epi* is individually applied to each of these groups. So, contrary to the claims of many, it clearly distinguishes **"as many as walk according to this rule"** and **"the Israel of God"** as two *different* groups.

And we are also plainly told of a future for Israel, that the partial blindness which has been inflicted upon them is only temporary. **"²⁵ For I do not desire, brethren, that you should be ignorant of this mystery, lest you should be wise in your own opinion, that blindness in part has happened to Israel until the fullness of the Gentiles has come in."** (Romans 11:25) So there is an **"until"** in the imposition of the **"blindness in part"** that has ben imposed upon them. And we are told in many scriptures that their spiritual vision will be restored, and that they will be brought back to faith, after the Lord returns.

And finally, the scriptures reveal that, even in heaven, **"the church"** and **"Israel"** will still be two different groups. We first see this in the words of the prophet John the Baptist:

> **"²⁷ John answered and said, 'A man can receive nothing unless it has been given to him from heaven. ²⁸ You yourselves bear me witness, that I said, "I am not the Christ," but, "I have been sent before Him." ²⁹ He who has the bride is the bridegroom; but the friend of the bridegroom, who stands and hears him, rejoices greatly because of the bridegroom's voice. Therefore this joy of mine is fulfilled.'"** (John 3:27-29)

Here we see, in the words, **"this joy of mine is fulfilled,"** that John clearly classified himself as a **"friend of the bridegroom,"** rather than as a part of **"the bride."**

And we see this again in the account of the wedding, as it takes place in heaven.

> "¹ **After these things I heard a loud voice of a great multitude in heaven, saying, 'Alleluia! Salvation and glory and honor and power** *belong* **to the Lord our God!** ² **For true and righteous** *are* **His judgments, because He has judged the great harlot who corrupted the earth with her fornication; and He has avenged on her the blood of His servants** *shed* **by her.'** ³ **Again they said, 'Alleluia! Her smoke rises up forever and ever!'** ⁴ **And the twenty-four elders and the four living creatures fell down and worshiped God who sat on the throne, saying, 'Amen! Alleluia!'** ⁵ **Then a voice came from the throne, saying, 'Praise our God, all you His servants and those who fear Him, both small and great!'** ⁶ **And I heard, as it were, the voice of a great multitude, as the sound of many waters and as the sound of mighty thunderings, saying, 'Alleluia! For the Lord God Omnipotent reigns!** ⁷ **Let us be glad and rejoice and give Him glory, for the marriage of the Lamb has come, and His wife has made herself ready.'** ⁸ **And to her it was granted to be arrayed in fine linen, clean and bright, for the fine linen is the righteous acts of the saints.** ⁹ **Then he said to me, 'Write: "Blessed** *are* **those who are called to the marriage supper of the Lamb!"'And he said to me, 'These are the true sayings of God.'"** (Revelation 19:1-9)

Here, we see the wedding taking place in heaven. But even as it takes place, there is **"a loud voice of a great multitude in heaven"** (verse 1) and again **"the voice of a great multitude, as the sound of many waters and as the sound of mighty thunderings,"** (verse 6) which clearly distinguish themselves from **"His wife,"** whom they call **"herself."** (verse 7) And we are explicitly told of **"those who are called to the marriage supper of the Lamb."**

So we see that, even as the wedding takes place, there will be a very large group that, while they are indeed in heaven, they are not part of **"the bride."** So, even as the last few articles demonstrated that the blessings promised to **"Israel"** are completely different from the blessings promised to **"the church,"** so also, even in heaven, there will be different groups of the Lord's own. Some will comprise **"the bride, the Lamb's wife."** (Revelation 21:9) But others will only be a **"friend of the bridegroom."** (John 3:29)

So we see that the idea that "there is only one people of God" is not only completely absent from scripture. It is contrary to scripture. And thus, we see that the many and extreme differences between the promises made by God to **"Israel"** and to **"the church"** indeed show us that these are two entirely different groups of the people of God.

JAMES C. MORRIS

The Millennium

The Bible could not be more clear in explicitly teaching that, following the coming restoration of the ancient nation of Israel, there will be a golden age on this earth, in which the resurrected saints will reign for **"a thousand years."** This time span is explicitly stated in the following passage:

> **"¹ Then I saw an angel coming down from heaven, having the key to the bottomless pit and a great chain in his hand. ² He laid hold of the dragon, that serpent of old, who is *the* Devil and Satan, and bound him for a thousand years; ³ and he cast him into the bottomless pit, and shut him up, and set a seal on him, so that he should deceive the nations no more till the thousand years were finished. But after these things he must be released for a little while.**
>
> **"⁴ And I saw thrones, and they sat on them, and judgment was committed to them. Then *I saw* the souls of those who had been beheaded for their witness to Jesus and for the word of God, who had not worshiped the beast or his image, and had not received *his* mark on their foreheads or on their hands. And they lived and reigned with Christ for a thousand years. ⁵ But the rest of the dead did not live again until the thousand years were finished. This *is* the first resurrection. ⁶ Blessed and holy *is* he who has part in the first resurrection. Over such the second death has no power, but they shall be priests of God and of Christ, and shall reign with Him a thousand years.**
>
> **"⁷ Now when the thousand years have expired, Satan will be released from his prison."** (Revelation 20:1-8)

THOUGHTS ABOUT PROPHETIC SUBJECTS

In spite of this time span being so explicitly stated, no less than six times in just the last six verses of this passage, many claim that this term, **"thousand years,"** is only a metaphorical expression meaning "a very long time." But is this claim correct?

The first place this term occurs in the Bible is Psalm 90:4, where we read, **"For a thousand years in Your sight *Are* like yesterday when it is past, And *like* a watch in the night."** In the Hebrew, the words here translated *a thousand years* are שנה אלף, *'elep shaneh* in our alphabet, word numbers 505 and 8141 in Strong's Hebrew Dictionary, which translate literally as *thousand-of years*.

The second place where we find this term in the scriptures is Ecclesiastes 6:6, where we read, **"even if he lives a thousand years twice."** In the Hebrew, the words here translated **"a thousand years twice"** are the same *'elep shaneh*, but with the added word פעם, *pa'am* in our alphabet, word number 6471 in Strong's Hebrew Dictionary, which literally means *two times*.

The third and fourth places where we find this term in the scriptures both occur in 2 Peter 3:8, where we read, **"But, beloved, do not forget this one thing, that with the Lord one day *is* as a thousand years, and a thousand years as one day."** In both of these cases, the Greek words translated **"a thousand years"** are χίλιοι ἔτος, *chilioi etos* in our alphabet, words numbered 5507 and 2094 in Strong's Greek Dictionary, which literally translate as *thousand years*.

This is all the places where this term is used in the Bible outside of Revelation 20. In each of these places it is obvious that, as these people argue, it is indeed simply a metaphorical expression meaning "a very long time." But now we need to examine the first eight verses of Revelation 20 in more detail. Here we find the term **"a thousand years"** three times. This is found in verses 2, 4, and 6. In each of these cases we find exactly the same Greek words as we saw in 2 Peter 3:8, *chilioi etos*, which literally translates as **"thousand years."**

But we need to notice that in each of the passages we have examined so far, the Holy Spirit did not use any article at all. Now anyone with even a smattering of knowledge of Hebrew and Greek knows that in both Hebrew and Greek, the use of an article is optional. So the translators were indeed correct in adding the indefinite article **"a"** in each of these cases without putting it in italics, for it is implied, even though it is not stated.

But there is a different term also used in verses 3, 5, and 7 of Revelation 20. In each of these, we find the English words **"the thousand years,"** as opposed to the term **"a thousand years"** we have been seeing. In each of these cases, the Greek words translated **"the thousand years"** are τα χίλιοι ἔτος, *ta chilioi etos* in our alphabet, words numbered 3588, 5507 and 2094 in Strong's Greek Dictionary. These words literally translate as **"the thousand years,"** not just the **"a thousand years"** that we saw in all the other cases. (The Greek word τα, *ta* in our alphabet, is a nominative form of the Greek word ὁ, ho in our alphabet, which literally means **"the."** In the Bible, in both Greek and Hebrew, when the definite article is used, it is normally used for stress. Thus, it refers to a *particular* thing, instead of just *something* in a general way. So the clause **"the thousand years"** means a *particular* period that will last **"a thousand years,"** not just some generic long period of time that may or may not literally last **"a thousand years."**

But whether this period will literally last **"a thousand years"** or will just last "a very long time" is really nothing but a detail used by false teachers to distract people, to keep them from noticing everything else our God has explicitly told us about this time. And the hard truth is that, although the length of time this coming earthly kingdom will last is only stated in Revelation 20, the kingdom itself is the subject of many prophecies. And most of these prophecies are explicitly stated in plain, clear words. That is, they are not parts of symbolic visions whose meanings can be debated endlessly, but instead are simple statements of coming events or conditions.

The first and most significant detail we need to notice about this future kingdom is that during this time Satan will be imprisoned Many think Satan is just a symbolic personification of evil, but the Bible could hardly be more clear in depicting him as an actual living being, a person, an individual. And the Bible explicitly tells us that this wicked individual will be imprisoned during this period, saying:

> "**¹ Then I saw an angel coming down from heaven, having the key to the bottomless pit and a great chain in his hand. ² He laid hold of the dragon, that serpent of old, who is *the* Devil and Satan, and bound him for a thousand years; ³ and he cast him into the bottomless pit, and shut him up, and set a seal on him, so that he should deceive the nations no more till the thousand years were finished.**" (Revelation 20:1-3)... "**⁷ Now when the thousand years have expired, Satan will be released from his prison.**" (Revelation 20:7)

It is amazing to hear people claiming that this imprisonment is currently in effect. While the manifest presence of evil throughout the world renders this claim obviously ridiculous, it is more than simply ridiculous. For it is directly contrary to explicitly stated scripture. We are explicitly told, "**³ But even if our gospel is veiled, it is veiled to those who are perishing, ⁴ whose minds the god of this age has blinded, who do not believe, lest the light of the gospel of the glory of Christ, who is the image of God, should shine on them.**" (2 Corinthians 4:3-4) And, "**⁸ Be sober, be vigilant; because your adversary the devil walks about like a roaring lion, seeking whom he may devour.**" (1 Peter 5:8) An individual that is presently imprisoned "**so that he should deceive the nations no more till the thousand years** were finished" would be unable to be currently blinding "**the minds**" of those "**who do not believe,**" and would be unable to currently walk about, "**seeking whom he may devour.**"

We remember that, as we saw in the article titled "**The Ancient Promises,**" the ancient nation of Israel will be brought back to its ancient homeland, This is explicitly stated in Ezekiel 36:1-12, where the "**mountains of Israel,**" along with "**the hills, the rivers, the valleys, the desolate wastes, and the cities that have been forsaken, which became plunder and mockery to the rest of the nations all around–**" (verse 4) are explicitly promised that "**[8b] you shall shoot forth your branches and yield your fruit to My people Israel, for they are about to come. [9] For indeed I *am* for you, and I will turn to you, and you shall be tilled and sown. [10] I will multiply men upon you, all the house of Israel, all of it; and the cities shall be inhabited and the ruins rebuilt. [11] I will multiply upon you man and beast; and they shall increase and bear young; I will make you inhabited as in former times, and do better *for you* than at your beginnings. Then you shall know that I *am* the LORD. [12] Yes, I will cause men to walk on you, My people Israel; they shall take possession of you, and you shall be their inheritance; no more shall you bereave them *of children.*"** (verses 8-12)

And as we saw, in Ezekiel 47:13-20 the Holy Spirit went so far as to specifically define the borders of the land of Israel in that day, and in the following chapter to specify which part of that *plot of real estate* would go to each of the twelve tribes of Israel, naming each of these twelve tribes as it specified the location of its individual *plot of real estate.*

But it is not only Israel that will be restored at that time. We are explicitly told that the whole world will be blessed. For, as we also saw in the article titled "**New Testament Prophecies of the Restoration of Israel,**" it says concerning Israel that "**if their** being cast away *is* the reconciling of the world, what *will* their acceptance *be* but life from the dead?" (Romans 11:15) And we read of this day that "**there shall be no more curse.**" (Revelation 22:3) This refers to Genesis 3:17, where the Lord told Adam, "**Because you have heeded the voice of your wife, and have eaten from the tree of which I commanded you, saying, 'You shall not eat of it': Cursed** *is* **the ground for your sake; In toil you shall eat** *of* **it All the days of your life.**" We see this again in Romans 8:19, where we read that "**the earnest expectation of the creation eagerly waits for the revealing of the sons of God.**"

The blessings of this wonderful time are described in glowing terms such as:

"**[6] The wolf also shall dwell with the lamb,**

The leopard shall lie down with the young goat,

The calf and the young lion and the fatling together;

And a little child shall lead them.

7 The cow and the bear shall graze;

Their young ones shall lie down together;

And the lion shall eat straw like the ox.

[8] The nursing child shall play by the cobra's hole,

And the weaned child shall put his hand in the viper's den.

[9] They shall not hurt nor destroy in all My holy mountain,

For the earth shall be full of the knowledge of the LORD

As the waters cover the sea." (Isaiah 11:6-9)

And:

"**[20] No more shall an infant from there** *live but a few* **days,**

Nor an old man who has not fulfilled his days;
For the child shall die one hundred years old,
But the sinner *being* one hundred years old shall be accursed.
²¹ They shall build houses and inhabit *them;*
They shall plant vineyards and eat their fruit.
²³ They shall not build and another inhabit;
They shall not plant and another eat;
For as the days of a tree, *so shall be* the days of My people,
And My elect shall long enjoy the work of their hands.
²³ They shall not labor in vain,
Nor bring forth children for trouble;
For they *shall be* the descendants of the blessed of the LORD,
And their offspring with them.
²⁴ It shall come to pass
That before they call, I will answer;
And while they are still speaking, I will hear.
²⁵ The wolf and the lamb shall feed together,
The lion shall eat straw like the ox,
And dust *shall be* the serpent's food.
They shall not hurt nor destroy in all My holy mountain,'
Says the LORD." (Isaiah 65:20-25)

We also read of that day that "**They shall beat their swords into plowshares, And their spears into pruning hooks; Nation shall not lift up sword against nation, Neither shall they learn war anymore.**" (Isaiah 2:4) This is repeated in Micah 4:3.

And, as we will see in more detail in the article titled **"The Worship During the Millennium,"** in Ezekiel 40-46, we are explicitly told of the worship in that day. Some have imagined that this cannot happen, because they think it would be a return to the law of Moses. But that is not the case. For, although all the sacrifices that were specified as perpetual in the law of Moses are again specified in Ezekiel, Both the sacrifices and the associated ordinances are significantly different from those specified by Moses.

And finally, we are told of a healing river that will flow out of the temple.

> "⁸ **This water flows toward the eastern region, goes down into the valley, and enters the sea. When it reaches the sea, its waters are healed. ⁹ And it shall be that every living thing that moves, wherever the rivers go, will live. There will be a very great multitude of fish, because these waters go there; for they will be healed, and everything will live wherever the river goes. ¹⁰ It shall be that fishermen will stand by it from En Gedi to En Eglaim; they will be places for spreading their nets. Their fish will be of the same kinds as the fish of the Great Sea, exceedingly many. ¹¹ But its swamps and marshes will not be healed; they will be given over to salt. ¹² Along the bank of the river, on this side and that, will grow all kinds of trees used for food; their leaves will not wither, and their fruit will not fail. They will bear fruit every month, because their water flows from the sanctuary. Their fruit will be for food, and their leaves for medicine."** (Ezekiel 47:8-12)

The fact that these scriptures describe reproduction, (and thus marriage) sin, death, and healing (indicating the presence of sickness) are hard proof that these are not descriptions of the resurrected state, where none of these things will exist, but of a future intermediate state, different from both the present time and the eternal state. And the end of this intermediate state is described in explicit words:

"⁷ **Now when the thousand years have expired, Satan will be released from his prison ⁸ and will go out to deceive the nations which are in the four corners of the earth, Gog and Magog, to gather them together to battle, whose number** *is* **as the sand of the sea. ⁹ They went up on the breadth of the earth and surrounded the camp of the saints and the beloved city. And fire came down from God out of heaven and devoured them. ¹⁰ The devil, who deceived them, was cast into the lake of fire and brimstone where the beast and the false prophet** *are*. **And they will be tormented day and night forever and ever.**" (Revelation 20:7-10) And then, just a few verses later, we read, "**¹ Now I saw a new heaven and a new earth, for the first heaven and the first earth had passed away. Also there was no more sea.**" (Revelation 21:1) We will examine that subject in the article titled **"The New Heavens and New Earth."**

THOUGHTS ABOUT PROPHETIC SUBJECTS

The Worship During the Millennium

The building of a new temple during the Millennium is distinctly prophesied in words too plain to misunderstand. For we read:

"[12b] **Behold, the Man whose name *is* the BRANCH!**
From His place He shall branch out,
And He shall build the temple of the LORD;
[13] **Yes, He shall build the temple of the LORD.**
He shall bear the glory,
And shall sit and rule on His throne;
So He shall be a priest on His throne,
And the counsel of peace shall be between them both." (Zechariah 6:12b-13)

And again, in Ezekiel 40 through 42, the prophet was shown a vision of a temple, in which a man with a measuring line took him everywhere, measuring all the details of a temple unlike anything that has ever been built. Finally, in chapter 43, Ezekiel was told, **"Son of man, *this is* the place of My throne and the place of the soles of My feet, where I will dwell in the midst of the children of Israel forever. No more shall the house of Israel defile My holy name, they nor their kings, by their harlotry or with the carcasses of their kings on their high places."** (Ezekiel 43:7)

And the worship in this new temple is described in great detail, including animal sacrifices. Many think this cannot happen, because it seems contrary to scriptures such as Hebrews 10:14, **"by one offering He has perfected forever those who are**

being sanctified." and Hebrews 10:18, **"Now where there is remission of these,** *there is* **no longer an offering for sin."** But our understanding of the result of one scripture cannot set aside the express statement of another scripture. When the Bible tells us something in plain words, it means exactly what it says. The people that claim this cannot happen are forgetting that the God who had the *right* to originally set up the system of worship instituted under Moses, and who had the *perfect right* to terminate *that* system of worship and to institute a *different* one when our Lord Jesus made His one great sacrifice at Calvary, *still* has the *absolute right* to change the present form of worship into something completely different, *whenever* that suits His purpose.

Like the construction of a new temple, worship in the form of animal sacrifice is prophesied in crystal clear language. These prophecies begin in Ezekiel 43:12, with the words, **"[12] This *is* the law of the temple: The whole area surrounding the mountaintop *is* most holy. Behold, this *is* the law of the temple."** An altar is then described, and Ezekiel is told **"These *are* the ordinances for the altar on the day when it is made, for sacrificing burnt offerings on it, and for sprinkling blood on it."** (Ezekiel 43:18)

Next follows a long and detailed description of various animal sacrifices that are to be offered on this altar. This goes into chapter 46. The language is all future, and is very explicit and detailed. The instructions in this section include every sacrifice specified as perpetual in the law of Moses, as well as most of the ordinances specified the same way.

These include a renewal of the command to keep the **"Sabbath,"** as given in Ezekiel 44:24, Ezekiel 45:17, and Ezekiel 46:1-5 and 12. This had been commanded as **"a perpetual covenant"** with **"the children of Israel"** in Exodus 31:16. Again, in Ezekiel 45:21-25 we find the keeping of the **"Passover,"** with its accompanying **"unleavened bread."** This had been commanded as **"an everlasting ordinance"** in Exodus 12:14 and 17, and **"forever"** in Exodus 12:24. In addition to these, we find the keeping of **"the appointed feasts"** in Ezekiel 46:9-11. These are detailed in Leviticus 23:4-43, where they are commanded to be kept **"forever"** in verses 14, 21, 31, and 41.

The last of these **"appointed feasts"** was a command to **"dwell in booths for seven days."** (Leviticus 23:42) This came to be called **"the Feast of Tabernacles."** (John 7:2) This is not named in Ezekiel, but Zechariah 14:16-19 goes into some detail about it, saying that not only Israel, but all the surrounding nations, will come up to Jerusalem to keep it every year, and that every **"family"** that fails to come up to that feast will be severely punished, either by a lack of rain or by a terrible plague, that is, the punishment will be inflicted by God himself.

We find the same thing in the renewed laws of the priesthood. Ezekiel 44:15 explicitly limits this to **"the sons of Zadok,"** because he was the only priest that remained faithful **"when the children of Israel went astray from"** the Lord. Zadok's descent from Aaron through Phinehas is traced in 1 Chronicles 6:3-8. This is significant because the priesthood was given to Aaron and his sons **"for a perpetual statute"** in Exodus 29:9, and with **"an everlasting priesthood"** in Exodus 40:15. Then Aaron's son Phinehas and **"his descendants after him"** were additionally given **"a covenant of an everlasting priesthood"** in Numbers 25:13. So a future appointment of **"the sons of Zadok"** as priests is a fulfillment of both of these eternal pledges.

Other perpetual laws about the priests are also repeated here. Their holy garments are mentioned in Ezekiel 42:14 and 44:17-19. These had been commanded to be worn **"always"** in Exodus 28:38 and as **"a statute forever"** in Exodus 28:43. Again, Ezekiel 44:21 says, **"No priest shall drink wine when he enters the inner court."** This is the same as in Leviticus 10:9, where it is commanded as **"a statute forever throughout your gener-**

ations." And Ezekiel 48:14 forbids them to sell their land. This might seem strange to us, but this was to preserve the land to them and their children for ever. This, again, is a repeat of what we find in Leviticus 25:32-34, where the priests could only sell their houses until **"the Jubilee"** (an equivalent of what we call a lease,) but they could not sell their land at all **"for it is their perpetual possession."**

Likewise, **"every sacrifice of any kind,"** including **"the best of all firstfruits of any kind"** were reserved as food for the priests in Ezekiel 44:29-30. These had been reserved as food for the priests **as "a statute forever"** in Exodus 29:28, and in Leviticus 6:18, 7:34 and 36, and 10:15, also **"as an ordinance forever"** in Numbers 18:11 and 19, and **"by a perpetual statute"** in Leviticus 24:9.

Thus we see that the commandments for this future worship repeat the perpetual ordinances originally given through Moses. But they are not a return to that law. For some of the laws in this section are different from those given through Moses. For instance, the daily **"burnt offering"** of a lamb every morning and every evening, with flour and oil, is commanded **"continually"** in Exodus 29:38 and 42, as well as **"throughout your generations"** in Exodus 29:42. This command is repeated in Ezekiel 46:13-15, but there it is only every morning, and the amount of flour and of oil specified in Ezekiel is different from the amount specified in Exodus.

But a more radical difference between this future worship and that under the law of Moses can be seen by referring to something that was done by Saul, God's anointed king over Israel. Saul offered up a burnt offering. **"¹³ And Samuel said to Saul, 'You have done foolishly. You have not kept the commandment of the LORD your God, which He commanded you. For now the LORD would have established your kingdom over Israel forever. ¹⁴ But now your kingdom shall not continue. The LORD has** sought for Himself a man after His own heart, and the LORD has commanded him *to be* commander over His people, because you have not kept what the LORD commanded you.'" (1 Samuel 13:13-14) Under the law of Moses, offerings were not to be made by rulers, but by priests. Again, in 2 Chronicles 26:16-21, king Uzziah was struck with leprosy because he offered incense. But the law of this future temple will be different:

> "**[17] Then it shall be the prince's part *to give* burnt offerings, grain offerings, and drink offerings, at the feasts, the New Moons, the Sabbaths, and at all the appointed seasons of the house of Israel. He shall prepare the sin offering, the grain offering, the burnt offering, and the peace offerings to make atonement for the house of Israel."** (Ezekiel 45:17)

As punishment for presuming to act as priests, Saul lost his kingdom and Uzziah was struck with leprosy. But this coming prince **"shall be a priest on His throne."** (Zechariah 6:13)

These clear and well defined differences between this future law and the one given by Moses are absolute proof that this was never intended to apply to a time before Jesus came. For when Jesus was here, He said, "**[17] Do not think that I came to destroy the Law or the Prophets. I did not come to destroy but to fulfill. [18] For assuredly, I say to you, till heaven and earth pass away, one jot or one tittle will by no means pass from the law till all is fulfilled.**" (Matthew 5:17-18) So, long after Ezekiel was given, Jesus himself said that not even the tiniest detail of the law would pass until He had fulfilled all of it.

A further and very marked difference between this future worship and that in the old system is clearly stated in Jeremiah 3:16.

> "'**Then it shall come to pass, when you are multiplied and increased in the land in those days,' says the LORD,**

'that they will say no more, "The ark of the covenant of the LORD." It shall not come to mind, nor shall they remember it, nor shall they visit *it*, nor shall it be made anymore.'"

But this new temple will not just be a place for the restored nation of Israel to worship. We are explicitly told that all the surrounding nations will also worship the LORD there.

"[20b] **Peoples shall yet come,**

Inhabitants of many cities;

[21] **The inhabitants of one** *city* **shall go to another, saying,**

'Let us continue to go and pray before the LORD,

And seek the LORD of hosts.

I myself will go also.'

[22] **Yes, many peoples and strong nations**

Shall come to seek the LORD of hosts in Jerusalem,

And to pray before the LORD." (Zechariah 8:20-22)

And:

"[16] And it shall come to pass *that* everyone who is left of all the nations which came against Jerusalem shall go up from year to year to worship the King, the LORD of hosts, and to keep the Feast of Tabernacles. [17] And it shall be *that* whichever of the families of the earth do not come up to Jerusalem to worship the King, the LORD of hosts, on them there will be no rain. [18] If the family of Egypt will not come up and enter in, they *shall have* no *rain;* they shall receive the plague with which the LORD strikes the nations who do not come up to keep the Feast of Tabernacles. [19] This shall be the punishment of Egypt and the punishment of all

the nations that do not come up to keep the Feast of Tabernacles." (Zechariah 14:16-19)

So now we are faced with a simple decision. Are we going to believe what our God has explicitly told us He will bring to pass? Or are we going to refuse to believe it. Our choice in this matter will have eternal consequences.

The New Heavens and the New Earth

At he end of the article titled **"The Millennium,"** we noticed the scriptures that describe the final rebellion of mankind at the end of that millennium, and the judgment of God that will fall upon the rebels, as described in Revelation 20:7-10. This will be followed by the second resurrection and the judgment of the wicked dead, as described in the rest of Revelation 20. (verses 11-25) Then, the next thing the Holy Spirit said, was, **"¹I saw a new heaven and a new earth, for the first heaven and the first earth had passed away. Also there was no more sea."** (Revelation 20:1) Here, there is no description of, and there are no details given about, the passing away of **"the first heaven and first earth."** All we are told is that, at the time of this vision, that will have already happened. But another scripture gives us a few details about that event. For we read in 2 Peter 3:10-12, **"¹⁰ But the day of the Lord will come as a thief in the night, in which the heavens will pass away with a great noise, and the elements will melt with fervent heat; both the earth and the works that are in it will be burned up. ¹¹Therefore, since all these things will be dissolved, what manner *of persons* ought you to be in holy conduct and godliness, ¹²looking for and hastening the coming of the day of God, because of which the heavens will be dissolved, being on fire, and the elements will melt with fervent heat?"** So the present (first) heavens will be burned, and the present (first) earth will **"melt with fervent heat."**

We remember that, after the great flood of Genesis, God promised Noah that **"Never again shall all flesh be cut off by** the waters of the flood; never again shall there be a flood to destroy the earth." (Genesis 9:11) And 2 Peter 3:6-7 reminds us of that promise, saying, "**⁶by which the world *that* then existed perished, being flooded with water. ⁷But the heavens and the earth which are now preserved by the same word, are reserved for fire until the day of judgment and perdition of ungodly men.**" So we are explicitly told that the present heavens and the present earth will be destroyed by fire. But that is not the end of the story. For 2 Peter goes on to say, "**¹³Nevertheless we, according to His promise, look for new heavens and a new earth in which righteousness dwells.**" (2 Peter 3:13)

We are told very few details about this "**new heavens**" and "**new earth.**" but in Revelation 21:1 we are told, as noted above, "**Also there was no more sea.**" And in Isaiah we are told:

"**⁴Every valley shall be exalted
And every mountain and hill brought low;
The crooked places shall be made straight
And the rough places smooth.**" (Isaiah 40:4)

Of course, when we think about it, this is exactly the result we would expect, when the earth will be melted "**with fervent heat.**" All high places and low places will be eliminated, for when everything is reduced to a liquid, the top becomes level. And when it cools, it will all be a vast plain, with neither hills nor valleys. Some have mistakenly assumed that this change will be made at the time of the millennium. But concerning the time of the millennium, we are explicitly told:

"**¹Now it shall come to pass in the latter days
That the mountain of the LORD'S house
Shall be established on the top of the mountains,
And shall be exalted above the hills; And peoples shall flow to it.**

² Many nations shall come and say,
'Come, and let us go up to the mountain of the LORD,
To the house of the God of Jacob;
He will teach us His ways,
And we shall walk in His paths.'
For out of Zion the law shall go forth,
And the word of the LORD from Jerusalem." (Micah 4:1-2)

So that cannot be the time when

"Every valley shall be exalted

And every mountain and hill brought low."

This change is mentioned in a few other scriptures. In Isaiah the Lord said, "**¹⁷ For behold, I create new heavens and a new earth; And the former shall not be remembered or come to mind.**" (Isaiah 65:17) And, " **²² For as the new heavens and the new earth Which I will make shall remain before Me,' says the LORD, 'So shall your descendants and your name remain.**" (Isaiah 66:22)

And in the epistle to the Hebrews, the Holy Spirit said::

"¹⁰ You, LORD, in the beginning laid the foundation of the earth,

And the heavens are the work of Your hands.

¹¹ They will perish, but You remain;

And they will all grow old like a garment;

¹² Like a cloak You will fold them up,

And they will be changed.

But You are the same,

And Your years will not fail." (Hebrews 1:10-12)

And finally, in Hebrews 12:26-27 the Holy Spirit quoted from His previous words in Haggai 2:6. *"Yet once more I shake not only the earth, but also heaven."* He then continues, saying, **"²⁷ Now this, 'Yet once more,' indicates the removal of those things that are being shaken, as of things that are made, that the things which cannot be shaken may remain."**

This is basically everything that our God has told us about this event. But one major question about it is how the righteous will be preserved at that time. And that is simply not directly revealed. But how it will be accomplished is indirectly revealed in the next detail we are given. For:

"² Then I, John, saw the holy city, New Jerusalem, coming down out of heaven from God, prepared as a bride adorned for her husband." (Revelation 21:2)

So the righteous will **"come down out of heaven"** to the new earth. This indirectly reveals that they will have been removed from the old earth before it was destroyed.

Finally, we see that the physical changes brought about by this event will be very great, as both mountains and valleys will be eliminated, and **"there was no more sea."** But the moral change that will occur at that time will be even greater, for 2 Peter 3:13 tells us that **"righteousness dwells"** there.

Concerning the time of the millennium, the Lord says:

"⁸ Early I will destroy all the wicked of the land,

That I may cut off all the evildoers from the city of the LORD." (Psalm 101:8)

The Hebrew word here translated **"early"** is בקר, *boqer* in our alphabet, word number 1242 in Strong's Hebrew Dictionary. This word translates literally as "morning," but it means *early morning*, as at the crack of dawn. And it seems to indicate that this will be a judgment of the wicked that will take place every morning. Further, we remember that Zechariah 14:17-19 tells us about the judgments of the nations that fail to take part in the annual worship at the feast of Tabernacles. And Isaiah 65:20 says that **"the sinner, *being* one hundred years old, shall be accursed." So during the millennium, evil will be restrained. But here, in the eternal state, it will be eliminated, and righteousness "dwells" there. But there is more.**

> ³ And I heard a loud voice from heaven saying, 'Behold, the tabernacle of God *is* with men, and He will dwell with them, and they shall be His people. God Himself will be with them *and be* their God. ⁴ And God will wipe away every tear from their eyes; there shall be no more death, nor sorrow, nor crying. There shall be no more pain, for the former things have passed away.'" (Revelation 21:3-4)

Evil having been permanently put away, it will now be possible for God to dwell in the midst of His people. He **"Himself will be with them *and be* their God."** Truly it will be heaven on earth. And **"there shall be no more death, nor sorrow, nor crying. There shall be no more pain, for the former things have passed away."** As **"the wages of sin is death,"** (Romans 6:23) sin being done away with, death also ceases to be. As we are told that **"²⁶ The last enemy *that* will be destroyed *is* death."** (1 Corinthians 15:26) So, in this **"new heavens and new earth," "there shall be no more death."**

And the description ends with the words:

> "⁵ Then He who sat on the throne said, 'Behold, I make all things new.' And He said to me, 'Write, for these words are true and faithful.' ⁶ And He said to me, 'It is done! I am the Alpha and the Omega, the Beginning and the End. I will give of the fountain of the water of life freely to him who thirsts. ⁷ He who overcomes

shall inherit all things, and I will be his God and he shall be My son. ⁸ But the cowardly, unbelieving, abominable, murderers, sexually immoral, sorcerers, idolaters, and all liars shall have their part in the lake which burns with fire and brimstone, which is the second death.'" (Revelation 21:5-8)

When Will Israel Be Brought Back to the Land?

Almost everyone who is even slightly acquainted with Bible prophecy knows that it clearly teaches that the ancient nation of Israel will eventually be brought back to its ancient homeland, and will there be blessed by God. But many earnest students of the scriptures seem to be almost totally unaware of *when* Our God has told us that this will happen. Like many other details of end time prophecy, this is defined far more accurately than most students even imagine.

One of the most common errors in modern discussion about Bible prophecy is the mistaken claim that this return has already happened. But the return that occurred in the twentieth century was not a return of Israel, but only of Judah. And the promised return is a return of **"all the house of Israel, all of it."** (Ezekiel 36:10) As the Lord said in another place:

> "[12] **I will surely assemble all of you, O Jacob,**
> **I will surely gather the remnant of Israel;**
> **I will put them together like sheep of the fold,**
> **Like a flock in the midst of their pasture;**
> **They shall make a loud noise because of** *so many* **people.**" (Micah 2:12)

There can be zero question that this has not yet happened.

We must remember that the wording of Bible prophecy is very precise. Jesus himself said, "[17] **Do not think that I came to destroy the Law or the Prophets. I did not come to destroy but to fulfill.** [18] **For assuredly, I say to you, till heaven and** earth pass away, one jot or one tittle will by no means pass from the law till all is fulfilled."** (Matthew 5:17-18) The jot and the tittle were the two smallest marks used in writing the Hebrew language. So here, Jesus was saying that, not only every word, but even the spelling of every word, was important. Why was this? Because the details of the spelling of the various words is what shows us things like whether the individual (or individuals) are mentioned in the first, second, or third person, whether they are the ones who do the action or the ones to whom the action is done, and whether the action is past, present, or future. And in that line, we must remember that, even as we often say, "Israel is not the church, and the church is not Israel," even so, "Israel is not Judah, and Judah is not Israel."

So when will this gathering of **"all the house of Israel, all of it"** take place? The answer to this question begins, as do many other prophetic details, in Isaiah, where we read:

" **^{15} For behold, the LORD will come with fire**

And with His chariots, like a whirlwind,

To render His anger with fury,

And His rebuke with flames of fire.

^{16} **For by fire and by His sword The LORD will judge all flesh;**

And the slain of the LORD shall be many.

'^{17} **Those who sanctify themselves and purify themselves,**

To go **to the gardens**

After an *idol* **in the midst,**

Eating swine's flesh and the abomination and the mouse,

Shall be consumed together,' **says the LORD.**

'^{18} **For I** *know* **their works and their thoughts. It shall be that I will gather all nations and tongues; and they** shall come and see My glory. ¹⁹ **I will set a sign among them; and those among them who escape I will send to the nations:** *to* **Tarshish and Pul and Lud, who draw the bow, and Tubal and Javan,** *to* **the coastlands afar off who have not heard My fame nor seen My glory. And they shall declare My glory among the Gentiles. ²⁰ Then they shall bring all your brethren for an offering to the LORD out of all nations, on horses and in chariots and in litters, on mules and on camels, to My holy mountain Jerusalem,' says the LORD, 'as the children of Israel bring an offering in a clean vessel into the house of the LORD.'** " (Isaiah 66:15-20)

Here we find a clear description of the great battle of Armageddon, although it is not named. And then it explicitly says, **"those among them who escape I will send to the nations... And they shall declare My glory among the Gentiles."** And then **"they shall bring all your brethren for an offering to the LORD out of all nations."**

So this return is after the Lord has returned **"with fire And with His chariots, like a whirlwind, To render His anger with fury, And His rebuke with flames of fire."** That is, it is not *before* this, it is *after* it. The time of this return is again stated in Micah 5, where we read:

> "Therefore He shall give them up,
> Until the time *that* she who is in labor has given birth;
> Then the remnant of His brethren
> Shall return to the children of Israel." (Micah 5:3)

The words **"the time *that* she who is in labor has given birth"** obviously mean when **"the great tribulation"** has finally ended.

We remember that Jesus himself said of this time, that:

THOUGHTS ABOUT PROPHETIC SUBJECTS

"²⁹ Immediately after the tribulation of those days the sun will be darkened, and the moon will not give its light; the stars will fall from heaven, and the powers of the heavens will be shaken. ³⁰ Then the sign of the Son of Man will appear in heaven, and then all the tribes of the earth will mourn, and they will see the Son of Man coming on the clouds of heaven with power and great glory. ³¹ And He will send His angels with a great sound of a trumpet, and they will gather together His elect from the four winds, from one end of heaven to the other." (Matthew 24:29-31)

Many have erroneously assumed that this is a description of the rapture. But that is described in other scriptures. For in the rapture, it is **"the Lord himself"** that will come for us, (1 Thessalonians 4:16-17) and here, **"He will send his angels"** to gather them. Those who make this error imagine that **"His elect"** means "the church." But the righteous remnant of Israel is also called His **"elect"** in scriptures such as:

"⁹ I will bring forth descendants from Jacob,

And from Judah an heir of My mountains;

My elect shall inherit it,

And My servants shall dwell there." (Isaiah 65:9)

And further on in the same prophecy:

"²² They shall not build and another inhabit;

They shall not plant and another eat;

For as the days of a tree, *so shall be* the days of My people,

And My elect shall long enjoy the work of their hands." (Isaiah 65:22)

So the scriptural designation, His **"elect"** is most certainly not limited to "the church."

We are also given specific details about this return. For although, as we have seen, the bulk of it will be accomplished by merely human means, there will be much work for the **"angels"** mentioned in Matthew 24:31. For we read, " **'14 Therefore behold, the days are coming,'** says the LORD, 'that it shall no more be said, "The LORD lives who brought up the children of Israel from the land of Egypt," 15 but, "The LORD lives who brought up the children of Israel from the land of the north and from all the lands where He had driven them."' For I will bring them back into their land which I gave to their fathers. 16 'Behold, I will send for many fishermen,' says the LORD, 'and they shall fish them; and afterward I will send for many hunters, and they shall hunt them from every mountain and every hill, and out of the holes of the rocks.'** " (Jeremiah 16:14-16)

And we read again, " **11 For thus says the Lord GOD: 'Indeed I Myself will search for My sheep and seek them out. 12 As a shepherd seeks out his flock on the day he is among his scattered sheep, so will I seek out My sheep and deliver them from all the places where they were scattered on a cloudy and dark day. 13 And I will bring them out from the peoples and gather them from the countries, and will bring them to their own land; I will feed them on the mountains of Israel, in the valleys and in all the inhabited places of the country. 14 I will feed them in good pasture, and their fold shall be on the high mountains of Israel. There they shall lie down in a good fold and feed in rich pasture on the mountains of Israel. 15 I will feed My flock, and I will make them lie down,'** says the Lord GOD. **16 'I will seek what was lost and bring back what was driven away, bind up the broken and** strengthen what was sick; but I will destroy the fat and the strong, and feed them in judgment.'" (Ezekiel 34:11-16)

And again we read:

> "[11] It shall come to pass in that day
> *That* the LORD shall set His hand again the second time
> To recover the remnant of His people who are left,
> From Assyria and Egypt, From Pathros and Cush,
> From Elam and Shinar, From Hamath and the islands of the sea.
> [12] He will set up a banner for the nations,
> And will assemble the outcasts of Israel,
> And gather together the dispersed of Judah
> From the four corners of the earth." (Isaiah 11:11-12)

But many of the individual Israelites are rebels. And God's dealing with them is detailed in the one other scripture that shows the timing of this return.

> "[33] *As* I live,' says the Lord GOD, 'surely with a mighty hand, with an outstretched arm, and with fury poured out, I will rule over you. [34] I will bring you out from the peoples and gather you out of the countries where you are scattered, with a mighty hand, with an outstretched arm, and with fury poured out. [35] And I will bring you into the wilderness of the peoples, and there I will plead My case with you face to face. [36] Just as I pleaded My case with your fathers in the wilderness of the land of Egypt, so I will plead My case with you,' says the Lord GOD. [37] 'I will make you pass under the rod, and I will bring you into the bond of the covenant; [38] I will purge the rebels from among you, and those who transgress against Me; I will bring them out of the country where they dwell, but they shall

not enter the land of Israel. Then you will know that I *am* the LORD.'" (Ezekiel 20:33-38)

As this scripture clearly says that the Lord will **"plead"** with them **"face to face,"** it shows that this will be after He has returned, and is therefore physically present on the earth.

But we also need to notice what this prophecy says about these **"rebels."** **"I will purge the rebels from among you, and those who transgress against Me; I will bring them out of the country where they dwell, but they shall not enter the land of Israel."** Dispensationalists are often falsely accused of teaching that the Lord will save people "just because of their DNA." But that is not what the prophetic scriptures teach. These **"rebels"** will have the same DNA as the rest of Israel. And they, like the rest of Israel, will be brought **"out of the country where they dwell"** But **"they shall not enter the land of Israel."** Other scriptures show us that this purging will be by death. For we also read:

> **"² In that day the Branch of the LORD shall be beautiful and glorious;**
> **And the fruit of the earth *shall be* excellent and appealing**
> **For those of Israel who have escaped.**
> **³ And it shall come to pass that *he who is* left in Zion and remains in Jerusalem will be called holy--everyone who is recorded among the living in Jerusalem.**
> **⁴ When the Lord has washed away the filth of the daughters of Zion, and purged the blood of Jerusalem from her midst, by the spirit of judgment and by the spirit of burning."** (Isaiah 4:2-4)

And, although Ezekiel 20:33-38 only speaks of those returning to the land at this time, we are told of a similar purging of those already in the land:

> "⁸And it shall come to pass in all the land,'
> Says the LORD,
> *That* two-thirds in it shall be cut off *and* die,
> But *one*-third shall be left in it:
> ⁹I will bring the *one*-third through the fire,
> Will refine them as silver is refined,
> And test them as gold is tested.
> They will call on My name,
> And I will answer them.
> I will say, "This *is* My people";
> And each one will say,
> "The LORD *is* my God." ' " (Zechariah 13:8-9)

This purging (by death) of all but the righteous remnant of Israel is what shows us the resolution to an apparent contradiction in the prophetic scriptures. For, although many scriptures, as we have seen, explicitly say that this restoration will involve **"all the house of Israel, all of it,"** other scriptures just as explicitly say that: **"²² For though your people, O Israel, be as the sand of the sea, A remnant of them will return."** (Isaiah 10:22) For by the time these two purges have been completed, the entirety of the nation of Israel of Israel will have been reduced to its righteous remnant. And that is how the Lord promised that in that day, **"³⁴ No more shall every man teach his neighbor, and every man his brother, saying, 'Know the LORD,' for they all shall know Me, from the least of them to the greatest of them, says the LORD. For I will forgive their iniquity, and their sin I will remember no more."** (Jeremiah 31:34)

JAMES C. MORRIS

The Timing of Ezekiel 38-39

There are numerous details in Ezekiel 38 and 39 that show when this great battle will take place. We will first see that this attack is unquestionably an end time event.

In Ezekiel 38:8 the LORD tells Gog, **"After many days you will be visited. In the latter years you will come into the land of those brought back from the sword** *and* **gathered from many people on the mountains of Israel."** Again, in verse 16 He plainly states that **"It will be in the latter days that I will bring you against My land, so that the nations may know Me, when I am hallowed in you, O Gog, before their eyes."** There has been no event even remotely similar to the one described in these chapters at any time in the sad history of this nation. So this event has to take place in the future. But these passages also plainly tell us that it will take place **"in the latter years"** and **"in the latter days."** So it is definitely an end time event.

But when, within the time line prophesied for the end times, will this great event take place? We will first examine several details that show that it cannot take place before the middle of the seventieth week of Daniel's famous prophecy of the seventy weeks.

In Ezekiel 39:7, after telling Gog he will be destroyed, the Lord says **"So I will make My holy name known in the midst of My people Israel, and I will not** *let them* **profane My holy name anymore."** But Daniel 9:27 tells us that **"in the middle of"** the seventieth week, the **"prince that shall come"** **"shall bring an end to sacrifice and offering. And on the wing of abominations shall be one who makes desolate."** There can be no reasonable doubt that the abomination referred to here, is when **"the man of sin," "the son of perdition, who opposes and** exalts himself above all that is called God or that is worshiped" "sits as God in the temple of God, showing himself that he is God." (I Thessalonians 2:3-4) Aside from their blasphemy against and crucifixion of Jesus, This will clearly be the worst profaning of the Lord's name ever done by this rebellious people. But after Gog is destroyed, the Lord **"will not *let*"** His people Israel **"profane"** His holy name **"anymore."** This shows us that Gog's destruction cannot take place before the middle of the seventieth week, the time when this abomination will be committed.

We just looked at the first part of Ezekiel 39:7. The rest of that verse is **"Then the nations shall know that I *am* the LORD, the Holy One in Israel."** But according to I Thessalonians 2:9-12, **"The coming of the *lawless one* is according to the working of Satan, with all power, signs, and lying wonders, and with all unrighteous deception among those who perish, because they did not receive the love of the truth, that they might be saved. And for this reason God will send them strong delusion, that they should believe the lie, that they all may be condemned who did not believe the truth but had pleasure in unrighteousness."** During the time of the Antichrist **"God will send them strong delusion, that they should believe the lie."** But beginning with Gog's destruction, **"Then the nations shall know"** that Israel's God is the Lord. This has to be after the time they are under a divinely sent **"strong delusion, that they should believe the lie."** This again shows that Gog's destruction cannot take place before the time of the Antichrist.

But simply knowing it cannot be before the middle of the seventieth week is still not very definitive. The time is shown more precisely than that.

In Ezekiel 39:29 the Lord says that after this great deliverance He **"will not hide"** His **"face from them anymore."** But during the great tribulation:

> **"Then they will cry to the Lord,**

> **But He will not hear them;**
> **He will even hide His face from them at that time,**
> **Because they have been evil in their deeds."**
> (Micah 3:4)

This shows that the deliverance from Gog cannot take place until after the great tribulation.

So now we know that Gog's attack has to be not only after the middle of the seventieth week, but also after the great tribulation, which is the last half of the seventieth week. But scripture gives us the timing even more precisely that this.

In Ezekiel 39:22, the Lord says, "**the house of Israel shall know that I *am* the LORD their God from that day forward**" But in John 5:43 Jesus told the Jews (see verses 18-19 of that chapter); "**I have come in My Father's name, and you do not receive Me; if another comes in his own name, him you will receive.**" This plainly shows that the Jews will receive the Antichrist, so at that time they will not know that the Lord is "**their God.**" But when Gog is destroyed, "**the house of Israel shall know that**" He is "**the LORD their God from that day forward.**" During the millennium "**No more shall every man teach his neighbor, and every man his brother, saying, 'Know the Lord,' for they all shall know Me, from the least of them to the greatest of them.**" (Jeremiah 31:34) So Gog will be destroyed before the millennium. From these two details we see that we really do not need anything more than this one verse to understand that Gog's destruction takes place after the time of the Antichrist (this is the third detail in this prophecy that shows that) and before the millennium.

This is how we know that Gog's attack and destruction will not only be and end time event, but within the end times it will be after the time of the Antichrist, (shown by three details) after the great tribulation, (shown by one detail) and before the millennium (shown by a final detail.)

There are also less obvious reasons for the conclusion that Ezekiel 38 and 39 take place after the seventieth week. The first of these is that throughout this prophecy the people being attacked are called **"Israel,"** not **"Judah."** In prophecies about suffering in the land during the seventieth week, the people who are suffering are never called **"Israel."** This is because only **"Judah"** will be in the land during that seventieth week. **"All Israel"** will not be in the land until **"Messiah"** comes and brings the rest of Israel back to the land. (see Isaiah 66:15-20, Micah 5:3, Matthew 24:29-31, and Ezekiel 20:33-38)

In Ezekiel 36:10, the Lord tells the **"mountains of Israel"** (verse 8) that He **"will multiply men upon you, all the house of Israel, all of it."** Again, in Micah 2:12, the Lord says **"I will surely assemble all of you, O Jacob, I will surely gather the remnant of Israel; I will put them together like sheep of the fold."** It is clear that this has not yet happened, for there are still Jews elsewhere in the world. But when will it happen?

We see this in Ezekiel 20:33-38, where we read: **"'As I live,'** **says the Lord GOD, 'surely with a mighty hand, with an outstretched arm, and with fury poured out, I will rule over you. I will bring you out from the peoples and gather you out of the countries where you are scattered, with a mighty hand, with an outstretched arm, and with fury poured out. And I will bring you into the wilderness of the peoples, and there I will plead My case with you face to face. Just as I pleaded My case with your fathers in the wilderness of the land of Egypt, so I will plead My case with you,' says the Lord GOD.**

"'I will make you pass under the rod, and I will bring you into the bond of the covenant; I will purge the rebels from among you, and those who transgress against Me; I

will bring them out of the country where they dwell, but they shall not enter the land of Israel. Then you will know that I *am* the LORD.'"

When the Lord brings Israel **"out from the peoples"** and gathers them **"out of the countries"** where they **"are scattered,"** He will plead His case with them **"face to face,"** Just as He did with their fathers **"in the wilderness of the land of Egypt."** And the transgressors among them will be brought **"out of the country where they dwell, but they shall not enter the land of Israel."** This is plainly after Messiah comes, so all Israel will not be in the land until that time.

All this agrees perfectly with the fact that those who have now returned to the land are called Jews. The word Jew does not mean an Israelite. It means a descendant of the ancient kingdom of Judah, that is, a member of either the tribe of Judah or the tribe of Benjamin. This can be seen from the Hebrew words translated "Jew" in the Old Testament. The one used most often is יהוד, *yeudiy* in our alphabet, word number 3064 in Strong's Hebrew Dictionary. The meaning of this word becomes obvious when we see the word it is derived from, יהודה, *yehudah* in our alphabet, word number 3063 in Strong's Hebrew Dictionary. This is the name transliterated *Judah*, the name of both the tribe and the kingdom of Judah. Thus we see that the original form of the word "*Jew*" was "*Judie*," that is, a citizen of the kingdom of Judah.

There is another detail only slightly more obvious, which shows that Gog's attack cannot be before the seventieth week. The prophecy repeatedly states that at the time of the attack, the people of Israel will be dwelling **"safely."** (Ezekiel 38:8,11,14) The Hebrew word translated *safely* in each of these places is בטח, *betach* in our alphabet, word number 983 in Strong's Hebrew Dictionary. This word doesn't only refer to the actual fact of safety. It also refers to a feeling of being safe. Whether the word refers to the fact or the feeling of safety can only be determined from the context.

THOUGHTS ABOUT PROPHETIC SUBJECTS

In this case, the meaning is plainly the feeling of safety, rather than the actual fact. This can be seen from verse 14: **"Therefore, son of man, prophesy and say to Gog, 'Thus says the Lord GOD: "On that day when My people Israel dwell safely, will you not know** *it?*"'" If the meaning was that Gog knew the people were *actually* safe, this would not make him decide to attack. But if the meaning was that Gog knew they *felt* safe, it would encourage him to attack. We see this more clearly in verse 11: **"You will say, 'I will go up against a land of unwalled villages; I will go to a peaceful people, who dwell safely, all of them dwelling without walls, and having neither bars nor gates'"** Thus we see that the word *safely* in this prophecy refers to *feeling* safe, not actually *being* safe.

In Daniel 9:27 we are told that The Roman prince will make a seven year covenant with Judah. This seven year period is the seventieth week. This covenant will give them a false sense of security. (Isaiah 28:14-18) It seems obvious that those who dwell in present day Israel will never feel safe until the Roman prince's treaty is confirmed. But that feeling of safety will be short lived. For we are clearly told that there will be a great attack that will come **"in the middle of he week,"** only three and a half years after the **"covenant"** is confirmed.

And the scriptures explicitly tell us that the enmity of **"Edom"** will never end.

> **"For three transgressions of Edom, and for four,**
> **I will not turn away its punishment,**
> **Because he pursued his brother with the sword,**
> **And cast off all pity;**
> **His anger tore perpetually,**
> **And he kept his wrath forever."**
> (Amos 1:11)

The anger and wrath of Edom will never cease. The ancient land of Edom covered the southern portion of today's Jordan and the north-western part of today's Saudi Arabia. Again, we read:

> **"For three transgressions of Gaza, and for four,**
> **I will not turn away its *punishment*,**
> **Because they took captive the whole captivity**
> **To deliver *them* up to Edom,"** (Amos 1:6)

This clearly shows that Gaza will join Edom in their wickedness. The next verse, 8, mentions that this is the land of the Philistines. (that is, the Palestinians) And verse 9 adds that Tyre (in present day Lebanon) will join in as well. Thus we see that until Edom is destroyed there will never be a time when Judah (which is now called Israel) will have reasonable cause to feel safe. But this will not happen until Messiah comes.

> **We know this because we also read:**
> **"Therefore hear the counsel of the LORD that**
> **He has taken against Edom,**
> **And His purposes that He has proposed against**
> **the inhabitants of Teman:**
> **Surely the least of the flock shall draw them out;**
> **Surely He shall make their dwelling places**
> **desolate with them.**
> **The earth shakes at the noise of their fall;**
> **At the cry its noise is heard at the Red Sea.**
> **Behold, He shall come up and fly like the eagle,**
> **And spread His wings over Bozrah;**
> **The heart of the mighty men of Edom in that day shall be**
> **Like the heart of a woman in birth pangs."**
> (Jeremiah 49:20-22)

THOUGHTS ABOUT PROPHETIC SUBJECTS

Again, we read:
> "For My sword shall be bathed in heaven;
> Indeed it shall come down on Edom,
> And on the people of My curse, for judgment.
> The sword of the LORD is filled with blood,
> It is made overflowing with fatness,
> With the blood of lambs and goats,
> With the fat of the kidneys of rams.
> For the LORD has a sacrifice in Bozrah,
> And a great slaughter in the land of Edom.
> The wild oxen shall come down with them,
> And the young bulls with the mighty bulls;
> Their land shall be soaked with blood,
> And their dust saturated with fatness.
> For *it is* the day of the Lord's vengeance,
> The year of recompense for the cause of Zion.
> Its streams shall be turned into pitch,
> And its dust into brimstone;
> Its land shall become burning pitch.
> It shall not be quenched night or day;
> Its smoke shall ascend forever.
> From generation to generation it shall lie waste;
> No one shall pass through it forever and ever."
> (Isaiah 34:5-10)

This judgment begins at Bozrah, about thirty miles south of the Dead Sea. It then goes some twenty-five miles south to Teman, and from there to within hearing of the Red Sea. Habakkuk 3:3 mentions the Lord's coming from Mount Paran, which is approximately one hundred and sixty miles southeast of Teman, and is on the shore of the Red Sea. This entire area will receive the same judgment as Sodom and Gomorrah.

This obviously takes place at the time when Messiah comes in power and glory, so we know Edom will not be destroyed until that time. And from this, we know that Israel will not dwell safely before that time, and therefore that Gog's invasion cannot be before that time.

So we see that the scriptures do indeed indicate, and very clearly indicate, that, rather being before the seventieth week, as many imagine, the great attack led by **"Gog"** in Ezekiel 38 ad 39 will take place after the end of the seventieth week, and before the Millennium.

Now many reject this conclusion due to faulty reasoning.

We read in Ezekiel 39:9-10, " **'Then those who dwell in the cities of Israel will go out and set on fire and burn the weapons, both the shields and bucklers, the bows and arrows, the javelins and spears; and they will make fires with them for seven years. They will not take wood from the field nor cut down** *any* **from the forests, because they will make fires with the weapons; and they will plunder those who plundered them, and pillage those who pillaged them,'** says the Lord GOD."

We also read that **"For seven months the house of Israel will be burying them, in order to cleanse the land."** (Ezekiel 39:12)

These people point out that if the attack described in these two chapters were to come after the seventieth week, this would make these two periods extend into the Millennium. Then they argue that, "since that obviously could not happen," this attack has to come before the seventieth week begins.

But this argument has a fatal flaw. While this *seems* obvious to them, they are totally unable to produce even a scrap of scriptur-

THOUGHTS ABOUT PROPHETIC SUBJECTS

al evidence that this "could not happen" during the Millennium. Not only does no scripture say this, there is no scripture that even implies such an idea. This is nothing but pure, unadulterated, human reasoning. And, as we have seen, it is contrary to what the scriptures actually say.

JAMES C. MORRIS

The Timing of the Sheep and Goats Judgment

There is no question about the fact that when the Lord comes, He will gather all nations before a throne, for a formal judgment. But when will that take place, in relation to the many other things we are told will happen when He comes? To learn this, we first need to read the entirety of the passage in question.

> "[31] When the Son of Man comes in His glory, and all the holy angels with Him, then He will sit on the throne of His glory. [32] All the nations will be gathered before Him, and He will separate them one from another, as a shepherd divides *his* sheep from the goats. [33] And He will set the sheep on His right hand, but the goats on the left. [34] Then the King will say to those on His right hand, 'Come, you blessed of My Father, inherit the kingdom prepared for you from the foundation of the world: [35] for I was hungry and you gave Me food; I was thirsty and you gave Me drink; I was a stranger and you took Me in; [36] I *was* naked and you clothed Me; I was sick and you visited Me; I was in prison and you came to Me.' [37] Then the righteous will answer Him, saying, 'Lord, when did we see You hungry and feed *You,* or thirsty and give *You* drink? [38] When did we see You a stranger and take *You* in, or naked and clothe *You?* [39] Or when did we see You sick, or in prison, and come to You?' [40] And the King will answer and say to them, 'Assuredly, I say to you, inasmuch as you did *it* to one of the least of these My brethren, you did *it* to Me.' [41] Then He will also say to those on the left hand, 'Depart from Me, you cursed, into the everlasting fire prepared for the devil and his

angels: **⁴²** for I was hungry and you gave Me no food; I was thirsty and you gave Me no drink; **⁴³** I was a stranger and you did not take Me in, naked and you did not clothe Me, sick and in prison and you did not visit Me.' **⁴⁴** Then they also will answer Him, saying, 'Lord, when did we see You hungry or thirsty or a stranger or naked or sick or in prison, and did not minister to You?' **⁴⁵** Then He will answer them, saying, 'Assuredly, I say to you, inasmuch as you did not do *it* to one of the least of these, you did not do *it* to Me.' **⁴⁶** And these will go away into everlasting punishment, but the righteous into eternal life."** (Matthew 25:31-46)

Here we clearly see the righteous and the wicked being clearly separated, and then the wicked being removed. **"These will go away into everlasting punishment."** So, after this judgment, there will be no wicked left in the world to continue their rebellion. And this detail alone is enough to show us the timing of this judgment. Since the wicked are removed at this time, it has to take place after all the rebellions and wars described in other scriptures about His coming. For after this judgment, there will be no wicked people left in the world.

Thus we see that this judgment has to take place after **"Armageddon,"** where the nations of the world will unite under the leadership of the Roman **"beast"** to oppose he coming of **"Messiah"**. And it has to be after Ezekiel 38 and 39, where the nations of the world will unite a second time under the leadership of **"Gog"** to make a second attempt to defeat Him.

This means that it also has to take place after all Israel is brought back to the land and settled there. For the battle of Ezekiel 38 and 39 will take place after Israel has been safely settled in her ancient homeland, as is demonstrated in the article about that. And it further means that it will take place after all the other battles against the enemies of Israel. For it will not be possible to settle Israel securely in her land until all her enemies have been defeated.

JAMES C. MORRIS

The Letters to the Seven Churches

In Revelation two and three, the Holy Spirit addressed seven letters to seven churches in the Roman province of Asia. But this suggests two questions. "Why this number of churches?" And, "Why these particular churches?" It is widely understood that in scriptural symbology, the number seven represents perfection. But is there more involved here than simple perfection? Why, for instance, did the list include neither Jerusalem, the early center of Christianity, nor Rome, the largest city in the world? There seems to be more involved than just letters to a few particular churches. But what is this greater something?

We remember that in the historical books of the Bible, vast spans of time are often passed over in just a few verses, while the lifetimes of certain individuals fill many chapters. So the point of these divinely inspired records is not just to satisfy the curiosity of the readers. Rather, certain stories were selected for inclusion, while most others were left out. We are not left to our own imaginations as to why this was done. For we are explicitly told that **"whatever things were written before were written for our learning, that we through the patience and comfort of the Scriptures might have hope."** (Romans 15:4) Even so, the letters to the seven churches have a far greater significance than simply letters to a few churches that existed thousands of years ago. But what is that significance?

We find our first hint about this in two statements from the first chapter. In verse 1 we read, **"The Revelation of Jesus Christ, which God gave Him to show His servants – things which must shortly take place."** And then in verse 19 we read,

THOUGHTS ABOUT PROPHETIC SUBJECTS

"**Write the things which you have seen, and the things which are, and the things which will take place after this.**"

So the book itself is about "**things which must shortly take place.**" And it is in three divisions. The first division was the things which John had just seen, that is, the vision of Jesus in the midst of the seven churches. The second division was "**the things which are.**" And the third division was "**the things which will take place after this.**" Then, immediately after the end of the seven letters, the next thing we read is "**After these things I looked, and behold, a door** *standing* **open in heaven. And the first voice which I heard** *was* **like a trumpet speaking with me, saying, 'Come up here, and I will show you things which must take place after this.'** " (Revelation 4:1) I have no explanation for why the translators of the NKJV, which we are using, rendered the last word in both Revelation 1:19 and Revelation 4:1 as "**this,**" for the Greek word used in both of these places was σαυτα, "tauta" in our alphabet. This Greek word (word number 5023 in Strong's Greek Dictionary) is plainly plural, so in English they should read, "things which will take place after these," not after "**this,**" as the NKJV renders them. In the KJV this Greek word was rendered in the plural 193 times, and as singular only 6 times. (And as a side note we should notice that this word is in the accusative case, so the preceding Greek word, which is μετα, "meta" in our alphabet, word number 3326 in Strong's Greek Dictionary, was properly translated as "**after,**" rather than its more common meaning of "with." So a literal translation of these two words, which occur in each of these two sentences, is "after these." or, more clearly, "after these *things,*" with the word *"things"* in italics to indicate that it had been added to complete the sense.)

So in the first place, the entire book is about "**things which must shortly take place,**" and the third division is about "**things which will take place after these,**" that is, "**things which will take place after**" "**the things which are.**" This is the first distinct hint, right in the Greek text of the Revelation, that the seven letters represent something more than just individual messages to seven local churches that existed thousands of years ago.

The rendering of the Greek word "tauta" as **"this,"** rather than "these," is an unfortunate error which occurs in several translations. For it masks what was actually said in these two passages. From chapter 4 onward, the Revelation is about things that were to take place after what was revealed in chapters 2 and 3. But the things presented from that chapter onward have still not happened, even to the present day. So, Revelation 1:19 and 4:1 together form a distinct hint that these seven letters speak of the period from when the Revelation was given until a time that has not yet arrived.

But after this clearly implied hint, we have four distinct statements of a passing of time.

The first of these that we will notice is in verse 19 of chapter 2, where we read, concerning the church of Thyatira, **"I know your works, love, service, faith, and your patience; and as for your works, the last are more than the first."** Here we see a time progression clearly stated. For **"the last" "works"** are said to be **"more than the first" "works."** After this, we will notice that in verse 4 of chapter 2 the church of Ephesus was told that **"you have left your first love."** Then, in verse 10 of the same chapter, the church in Smyrna was told that **"you will have tribulation ten days."** Then, in verse 21, it was said of the church in Thyatira, that, **"I gave her time to repent of her sexual immorality, and she did not repent."** In each of these four places a passing of time is not just hinted at, but is distinctly stated.

So we have a total of five separate statements showing that these letters speak of periods of time. There are also other hints that are not directly stated, but are just as real.

One of these is the manifest progression of evil in the sequence of these letters. This clearly, even though not directly, indicates a

THOUGHTS ABOUT PROPHETIC SUBJECTS

time sequence. For, contrary to what some imagine, the scriptures very clearly teach that the church will progressively grow more evil. We read, for instance, **"For I know this, that after my departure savage wolves will come in among you, not sparing the flock. Also from among yourselves men will rise up, speaking perverse things, to draw away the disciples after themselves."** (Acts 20:29-30) We also read, **"But know this, that in the last days perilous times will come: For men will be lovers of themselves, lovers of money, boasters, proud, blasphemers, disobedient to parents, unthankful, unholy, unloving, unforgiving, slanderers, without self-control, brutal, despisers of good, traitors, headstrong, haughty, lovers of pleasure rather than lovers of God, having a form of godliness but denying its power. And from such people turn away!"** (2 Timothy 3:1-5) This warning led to a crescendo eight verses later, where the Holy Spirit declared that **"evil men and impostors will grow worse and worse, deceiving and being deceived."** (2 Timothy 3:13) And finally, our Lord himself asked the rhetorical question, **"when the Son of Man comes, will He really find faith on the earth?"** (Luke 18:8) So the scriptures plainly teach us to expect the church to become **"worse and worse,"** until, when the Lord finally arrives, He will not even **"find faith on the earth."**

So the steady progression of evil in these letters is indeed an indication that they represent a sequence of time. There were two exceptions to this steady progression of evil, one near the beginning and one near the end. We will deal with these exceptions later.

In the first letter, the only complaint made by the Holy Spirit was **"that you have left your first love."** (Revelation 2:4) In the third letter the complaint was that they were tolerating those who held wicked doctrines in their midst. (Revelation 2:15) The first group, **"the church of Ephesus,"** hated **"the deeds of the Nicolaitans,"** (verse 6) and in the third group, **"the church in**

Pergamos," there were some that held their evil doctrine. (verse 14) But the fourth group, **"the church in Thyatira,"** not only tolerated those that held these wicked doctrines, they were allowing such persons to teach those evil doctrines. (verse 20) Scripture does not tell us what their wicked deeds and doctrines were. These were clearly stated by many ancient Christian writers. But we will not go into what they said, as that is not the point of these letters.

The decline then accelerates in the fifth group, **"the church in Sardis,"** where the Holy Spirit declares, **"you have a name that you are alive, but you are dead."** (Revelation 3:1) And it is finally complete in the last group, **"the church of the Laodiceans,"** Where the Lord is on the outside, knocking on the door. (verse 20) The Holy spirit tells that church **"you are neither cold nor hot. I could wish you were cold or hot. So then, because you are lukewarm, and neither cold nor hot, I will vomit you out of My mouth."** (verses15-16)

Thus we see a steady progression from everything still being outwardly right, but having lost their first love, to everything being so wrong that the Lord himself is on the outside, not even in the church. Indeed, the last church is not even called the church of, or in, whatever city was being addressed, but instead of this terminology, which was used for all the other churches in this series, the last one is only called **"the church of the Laodiceans."** (Revelation 3:14) In other words, the Lord was denying that this last church was even his own. He only called it *their* church, not *His* church.

Other hints about this time sequence are to be found in a comparison of the details in these seven letters. There are two systematic differences in these seven letters. The most noticeable of these is that the first three of these letters all speak of their times ending, while the last four ones all speak distinctly of them still being present at the time of the Lord's coming. We will examine this in greater detail below.

THOUGHTS ABOUT PROPHETIC SUBJECTS

And finally, there is a systematic difference in the promises to the overcomers in these seven churches. In each of the first three, the promise comes before the words, **"He who has an ear, let him hear what the Spirit says to the churches,"** which are said to all seven. (See chapter 2, verses 7, 11, and 17.) But in each of the last four, the promise comes after these words. (See chapter 2, verses 26-28 and chapter 3, verses 5, 12, and 21.) It has been pointed out that this seems to indicate that in the first three, all are called to heed the exhortation to hear, while in the last four, the overall body is given up as already lost, and this exhortation is only addressed to the overcomers.

So we see that there are a total of six hints buried within the very wording of the Greek text of the Revelation, that these seven letters speak of the time between the time the Revelation was given and the time the Lord will return.

Now all of this is only interpretation. And *all* interpretations of scripture are subject to error. So we cannot positively insist that "this is what the Bible teaches." But These details most certainly *seem* to indicate that these letters at least speak in some general way of the entire span of time from when the Revelation was given until when the Lord returns.

But in addition to these distinctly stated hints in the text of scripture itself, we find a remarkable parallel between the details found in these letters and the historical records of the church.

In verse 5 of chapter 2, **"the church of Ephesus"** was told that unless they repented, the Lord would **"come to you quickly and remove your lampstand from its place."** This has indeed happened, as what was once the thriving city of Ephesus has shrunk to a mere village. And that village is 100% Muslim. There is not even one person in Ephesus that even pretends to be a Christian. The candlestick has been removed out of its place. For the glorious light of the gospel no longer has even a glimmer or glow in Ephesus.

In verse 10 of chapter 2, **"the church in Smyrna"** was told **"you will have tribulation ten days."** And after its post apostolic period, the church passed through ten periods of persecution. Some might complain that it does not say ten periods, but **"ten days."** But the word **"day"** is often used in the scriptures to represent a general period of time. We find this, for instance, in the Old Testament in Isaiah 19:18-25, in which a future period of time is called **"that day"** no less than five times. Likewise, in the New Testament, in Luke 6:23 a generic time of persecution is called **"that day,"** in John 16:23 the future in general is called **"that day,"** and in 2 Corinthians 6:2 The present age is called **"the day of salvation,"** saying, **"Behold, now *is* the accepted time; behold, now *is* the day of salvation."**

But after this church, the message changes. In verses 22 to 25, **"Jezebel"** and her adulterous lovers are told they will be **"cast" "into great tribulation"** unless they repent, and the faithful of **"Thyatira"** are told to **"hold fast what you have till I come."** Then, in chapter 3, in verse 3 **"the church in Sardis"** was told that unless they repented and watched, **"I will come upon you as a thief, and you will not know what hour I will come upon you."** and in verse 10 **"the church in Philadelphia"** was told that **"I also will keep you from the hour of trial which shall come upon the whole world, to test those who dwell on the earth."** the Greek word here translated **"from"** is εκ, *"ek"* in our alphabet, word number 1537 in String's Greek Dictionary. This Greek word literally means **"from,"** but in the sense of "away from," or "out of." So we see that in these details, the Holy Spirit was indicating that the first three churches would come to an end, but the next three would continue down to the Lord's coming. And the last one, which was a church in name only, will be vomited out of His mouth when He comes.

In the immediate post-Apostolic era, all seemed to be going on well in the church as a whole. But it is very revealing to compare the praise **"the church of Ephesus"** received with the praise the Holy Spirit heaped on the church at Thessalonica during the Apostolic era. There we read of **"your work of faith, labor of love, and patience of hope."** (1 Thessalonians 1:3) But here we read only of **"your works, your labor, your patience."** (Revelation 2:2) They still worked. But it was no longer a **"work of faith."** they still labored, but it was no longer a **"labor of love."** and they still had patience, but it was no longer a **"patience of hope."** But what was the *basic* problem? **"you have left your first love."** (Revelation 2:4) This is like the complaint in the old favorite song by Frank Sinatra, "You never seem to want my romancing. The only time you hold me is when we're dancing." Everything in **"the church of Ephesus"** was still outwardly right and proper. But God, who knows the hearts, knew that they no longer loved him with the fervor that had once burned in their hearts. **"The cares of this world, and the deceitfulness of riches"** (Matthew 13:22, Mark 4:19, see also Luke 8:14) was choking the word in their hearts. And this grieved their Savior, who had shed his blood for them.

But soon widespread persecution arose. There had always been persecutions. But they had mostly been local. But now a persecution against the church rose from the great Roman Empire itself. History tells us that there were a total of ten successive persecutions launched by various Roman Emperors. So **"the church in Smyrna"** was told **"you will have tribulation ten days."** (Revelation 2:10) As we have already noticed, in the scriptures, the word **"day"** is often used to represent an undefined period of time, as in the oft repeated expression, **"the last days,"** or the Holy Spirit's words, **"now is he day of salvation."** (2 Corinthians 6:2) We should also note here that, as this church was suffering, our Lord had nothing but comfort and encouragement for them. This should not be interpreted as meaning that there was nothing wrong in this church, but only demonstrates our Savior's compassion. When his own are suffering, He does not correct or rebuke them, but only comforts and encourages them.

But the persecutions finally ended, In the year 313 Constantine and Licinius issued the Edict of Milan decriminalizing Christian worship. And the church settled down in the world. It had become comfortable to be a Christian. This is treated at length in the third of these seven letters, the one to **"the church in Pergamos."** They were told that **"you dwell where Satan's throne *is*."**

This concept of "dwelling" in the Revelation does not simply imply their address, as it were, but the place where their hearts were occupied. Revelation 3:10, 11:10, 13:8, 13:12, 13:14 (twice) 14:6 and 17:8 all speak of **"those who dwell on the earth."** and always in the light of people who will receive the judgment of God. So their dwelling **"where Satan's throne *is*"** was not a commendation or an encouragement, but a criticism. But there was also a second problem in this church. They not only dwelt **"where Satan's throne *is*,"** but they were tolerating teachers of wicked doctrine in their very midst. And this is exactly what happened in the church at that time. The wicked teachers who had previously been cast out of the church became tolerated in her very bosom. Teachers who had previously been condemned as heretics began to be studied, so their evil opinions began to spread throughout the church.

Within 200 years this had disastrous results, which we find discussed at length in the fourth letter, the one to **"the church in Thyatira."** these wicked teachers began to not only be tolerated in the church, but to be allowed to openly teach their wicked doctrines. The time when this phase of church history began is not well defined, but some equate it with an ascendence of Monasticism, credited mainly to Boniface in around the year 530. This is the first church for which a protracted period of time is explicitly mentioned, in the words, **"I gave her time to repent of her sexual** immorality, and she did not repent."²¹ And, as explained in detail in the footnote, the Greek text does not simply say that she "**did not repent**," but that she "does not wish to repent." That is, that she loves her sinfulness, and has no intention of repenting. So what is the Lord's response go her stubborn rebellion?

"**Indeed I will cast her into a sickbed, and those who commit adultery with her into great tribulation, unless they repent of their deeds.**" (Revelation 2:22) Here we see an indication of this church continuing until the end. For the Lord "**will cast her**" "**into great tribulation.**" That is, these unrepentant sinners, being Christians in name only, will not be "**caught up**" in the rapture, but will be left behind to go through the "**great tribulation.**" But there is more. "**I will kill her children with death, and all the churches shall know that I am He who searches the minds and hearts. And I will give to each one of you according to your works.**" (Revelation 2:23)

These words, "**I will kill her children with death,**" *sounds* redundant. But it is not. As with much of what God says, the meaning here goes deeper than the superficial statement.

We remember God's words that, "**they did not receive the love of the truth, that they might be saved. And for this reason God will send them strong delusion, that they should believe the lie, that they all may be condemned who did not believe the truth but had pleasure in unrighteousness.**" (2 Thessalonians 2:10-12) And what He had previously told the rebels of Judah:

"**Just as they have chosen their own ways,**

---

21. The Greek words here translated "did not repent," are ου θελει μετανοησαι, "ou thelei metansai" in our alphabet. "Ou," word number 3756 in Strong's Greek Dictionary, translates literally as "not." And "thelei" is an indicative form of θελο, "thelo" in our alphabet, word number 2309 in Strong's Greek Dictionary, which translates literally as "wish." And "metansai" is a form of the Greek word μετανοεω, "metanoeo" in our alphabet, word number 3340 in Strong's Greek Dictionary. This word means "repent," but it is in an infinitive form, which makes it mean "to repent." So the actual Greek text literally says "not wish to repent," or, as the CSB version renders it, "not want to repent."

> **And their soul delights in their abominations,**
> **So will I choose their delusions,**
> **And bring their fears on them;**
> **Because, when I called, no one answered,**
> **When I spoke they did not hear;**
> **But they did evil before My eyes,**
> **And chose that in which I do not delight."**
> (Isaiah 66:3-4)

Even so, these false Christians, who loved their sin and did "not wish to repent," will be killed with something far worse than merely being *physically* killed, but with a *spiritual* death. They will be turned over to **"believe the lie."** That is, to believe the lie of the **"Antichrist,"** that **"the beast"** is God, and that he is God's messenger.

The period of church history covered by this letter has come to be called "the dark ages," or, more formally, "the middle ages." This gave way to "the Reformation," which, like the last age, did not have a distinct beginning. There were "reformers" as early as the mid 1300s, but this movement did not become widespread until the 1500s. A true gospel began to be preached again, and many came to faith in Christ. But this revival was short lived. And in time, the great movements that had been founded by the reformers slipped into the mere formality of the mainstream protestant churches, and from there into apostasy. So before long, the Lord's word to these remnants of what had once been a great movement of God, was: **"I know your works, that you have a name that you are alive, but you are dead. Be watchful, and strengthen the things which remain, that are ready to die, for I have not found your works perfect before God. Remember therefore how you have received and heard; hold fast and repent."** (Revelation 3:1-3)

This was an even more severe condemnation than the one received by the openly wicked **"church in Thyatira,"** to whom the Lord only said **"I have a few things against you."** But now, to these that had received His word, and had turned away from it, He said, **"you have a name that you are alive, but you are dead."** This is like the time when our Lord himself told **"the chief priests and the elders of the people"** (Matthew 21:23) **"that tax collectors and harlots enter the kingdom of God before you."** (Matthew 21:31) As the Holy Spirit said through Peter, **"For it would have been better for them not to have known the way of righteousness, than having known it, to turn from the holy commandment delivered to them."** (2 Peter 2:21)

The Lord had only addressed **"the rest in Thyatira, as many as do not have this doctrine, who have not known the depths of Satan, as they say,"** telling them that **"I will put on you no other burden. But hold fast what you have till I come."** (Revelation 2:24-25) But here He says, **"You have a few names even in Sardis who have not defiled their garments; and they shall walk with Me in white, for they are worthy."** (Revelation 3:4) These words **"even in Sardis"** are yet another indication that our Lord considered **"the church in Sardis"** to be worse than **"the church in Thyatira."**

But to this church, after telling them, **"Remember therefore how you have received and heard; hold fast and repent,"** the Lord said, **"Therefore if you will not watch, I will come upon you as a thief, and you will not know what hour I will come upon you."** (Revelation 3:3) So this church, like **"the church in Thyatira,"** is warned of judgment when the Lord comes.

After centuries of the apostasy of the church of the reformation, in the nineteenth century there came another revival. This began in movements such as the Plymouth brethren and churches of the Moody genre, and continues to this day in "Bible" churches and "community" churches, along with some churches of other types. These groups, with varying levels of Biblical understanding, faithfully follow the scriptures as they understand them. To these, **"the church in Philadelphia,"** the Lord says, **"I know your works. See, I have set before you an open door, and no one can shut it; for you have a little strength, have kept My word, and have not denied My name."** (Revelation 3:7) And from this, we know that Satan will not be able close the open door to proclaim the gospel, which God has **"set before"** this church. For **"no one can shut it."**

And, even as **"the church in Thyatira"** and **"the church in Sardis"** are warned of judgment when the Lord comes, the faithful few of **"the church in Philadelphia"** are promised the opposite. For the Lord had said of the wicked in Thyatira, **"Indeed I will cast her into a sickbed, and those who commit adultery with her into great tribulation, unless they repent of their deeds."** (Revelation 2:22) And He had said of the apostates in Sardis, that **"if you will not watch, I will come upon you as a thief, and you will not know what hour I will come upon you."** (Revelation 3:3) He now says of the faithful in Philadelphia, **"Because you have kept My command to persevere, I also will keep you from the hour of trial which shall come upon the whole world, to test those who dwell on the earth."** (Revelation 3:10) So the Lord here promises to keep His faithful ones **"from,"** not "through," not just the **"great tribulation,"** but **"the hour of trial."** That is, our Lord promised to keep these faithful ones out of the time during which the **"the whole world"** will be tested.

But finally, we come to the last church, which our Lord calls by an entirely different name. He no longer calls it **"the church of Ephesus,"** as He called the first one, or **"the church in"** such-and-such a place, as He called all the others, but only **"the church of the Laodiceans."** That is, he does not recognize it as His church, but only as their own. And what does He say to them? **"I know your works, that you are neither cold nor hot. I could wish**

THOUGHTS ABOUT PROPHETIC SUBJECTS

you were cold or hot. So then, because you are lukewarm, and neither cold nor hot, I will vomit you out of My mouth. Because you say, 'I am rich, have become wealthy, and have need of nothing'--and do not know that you are wretched, miserable, poor, blind, and naked– I counsel you to buy from Me gold refined in the fire, that you may be rich; and white garments, that you may be clothed, *that* **the shame of your nakedness may not be revealed; and anoint your eyes with eye salve, that you may see."** (Revelation 3:15-18)

Who can deny that this is the sad state of the bulk of what claims to be Christian today? This is an apt description of what has come to be called "Modernism." And where is the Lord in all this? he is not even there. He is on the outside, knocking on the door. For He says, **"Behold, I stand at the door and knock."** (Revelation 3:20) And we again see our Lord's coming in this letter, when he says, **"because you are lukewarm, and neither cold nor hot, I will vomit you out of My mouth."** (Revelation 3:16)

And finally, as was mentioned earlier, there is one more hint buried in the text of these seven letters, showing that this is a veiled prophecy of the sad history of **"the church."** And that is the location of the universal call, **"He who has an ear, let him hear what the Spirit says to the churches."** These same words were said to each of the seven churches. (Revelation 2:7, 11, 17, 29 and 3:6, 13, and 22) But for the first three churches, these words come before the promises to the overcomers, and for the last four, they come after those promises. It has been suggested that, for the first three churches, Our Lord directed His call to hear to all of them. But for the last four, the overall body had become so evil that His call was only addressed to the few overcomers within those churches.

Thus we see that these seven letters do indeed contain a veiled prophetic history of the church, written long ago, but aptly describing what actually took place during the almost two thousand years since these words were given through the Apostle John.

JAMES C. MORRIS

The Pseudo-science of Hermeneutics

Hermeneutics is defined as the science of interpretation. And when applied in accordance with scripture, it is both good and appropriate. But, as it is applied by those that do not wish to believe what God has revealed, it has become a seriously false pseudo-science. There are several false "principles" that these deceivers use to try to "get rid of" much of what our God has explicitly told us.

The first of these false "principles" they use is "authorial intent." This *sounds* good. What could be more basic than trying to understand what the author was really trying to say? But it involves a serious error, which, unfortunately, is not noticed, even by many who love and value the truth of God. And that error is that the human instruments that were used to produce the original written texts of the Bible were not the real authors. The real author of the Bible is the Holy Spirit of God. This is clearly stated in the Bible itself, saying, **"All Scripture is given by inspiration of God, and is profitable for doctrine, for reproof, for correction, for instruction in righteousness, that the man of God may be complete, thoroughly equipped for every good work."** (2 Timothy 3:16-17)

But the error here is not merely that these evil "teachers" neglect who is the real author of the scriptures, they also neglect what the scriptures explicitly tell us about the human writers. For several passages in the Bible explicitly say that the human writers of parts of the Bible did not themselves understand what they were being instructed to write.

One of these places is Daniel 12:8-9, where Daniel wrote, **"Although I heard, I did not understand. Then I said, 'My** lord, what shall be the end of these things?' And he said, 'Go your way, Daniel, for the words are closed up and sealed till the time of the end.'"** Here we see that, not only did Daniel *not* understand the message he had been instructed to convey, but when he asked about it, he was not told what it meant. Again, in Zechariah 4, Zechariah was shown a vision that he did not understand. But there, he was told what it meant.

But the key scripture about this is **"Of this salvation the prophets have inquired and searched carefully, who prophesied of the grace** *that would come* **to you, searching what, or what manner of time, the Spirit of Christ who was in them was indicating when He testified beforehand the sufferings of Christ and the glories that would follow. To them it was revealed that, not to themselves, but to us they were ministering the things which now have been reported to you through those who have preached the gospel to you by the Holy Spirit sent from heaven--things which angels desire to look into."** (1 Peter 1:10-12)

Here, we are explicitly told that, not only Daniel and Zechariah, but the prophets generally, were perplexed by the apparent contradictions in the messages they were being instructed to relay to the people. And what was this apparent contradiction? **"The sufferings of Christ and the glories that would follow."** Some of the prophecies, such as Isaiah 53, depicted the promised Messiah as a meek, suffering servant who would die for His people. But others, such as Psalm 45, depicted Him as a great, conquering warrior-king who would reign forever. How could someone who died for His people reign forever?

The Old Testament scriptures never, even once, revealed the resolution to this apparent contradiction. So *of course* the Old Testament prophets were unable to understand it. And **"the glories that would follow,"** the glorious restoration of the ancient nation of Israel to her ancient homeland, and her glorious kingdom in that ancient homeland, is the part of the message of the Old Testament prophets that many people try to "get rid of" with the pseudo-science they call "hermeneutics."

A second false "principle" they use is to ask the question, "how would the message have been perceived by its original audience"? Again, this *sounds* good. What could be more basic than trying to understand what the original audience would have thought the writer (or speaker) meant? But again, this involves a serious error, which, unfortunately, is not noticed by many who love and value the truth of God. For the scriptures explicitly and repeatedly tell us that at least parts of the messages of the Old Testament were not intended to be understood by their original audiences.

Two places where this is found are the last parts of two scriptures we have already examined. For when Daniel was denied an explanation to the message he did not understand, he was told, as we noticed, that:

"the words are closed up and sealed till the time of the end." (Daniel 12:9) (And Daniel had previously been told to **"shut up the words, and seal the book until the time of the end."** - Daniel 12:4) Again, as we also previously noticed, 1 Peter 1:12 says, concerning the Old Testament prophets, **"To them it was revealed that, not to themselves, but to us they were ministering the things which now have been reported to you."** We really do not need any more testimony from scripture than these. But other places also say this, like Isaiah 6:9-10, where we read:

"And He said, 'Go, and tell this people:
"Keep on hearing, but do not understand;
Keep on seeing, but do not perceive.'
"Make the heart of this people dull,
And their ears heavy,
And shut their eyes;
Lest they see with their eyes,

THOUGHTS ABOUT PROPHETIC SUBJECTS

> And hear with their ears,
> And understand with their heart,
> And return and be healed."

And again, when the disciples asked Jesus, **"Why do You speak to them in parables?"** (Matthew 13:10) He answered them by saying, **"Because it has been given to you to know the mysteries of the kingdom of heaven, but to them it has not been given. For whoever has, to him more will be given, and he will have abundance; but whoever does not have, even what he has will be taken away from him. Therefore I speak to them in parables, because seeing they do not see, and hearing they do not hear, nor do they understand. And in them the prophecy of Isaiah is fulfilled, which says:**

> *'Hearing you will hear and shall not understand,*
> *And seeing you will see and not perceive;*
> *For the hearts of this people have grown dull.*
> *Their ears are hard of hearing,*
> *And their eyes they have closed,*
> *Lest they should see with their eyes and hear with their ears,*
> *Lest they should understand with their hearts and turn,*
> *So that I should heal them.'"* (Matthew 13:10-15)

So there can be no doubt that both of these "principles of hermeneutics" are not only nothing but mere human reasoning, (which is useless in spiritual matters,) but are directly contrary to explicitly stated scripture

But their erroneous application of hermeneutics does not end there. These people, who do not wish to believe what our God has so explicitly said, have two more methods by which they vainly attempt to "get around" what the prophetic scriptures teach.

One of these dodges is to consider the time when a prophecy was given. While this, again, sounds like a reasonable concept, it is not even close to reasonable, when applied to the prophecies in the Bible. For when God said something was going to happen, the time when He said it is totally inconsequential. As an example, the words said to the serpent in the garden of Eden spoke of our Lord's victory over Satan, which took place roughly 4000 years later.

> "**I will put enmity**
> **Between you and the woman,**
> **And between your seed and her Seed;**
> **He shall bruise your head,**
> **And you shall bruise His heel.**" (Genesis 3:15)

Yet the pronouncements made at the same time to Eve and to Adam went into effect immediately.

> "**I will greatly multiply your sorrow and your conception;**
> **In pain you shall bring forth children;**
> **Your desire *shall be* for your husband,**
> **And he shall rule over you.**" (Genesis 3:16)

And:

> "**Because you have heeded the voice of your wife, and have eaten from the tree of which I commanded you, saying, 'You shall not eat of it:'**
> **'Cursed *is* the ground for your sake;**
> **In toil you shall eat *of* it**
> **All the days of your life.**
> **Both thorns and thistles it shall bring forth for you,**
> **And you shall eat the herb of the field.**
> **In the sweat of your face you shall eat bread**

> **Till you return to the ground,**
> **For out of it you were taken;**
> **For dust you *are*,**
> **And to dust you shall return."** (Genesis 3:17-19)

The people who so misuse the pseudo-science of hermeneutics use this "principle" of considering the time when a prophecy was made to pretend that all the prophecies about a return to the land made before the return from Babylon refer to *that* return. And they stubbornly maintain that false "principle," even in the face of hard proof that the prophecies in question do not even approximately match their alleged "fulfillment" in the return from Babylon. Several examples of that stubbornness are:

A flat refusal to admit that the return described in Ezra 2:64-65 of a very small part of only the ancient sub-nation of Judah, does not even approximately match the promise in Ezekiel 36:1-11, that, **"all the house of Israel, all of it"** will again inhabit the **"mountains of Israel,"** with **"the hills, the rivers, the valleys, the desolate wastes, and the cities that have been forsaken."**

And a flat refusal to admit that the temple whose dimensions are given in Ezra 6:3 as **"its height sixty cubits and its width sixty cubits,"** does not even approximately match the temple prophesied in Ezekiel 41:13-14 as **"one hundred cubits"** square. These are just two examples of the unreasonableness with which this "heremeunitic principle" is being applied.

Another of these dodges is context. Now context, in and by itself, is an all important concept. But, in considering the prophetic scriptures, they use this concept, not to understand the ancient prophecies, but to dodge what they say. For many prophecies in the Bible combine statements concerning different times. One example of this is the woman who is seen in Revelation 12, who **"bore a male Child who was to rule all nations with a rod of** iron. And her Child was caught up to God and His throne." (Revelation 12:5) Regardless of who the woman represents, there can be zero doubt that the **"male Child who was to rule all nations with a rod of iron"** could be no one but Jesus. And Jesus was not **"caught up to God and His throne"** until about 33 years after He was born.

Again, when Jesus read the scriptures in the synagogue, **"And He was handed the book of the prophet Isaiah. And when He had opened the book, He found the place where it was written:**

The Spirit of the LORD is upon Me,

Because He has anointed Me

To preach the gospel to the poor;

He has sent Me to heal the brokenhearted,

To proclaim liberty to the captives

And recovery of sight to the blind,

To set at liberty those who are oppressed;

To proclaim the acceptable year of the LORD.'

Then He closed the book, and gave it back to the attendant and sat down. And the eyes of all who were in the synagogue were fixed on Him. And He began to say to them, 'Today this Scripture is fulfilled in your hearing.'" (Luke 4:17-21)

When Jesus read this passage, which was Isaiah 61:1 and the first line of Isaiah 61:2, He omitted the rest of the passage, which continued with the words **"And the day of vengeance of our God."** (The rest of Isaiah 61:2) This passage in Isaiah then went on to describe the future restoration of the nation of Israel. Now if Jesus himself so divided up a prophecy from the Old Testament into parts which had and had not been fulfilled, how can these people justify criticizing students of the scriptures for doing likewise?

THOUGHTS ABOUT PROPHETIC SUBJECTS

Another example of this is Zechariah 14:7-9, where we read:

> " 'Awake, O sword, against My Shepherd,
> Against the Man who is My Companion,'
> Says the LORD of hosts.
> 'Strike the Shepherd,
> And the sheep will be scattered;
> Then I will turn My hand against the little ones.
> And it shall come to pass in all the land,'
> Says the LORD,
> *'That* two-thirds in it shall be cut off *and* die,
> But *one*-third shall be left in it:
> I will bring the *one*-third through the fire,
> Will refine them as silver is refined,
> And test them as gold is tested.
> They will call on My name,
> And I will answer them. I will say,
> "This *is* My people;"
> And each one will say,
> "The LORD *is* my God." ' " (Zechariah 13:7-9)

There can be absolutely zero question that this prophecy speaks of different times. For, even if the naysayers were correct, that the last part of this prophecy speaks of AD 70 (which is not the case,) that was long after the **"Shepherd"** was struck, which happened about 40 years before AD 70. And the *hard truth* is, that, even to this day, there has *never* been a time when two-thirds of all the inhabitants of the land were killed, and the other third was not only physically saved, but restored to a true and living relationship with their God.

So their "hermeneutic principle"of paying attention to the context, while appropriate when used properly, is used by these people only as a way to "dodge" what the prophetic scriptures explicitly say, in plain, clear words.

Finally, they falsely claim a "hermeneutic principle" that all prophetic language is symbolic. So they claim, for instance, that **"Israel"** means **"the church," "the land"** means **"heaven,"** etc. Like the first two "principles of hermeneutics" we discussed, this is directly contrary to explicitly stated scripture. For when Jesus was here he said that **"one jot or one tittle will by no means pass from the law till all is fulfilled."** (Matthew 5:18) The **"jot"** and the **"tittle"** were the two smallest marks used in writing the Hebrew language. So here, our Lord was saying that, not only every single word in the Bible, but even the spelling of every word, is significant. Further, Our God has said:

> **"God is not a man, that He should lie,**
> **Nor a son of man, that He should repent.**
> **Has He said, and will He not do?**
> **Or has He spoken, and will He not make it good?"**
> (Numbers 23:19)

And:

> **"Thus says the LORD,**
> **Who gives the sun for a light by day,**
> **The ordinances of the moon and the stars for a light by night,**
> **Who disturbs the sea,**
> **And its waves roar (The LORD of hosts is His name):**
> '**If those ordinances depart**
> **From before Me, says the LORD,**
> ***Then*** **the seed of Israel shall also cease**
> **From being a nation before Me forever.'**
> **Thus says the LORD:**

> 'Of heaven above can be measured,
> And the foundations of the earth searched out beneath,
> I will also cast off all the seed of Israel
> For all that they have done,' says the LORD."
> (Jeremiah 31:35-37)

Some of these people try to defend this wresting of scripture by falsely claiming that the promises were all conditional, so that, Israel, having failed to meet the conditions, lost the promises. But what did God say about that? He said of His promise to David:

> "**If his sons forsake My law**
> **And do not walk in My judgments,**
> **If they break My statutes**
> **And do not keep My commandments,**
> *Then* **I will punish their transgression with the rod,**
> **And their iniquity with stripes.**
> **Nevertheless My lovingkindness I will not**
> **utterly take from him,**
> **Nor allow My faithfulness to fail.**
> **My covenant I will not break,**
> **Nor alter the word that has gone out of My lips."**
> (Psalm 89:30-34)

We need to notice that these words, **"My covenant I will not break, Nor alter the word that has gone out of My lips,"** were declared in explicit reference to His previous words **"If his sons forsake My law And do not walk in My judgments, If they break My statutes And do not keep My commandments."**

So God was here explicitly declaring that *even sin* could not cause Him to alter the word that had gone out of His lips. For that would be breaking His covenant, which was unconditional. Sin, if it came, would be dealt with. But the punishment would not be a cancellation of the promises, for they were **"irrevocable,"** as Romans 11:29 puts it.

So we see that all of these alleged "hermeneutic principles" that are used in a vain attempt to escape the force of what God said, in plain, clear words, are either directly contrary to explicitly scripture or are being grossly misused.

These people claim that their conclusions are all based on scripture, particularly on the writings of Paul, But the Apostle Peter said that, **"our beloved brother Paul, according to the wisdom given to him, has written to you, as also in all his epistles, speaking in them of these things, in which are some things hard to understand, which untaught and unstable people twist to their own destruction, as they do also the rest of the Scriptures."** (2 Peter 3:15-16) And when anyone claims that a literal host of explicitly stated scriptures do not mean what they so explicitly say, that person is twisting the scriptures.

And sadly they do this **"to their own destruction."** If they have truly trusted Jesus for the salvation of their souls, they will still be in heaven, for they will be covered by the scripture that says, **"If anyone's work is burned, he will suffer loss; but he himself will be saved, yet so as through fire."** (1 Corinthians 3:15) But if they have not truly trusted the blood of Jesus as the only and total sacrifice for their sins, they will fall under the judgment pronounced in Revelation 22:19: **"if anyone takes away from the words of the book of this prophecy, God shall take away his part from the Book of Life, from the holy city, and *from* the things which are written in this book."**

But, in all the talk about hermeneutics that I have ever heard or read, I have never, even once, known even one of these professed "scholars" to set forth what I personally consider the two most important questions we can ask about any scripture. These are:

THOUGHTS ABOUT PROPHETIC SUBJECTS

What was the Holy Spirit really saying in the passage being considered?

And:

How does that relate to what the Holy Spirit said in the rest of the Bible?

These two questions get to the central point of the entire message of the Bible. For they are based on two foundation principles. These are:

The Bible is the word of God, not the words of mere men, regardless of how godly they might have been.

And:

The Bible is a composite whole, a unified message. So all of its various parts relate to each other.

I have personally found these two simple questions to be more revealing than all of the alleged "principles of hermeneutics" taught by these self-proclaimed "scholars."

JAMES C. MORRIS

The Errors of Amillennialism

Amillennialists argue that the use of the term **"thousand years,"** which occurs six times over in Revelation 20, is only a metaphorical expression meaning "a very long time." The error of this claim is treated at length in the article titled **"The Millennium,"** but to review:

In Revelation 20 we find the same term **"a thousand years"** three times. This is used in verses 2, 4, and 6. In each of these cases the Holy Spirit did not use an article. And anyone with even a smattering of knowledge of Hebrew and Greek knows that in both Hebrew and Greek, the use of an article is optional. But there is also a different term used in Revelation 20, verses 3, 5, and 7. In each of these, we find the words **"the thousand years"** as opposed to the term **"a thousand years."** In each of these, the Greek words translated **"the thousand years"** are τα χίλιοι ἔτος, *ta chilioi etos* in our alphabet, words numbered 3588, 5507 and 2094 in Strong's Greek Dictionary, which literally translate as *the thousand years*. (The Greek word τα, *ta* in our alphabet, is a nominative form of the Greek word ὁ, *ho* in our alphabet, which literally means **"the."** In both Greek and Hebrew, when the definite article is used, it is normally used for stress. Thus, it refers to a *particular* thing, instead of just *something in general*. So the clause **"the thousand years"** means a *particular* period of **"a thousand years,"** not just some generic period of time that may or may not literally last **"a thousand years."**

So there is a significant difference between the generic usage of the term **"a thousand years,"** as we see in Revelation 20:2, 4, and 6, and the specific use of the term **"the thousand years"** we find in Revelation 20:3, 5, and 7. In the generic usage of the term

THOUGHTS ABOUT PROPHETIC SUBJECTS

"a thousand years," it indeed can simply mean, as the amillennialists argue, "a long period of time." But the repeated usage of the definite article in Revelation 20 stresses that the reference is to a *particular* period that will last **"a thousand years."**

So the Holy Spirit told us six times in just six verses that this period would last **"a thousand years."** Yet in spite of this, the amillennialists claim that He did not mean that this period would actually last **"a thousand years."** Instead, they claim that we are in this period now. For that reason, some of them have lately been styling themselves as "now millennialists," instead of "amillennialists."

Amillennialists defend their claim that the **"thousand years"** in Revelation 20 is only figurative with a secondary claim that the scriptures plainly teach that all the end time events prophesied in the scriptures will take place in a single day, that is, within a period of twenty-four hours, as humans measure time. This is based on a false claim that the terms **"the day of the Lord," "the day of judgment," "the last day," "that day,"** and similar terms used in the scriptures, all refer to a single literal **"day."** They do not even seem to realize the contradiction between their claiming that the statements of time in Revelation 20 are only symbolic, while all these *alleged* statements of time are literal. But, ignoring that logical contradiction, this claim neglects the unquestionable fact that the scriptures often use the word **"day"** as a figure of speech representing a period of time whose length is not defined. The scriptures use it this way both with and without a definite article.

The term **"the day of the Lord"** occurs 22 times in the Old Testament, plus 6 more times as a possessive statement, that is, **"the day of the Lord's vengeance," "the day of the Lord's wrath," "the day of the Lord's anger,"** etc. And every time it is used, the Hebrew word which is translated **"day"** is יוֹם, '*yom* in our alphabet, word number 3117 in Strong's Greek dictionary. This Hebrew word is defined by Strong as follows:

"From an unused root meaning to be hot; a day (as the warm hours), whether literally (from sunrise to sunset, or from one sunset to the next), or figuratively (a space of time defined by an associated term), (often used adverbially):—age, + always, + chronicles, continually (-ance), daily, ([birth-], each, to) day, (now a, two) days (agone), + elder, X end, + evening, + (for) ever (-lasting, -more), X full, life, as (so) long as (. . . live), (even) now, + old, + outlived, + perpetually, presently, + remaineth, X required, season, X since, space, then, (process of) time, + as at other times, + in trouble, weather, (as) when, (a, the, within a) while (that), X whole (+ age), (full) year (-ly), + younger."

So we clearly see that, although *yom* often means a literal 24 hour day, it is also often used figuratively to designate an undefined period of time. Here is one of the numerous times this was done.

> **"And in that day it shall be**
> **That living waters shall flow from Jerusalem,**
> **Half of them toward the eastern sea**
> **And half of them toward the western sea;**
> **In both summer and winter it shall occur.**
> **And the LORD shall be King over all the earth.**
> **In that day it shall be--**
> **'The LORD is one,' And His name one."**
> (Zechariah 14:8-9)

In this example **"that day "** is explicitly stated to be a period of time that includes both **"summer and winter."**

Here are two more times when the phrase **"that day"** was obviously used figuratively to indicate a period of time.

> **"In that day five cities in the land of Egypt will speak the language of Canaan and swear by the LORD of hosts; one will be called the City of Destruction. In that day there will be an altar to the LORD in the**

midst of the land of Egypt, and a pillar to the LORD at its border." (Isaiah 19:18-19)

"In that day there will be a highway from Egypt to Assyria, and the Assyrian will come into Egypt and the Egyptian into Assyria, and the Egyptians will serve with the Assyrians.

In that day Israel will be one of three with Egypt and Assyria--a blessing in the midst of the land, whom the LORD of hosts shall bless, saying, 'Blessed is Egypt My people, and Assyria the work of My hands, and Israel My inheritance.'" (Isaiah 19:23-25)

Further, the expression **"the day of the Lord"** is used in Ezekiel 30:3 in regard to an attack by Nebuchadnezzar upon **"Egypt,"** and **"Ethiopia, Libya, Lydia, all the mingled people, Chub, and the men of the lands who are allied."** (Ezekiel 30:1-19) We know for a fact that this attack took place in ancient times. Yet the Holy Spirit called it **"the day of the Lord."**

Again, the expression **"the day of the Lord"** occurs 3 times in the New Testament, plus 2 more times when it is modified to **"the day of the Lord Jesus."** Like the Hebrew word translated **"day,"** the Greek word translated *day* in each of these cases is ημερα, *hemera* in our alphabet, word number 2250 in Strong's Greek Dictionary. Strong defines this word as follows:

"Feminine (with G5610 implied) of a derivative of ἡμαι hemai (to sit; akin to the base of G1476) meaning tame, that is, gentle; day, that is, (literally) the time space between dawn and dark, or the whole 24 hours (but several days were usually reckoned by the Jews as inclusive of the parts of both extremes); figuratively a period (always defined more or less clearly by the context):—age, + alway, (mid-) day (by day, [-ly]), + for ever, judgment, (day) time, while, years."

The figurative use of this word as a period of time is found in Luke 6:22-23:

> **"Blessed are you when men hate you,**
> **And when they exclude you,**
> **And revile you, and cast out your name as evil,**
> **For the Son of Man's sake.**
> **Rejoice in that day and leap for joy!**
> **For indeed your reward is great in heaven,**
> **For in like manner their fathers did to the prophets."**

When they were hated, and separated from the company of the others, and reproached, and vilified as evil, then they should rejoice. And the time when they should so rejoice is called **"that day."**

We see this again in John 16:23-27, where Jesus twice called the time *after* His resurrection **"that day." "And in that day you will ask Me nothing. Most assuredly, I say to you, whatever you ask the Father in My name He will give you. Until now you have asked nothing in My name. Ask, and you will receive, that your joy may be full.**

"These things I have spoken to you in figurative language; but the time is coming when I will no longer speak to you in figurative language, but I will tell you plainly about the Father. In that day you will ask in My name, and I do not say to you that I shall pray the Father for you; for the Father Himself loves you, because you have loved Me, and have believed that I came forth from God."

This is not all the examples we could examine, but we will stop with 2 Corinthians 6:2:

> "For He says:
>
> *'In an acceptable time I have heard you,*
> *And in the day of salvation I have helped you.'*

Behold, now is the accepted time; behold, now is the day of salvation."

All this is conclusive proof that neither the term **"the day of the Lord"** nor the term **"the last day"** refers to a specific 24 hour period, and that many other scriptures clearly show that both of these terms refer to a period of time, not to a specific day.

But what about the other terms claimed by the Amillennialists as proof that everything prophesied will take place in a single 24 hour day? Specifically, what about the scriptural term **"the day of judgment?"** This term occurs nine times, in the New Testament only, and all nine times the Greek word translated **"day"** is the same *"hemera"* we have been discussing. This is also true of the term **"the day of wrath and revelation of the righteous judgment of God,"** found in Romans 2:5

This leaves only the scriptural term **"the last day,"** which truly, if it were to be considered in isolation from the rest of scripture, *sounds* like it might actually mean a single 24 hour period. This term, which occurs only in the gospel of John, is found there six times. And all six times, the Greek word translated **"day"** is again the same word *"hemera."* But more than that, the first five times this term is used, it is used of the resurrection of the righteous. (John 6:39, 40, 44, and 54, and 11:24) But the last time it is used, our Lord said, **"He who rejects Me, and does not receive My words, has that which judges him--the word that I have spoken will judge him in the last day."** (John 12:48) And we know from Revelation 20 that the judgment of the wicked will be long after the resurrection of the righteous, even if the Amillennialists were correct in claiming that the **"thousand years"** of that chapter only mean "a very long time."

So in the end, there is zero basis for the claim that the Bible even implies, much less says, that all end time prophecy will take place in a single 24 hour period of time.

It is indeed correct that the wrath of God poured out in the destruction of the nations and the burning up of the earth *could* take place in mere moments. It is also indeed correct that God *could* bring to pass the resurrection of the dead, the judgment, and the establishment of new heavens and a new earth in mere moments. There can be no doubt that all these things are within the power of God. But is this what God has said He will do? The answer is a very definite no. God has not only told us that He will do all these things, He has also very explicitly told us that He will do many other things. And He has very explicitly told us how much time some of these events will occupy. Aside from the millennium, whose length we are discussing, the time periods that God has defined range from three days to multiple years.

But even without considering these time periods, the scriptures explicitly say, in a great many places, that God will bring the ancient nation of Israel back to its ancient homeland and establish a kingdom there. For amillennialism to be correct, every one of these prophecies has to have only symbolic meaning. But many of them are stated in language that leaves absolutely zero room for symbolic interpretation. Amillennialists claim that pre-millennialists are "interpreting" these prophecies. But that is simply not true. Pre-millennialists simply believe what these prophecies say. That is not interpretation. Claiming that the words do not *mean* what they *say* is interpretation. But simply *believing* what the Bible *explicitly* says, in *plain, clear*, words, is not interpretation. It is faith.

And in Revelation 20, the Holy Spirit didn't only tell us that this period would last a thousand years. He also said that during this period Satan would be **"bound,"** and **"cast" "into the bottomless pit, and shut... up,"** and that a seal would be set on him, **"so that he should deceive the nations no more till the thousand years were finished."** (Revelation 20:2-3) Amillennialists pretend that this has already happened, and that Satan is currently bound. But that is obvious nonsense. From the all pervasive sexual depravity that we have to go out of our ways to avoid being exposed to, through the violence that continually takes place all over the world, and the outright persecution of believers that exists in most of the world today, and has existed in most of the world until the last few hundred years, Satan's work is evident all around us.

But this claim is not only obviously incorrect. It is contrary to explicitly stated scripture. For Ephesians 2:2 calls Satan **"the prince of the power of the air, the spirit that now works in the children of disobedience."** And 1 Peter 5:8 instructs us to **"Be sober, be vigilant; because your adversary the devil walks about like a roaring lion, seeking whom he may devour."** The two facts that he is **"now"** working **"in the children of disobedience,"** and that he currently **"walks about... seeking whom he may devour,"** clearly show that he is most certainly *not* at the present time **"bound,"** and **"cast" "into the bottomless pit, and shut... up,"** and sealed **"so that he should deceive the nations no more."**

The footnote below [22] goes into details of the Greek word forms used in these two verses to clearly demonstrate that the present tenses used in these two English sentences were not just the opinions of some boards of translators, but were the actual tenses used in the Greek texts of these two scriptures.

Amillennialists not only claim that Satan is currently bound. They also claim that Jesus is currently reigning over everything.

---

22. In Ephesians 2:2, the Greek words translated "now works" are νυν ενεργουντος, nun energountos in our alphabet. The Greek word νυν is word number 3568 in Strong's Greek Dictionary, and translates literally as "now." And the Greek word ενεργουντος is a present tense form of the Greek verb ενεργεω, energeo in our alphabet, word number 1754 in Strong's Greek Dictionary. In the form used, this Greek word literally means "is working." So the translator's use of the present tense in the clause "now works" is unquestionably correct. And in 1 Peter 5:8. the Greek word translated "walks about" is περιπατει, peripatei in our alphabet, which is a present tense form of the Greek verb περιπατεω, peripateo in our alphabet, word number 4043 in Strong's Greek Dictionary. In this form, this Greek word literally means "is walking around" And the Greek word translated "seeking" is ζητων, zeton in our alphabet. This is a present form of the Greek verb ζητεω, zeteo in our alphabet, word number 2212 in Strong's Greek Dictionary. In the form used, this Greek word literally means "seeking." So the translator's use of the present tense in the clause "walks about... seeking" is also unquestionably correct.

This, again, is contrary to explicitly stated scripture. For Hebrews 2:8 quotes the last line of Psalm 8:6, saying, " *You have put all things in subjection under his feet.* **'For in that He put all in subjection under him, He left nothing that is not put under him. But now we do not yet see all things put under him."** Here, the Holy Spirit specifically and explicitly told us that **"all things"** are **"not yet" "put under"** our Lord.

Again, Amillennialists claim that Revelation 20 is a prophetic vision, and such visions are always symbolic, rather than literal. This would indeed be a significant argument if it were not for the specific words used in verses 7 and 8, where we read, **"Now when the thousand years have expired, Satan will be released from his prison and will go out to deceive the nations which are in the four corners of the earth, Gog and Magog, to gather them together to battle, whose number** *is* **as the sand of the sea."**

Here the Holy Spirit changed the wording from **"I saw"** to **"will be."** Thus, the wording changed from symbolic language to explicit statements of coming events. **"When the thousand years have expired, Satan will be released from his prison"** is an explicit statement of a coming event. There is no room for interpretation here. This is either a true statement, or it is not. If it is true, then **"when the thousand years have expired, Satan will be released from his prison."** If this statement is not true, then one of two other things is unquestionably true. Either the Revelation is not the word of God or God is a liar. As both of these options are unacceptable as Christian doctrine, we are forced to conclude that it is true, and thus, that **"when the thousand years have expired, Satan will be released from his prison,"** and thus, that in the future there will indeed be a millennium.

So we see that almost all of the arguments used in trying to defend Amillennialism are incorrect, and most of them are directly contrary to explicitly stated scripture.

The Errors of Replacement Theology

Amillennialists and many others interpret the many Biblical prophecies about the future blessing of **"Israel"** to mean **"the church."** Although those who hold this erroneous doctrine prefer to call it "Supersessionism," we call it "Replacement Theology," from the idea that **"the Church"** has replaced **"Israel"** in the promises of God. But Romans 11 clearly states that God has not cast Israel away, (verse 1) that Israel's fall is only temporary, (verses 11-25) and that **"all Israel will be saved"** (verse 26) because **"the gifts and calling of God are irrevocable."** (verse 29) Zechariah 10:6 tells us that **"the house of Judah"** and **"the house of Joseph"** **"shall be as though I had not cast them aside,"** and the next verse (7) extends this to include **"Ephraim."** We should note here that no scripture even hints at an idea that the church is ever referred to by any of these last three names. This national restoration of Israel is described often in the prophets, but nowhere as clearly or as fully as in the last twelve chapters of Ezekiel.

A most unusual prophecy in Ezekiel 36 is addressed to a *plot of real estate*, which is defined as, **"The mountains of Israel,"** along with **"the hills, the rivers, the valleys, the desolate wastes, and the cities that have been forsaken."** This *plot of real estate* is promised that it will again be inhabited by **"all the house of Israel, all of it."** (verses 1-15) **"The house of Israel"** is then promised that they will be taken **"from among the nations,"** gathered **"out of all countries,"** and **"shall dwell in the land that I gave to your fathers."** (verses 16-28) In chapter 37 **"the children of Israel"** are promised that they will be brought back **"into their own land"** and made into **"one nation in the land,"** "**nor shall they ever be divided into two kingdoms again.**" (verses 15-28) In chapter 38 **"Gog"** comes **"against my people Israel like a cloud, to cover the land."** (verse 16) In chapter 39 **"the house of Israel"** is occupied seven months burying Gog's dead. (verse 12) Chapter 40 begins a highly detailed description of a temple unlike any that has ever been built. This continues into chapter 43, where the Lord says *"this is* **the place of My throne and the place of the soles of My feet, where I will dwell in the midst of the children of Israel forever."** (verse 7) Then verse 18 of chapter 43 begins a similarly detailed account of **"the ordinances for the altar on the day when it is made,"** which continue through chapter 44. Chapters 45 and 46 specify various laws which will apply when all this takes place. Finally, chapters 47 and 48 return to the *plot of real estate* described in chapter 36, specifying in detail **"the borders by which you shall divide the land as an inheritance among the twelve tribes of Israel."** (47:13-20) Then they state what portion of that *plot of real estate* will be inherited by each of the twelve tribes. (48:1-29) All this detail makes it abundantly clear that the meaning is the literal ancient **"nation"** of "Israel," not **"the church."**

This can also be seen in Jeremiah 32:6-33:14. In this passage, just as Jerusalem was about to be destroyed, the Lord told Jeremiah to purchase a piece of land. (chapter 32, verses 7-9 and 25) He then explained the reason (verse 37) for this.

The reason was that "**'fields will be bought in this land of which you say, "It is desolate, without man or beast; it has been given into the hand of the Chaldeans." Men will buy fields for money, sign deeds and seal them, and take witnesses, in the land of Benjamin, in the places around Jerusalem, in the cities of Judah, in the cities of the mountains, in the cities of the lowland, and in the cities of the South; for I will cause their captives to return,' says the LORD."** (verses 43-44)

Again, in Jeremiah 33 the Lord says **"concerning the houses of this city and the houses of the kings of Judah,"** (verse 4) that He **"will cause the captives of Judah and the captives of Israel to return, and will rebuild those places as at the first."** (verse 7) He concludes with the words **"'In this place which is desolate, without man and without beast, and in all its cities, there shall again be a dwelling place of shepherds causing their flocks to lie down. In the cities of the mountains, in the cities of the lowland, in the cities of the South, in the land of Benjamin, in the places around Jerusalem, and in the cities of Judah, the flocks shall again pass under the hands of him who counts them,' says the LORD. 'Behold, the days are coming,' says the LORD, 'that I will perform that good thing which I have promised to the house of Israel and to the house of Judah.'"** (Jeremiah 33:12-14) And in Jeremiah 30:18, the Lord says **"Behold, I will bring back the captivity of Jacob's tents, And have mercy on his dwelling places; The city shall be built upon its own mound, And the palace shall remain according to its own plan."**

Yet again, we read in Isaiah 66:15-16 that **"the LORD will come with fire And with His chariots, like a whirlwind, To render His anger with fury, And His rebuke with flames of fire. For by fire and by His sword The LORD will judge all flesh; And the slain of the LORD shall be many."** In verses 18 to 22 the Lord continues, **"'It shall be that I will gather all nations and tongues; and they shall come and see My glory. I will set a sign among them; and those among them who escape I will send to the nations: to Tarshish and Pul and Lud, who draw the bow, and Tubal and Javan, to the coastlands afar off who have not heard My fame nor seen My glory. And they shall declare My glory among the Gentiles. Then they shall bring all your brethren for an offering to the LORD out of all nations, on horses and in chariots and in litters, on mules and on camels, to My holy mountain**

Jerusalem,' says the LORD, 'as the children of Israel bring an offering in a clean vessel into the house of the LORD. And I will also take some of them for priests and Levites,' says the LORD. 'For as the new heavens and the new earth Which I will make shall remain before Me,' says the LORD, 'So shall your descendants and your name remain.'" The words **"your descendants"** are final proof that the meaning is the physical offspring of the ancient nation of Israel.

This statement in Ezekiel 36 that **"the children of Israel"** will again be made into **"one nation in the land"** is closely related to the promise of Jeremiah 31:35-36, where we read:

"[35] **Thus says the LORD,**

Who gives the sun for a light by day,

The ordinances of the moon and the stars for a light by night,

Who disturbs the sea, And its waves roar

(The LORD of hosts is **His name):**

'[36] **If those ordinances depart From before Me,' says the LORD,**

Then **the seed of Israel shall also cease**

From being a nation before Me forever.'"

Both of these passages clearly call the revived Israel a **"nation."** This excludes even the possibility that this is speaking of anything other than a physical restoration of the ancient **"nation"** of **"Israel."**

Now many of these people imagine that these prophecies were fulfilled in the return from **"Babylon,"** which took placed in the days of Ezra and Nehemiah. But *that* return did not include the ancient sub-kingdom of **"Ephraim,"** which, even to this day, has never returned. The return from **"Babylon"** was only the ancient sub-kingdom of Judah, and only a very small part of that. For

"**Altogether the whole assembly** *was* **forty-two thousand three hundred and sixty, besides their male and female servants, of whom** *there were* **seven thousand three hundred and thirty-seven; and they had two hundred and forty-five men and women singers.**" (Nehemiah 7:66-67) That is a total of only forty-nine thousand nine hundred and ninety two persons. By comparison, 2 Chronicles 17:12-19 informs us that, in the days of Jehoshaphat, the army of Judah totaled one million, one hundred and sixty thousand men, to say nothing of those that were not in the army. Compare this very small return with the return that God had promised:

> "**I will surely assemble all of you, O Jacob,**
>
> **I will surely gather the remnant of Israel;**
>
> **I will put them together like sheep of the fold,**
>
> **Like a flock in the midst of their pasture;**
>
> **They shall make a loud noise because of** *so many* **people.**" (Micah 2:12)

Compare this also with the promise in Ezekiel 36 which we have already considered, made to *a plot of real estate,*, telling the "**mountains of Israel,**" along with "**the hills, the rivers, the valleys, the desolate wastes, and the cities that have been forsaken,**" (verse 4) that it would again be inhabited by "**all the house of Israel, all of it.**"

A return of "**all of you, O Jacob**" and of "**all the house of Israel, all of it**" was most certainly not fulfilled in the return of only a very small part of only "**the house of Judah.**"

Again, Isaiah 4:3 tells us that "**it shall come to pass that** *he who is* **left in Zion and remains in Jerusalem will be called holy – everyone who is recorded among the living in Jerusalem.**" and

Zechariah 12:10-14 just as plainly tells us that **"all the families that remain"** will repent with bitter weeping. And is clear that neither of these has *ever* happened.

So, even as it is clear that the promised return of **"all Israel,"** accompanied with the conversion of all the survivors, meant the literal ancient **"nation"** of **"Israel,"** not **"the church,"** it is also clear that this promise was most certainly *not* fulfilled in the ancient return from **"Babylon."**

Thus it is clear that Replacement Theology, which is also called Supersessionism, is contrary to scripture.

THOUGHTS ABOUT PROPHETIC SUBJECTS

The Errors of Preterism

Preterism is the false doctrine that all of Bible prophecy was fulfilled in ancient times. (But some, who call themselves "Partial Preterists," only say that most of Bible prophecy was fulfilled in ancient times.) This idea is based on the many New Testament passages that say things like **"Blessed *is* he who reads and those who hear the words of this prophecy, and keep those things which are written in it; for the time *is* near."** (Revelation 1:3) and **"Behold, I am coming quickly! Blessed *is* he who keeps the words of the prophecy of this book."** (Revelation 22:7) Preterists insist that these scriptures, and others like them, prove that the prophesied events were to happen very soon after the prophecies were given.

There can be no doubt that this is correct, for the scriptures plainly declare it, not only in these places, but in many others as well. The prophesied events **"must shortly take place."** (Revelation 1:1) But words such as **"shortly"** and **"quickly"** should be interpreted on a *divine* time scale, not a *human* one. For **"with the Lord one day *is* as a thousand years, and a thousand years as one day."** (2 Peter 3:8)

Preterists complain that this answer is "unsatisfying." But this is not a *human* answer. When this statement is examined in its context, its meaning becomes absolutely clear. The Holy Spirit said this in answer to **"scoffers"** who **"will come in the last days, walking according to their own lusts, and saying, 'Where is the promise of His coming? For since the fathers fell asleep, all things continue as *they were* from the beginning of creation.'"** [23] (2 Peter 3:3-4) The Holy Spirit's answer was:

---

[23]. This scoffing is one of the chief arguments of Preterists. They claim that if we admit that New Testament prophecies were not fulfilled in ancient times, we justify such scoffing. But the Holy Spirit gives these scoffers an entirely different answer.

"For this they willfully forget: that by the word of God the heavens were of old, and the earth standing out of water and in the water, by which the world *that* then existed perished, being flooded with water. But the heavens and the earth *which* are now preserved by the same word, are reserved for fire until the day of judgment and perdition of ungodly men. But, beloved, do not forget this one thing, that with the Lord one day *is* as a thousand years, and a thousand years as one day. The Lord is not slack concerning *His* promise, as some count slackness, but is longsuffering toward us, not willing that any should perish but that all should come to repentance. But the day of the Lord will come as a thief in the night, in which the heavens will pass away with a great noise, and the elements will melt with fervent heat; both the earth and the works that are in it will be burned up." (2 Peter 3:5-10)

Thus we see that the statement **"with the Lord one day *is* as a thousand years, and a thousand years as one day"** was a *divine* explanation for apparent delay in the fulfillment of prophecy. This is also stated in the Old Testament, where, in speaking of judgment, the Holy Spirit said, **"a thousand years in Your sight *Are* like yesterday when it is past, And *like* a watch in the night."** (Psalm 90:4, see verses 3-9) *God's* answer is that **"The Lord is not slack concerning *His* promise, as some count slackness, but is longsuffering toward us, not willing that any should perish but that all should come to repentance."**

A second argument often pressed by Preterists is that the New Testament taught that its prophecies were to be fulfilled within the lifetimes of those who first received them. They quote passages such as **"Then we who are alive *and* remain shall be caught up together with them in the clouds to meet the Lord in the air."** (1 Thessalonians 4:17) **"and to *give* you who are troubled** rest with us when the Lord Jesus is revealed from heaven with His mighty angels." (2 Thessalonians 1:7) They claim that the "**we**" and "**you**" in these and many similar prophecies refer to the individuals who first received them. Taken by themselves, such passages could well have this meaning. But other *literal* interpretations are also possible. The "**we**" and "**you**" in these passages could also refer to the church as a whole, instead of simply the original hearers of these statements. We can only determine which of these *literal* interpretations is correct by examining the rest of scripture.

This also applies to the two proof texts they quote more often than any other. In the prophecy called the Olivet discourse, Jesus said, "**this generation will by no means pass away till all these things take place.**" (Matthew 24:34) Again, He said, "**there are some standing here who shall not taste death till they see the Son of Man coming in His kingdom.**" (Matthew 16:28) When taken out of their contexts, each of these statements appears to conclusively prove that many events commonly expected in the end times were to take place within the generation which first heard Jesus say these things. But when these statements are examined within their contexts, it becomes plain that this is an error.

Looking first at the passage in Matthew 24, we read:

> "**Learn this parable from the fig tree: When its branch has already become tender and puts forth leaves, you know that summer *is* near. So you also, when you see all these things, know that it is near; at the doors! Assuredly, I say to you, this generation will by no means pass away till all these things take place.**" (Matthew 24:32-34)

This passage could mean that the generation our Lord was addressing would not "**pass away till all these things take** place." But it could also mean that the words "**this generation**" were intended to mean the generation that would "**see all these things.**" We can only tell which of these *literal* interpretations is correct by examining the rest of scripture.

And looking the second passage in its context we read:

> "**For the Son of Man will come in the glory of His Father with His angels, and then He will reward each according to his works. Assuredly, I say to you, there are some standing here who shall not taste death till they see the Son of Man coming in His kingdom.**
>
> "**Now after six days Jesus took Peter, James, and John his brother, led them up on a high mountain by themselves; and He was transfigured before them. His face shone like the sun, and His clothes became as white as the light.**" (Matthew 16:27-17:2)

We need to notice the very next words after our Lord said "**there are some standing here who shall not taste death till they see the Son of Man coming in His kingdom.**" These words were "**Now after six days... He was transfigured before them. His face shone like the sun, and His clothes became as white as the light.**" Only six days after the Lord said this, "**Peter, James, and John his brother**" saw Him "**in the glory of His Father,**" the glory of "**His Kingdom.**" It is important to notice that this context is preserved in both of the other gospels that present this account. (See Mark 9:1-4 and Luke 9:27-29) Peter said of this event that "**we did not follow cunningly devised fables when we made known to you the power and coming of our Lord Jesus Christ, but were eyewitnesses of His majesty. For He received from God the Father honor and glory when such a voice came to Him from the Excellent Glory: 'This is My beloved Son, in whom I am well pleased.'**

THOUGHTS ABOUT PROPHETIC SUBJECTS

And we heard this voice which came from heaven when we were with Him on the holy mountain." (2 Peter 1:16-18)

From all this it seems that Jesus was speaking of this event when He said **"there are some standing here who shall not taste death till they see the Son of Man coming in His kingdom."** While this is only an interpretation, it is a possible *literal* interpretation o these words of Jesus. So again, the only way we can determine if it is correct is by examining the rest of scripture.

"The rest of scripture" is too big a subject to cover in such a short article as this. But there are many prophecies that definitely were not fulfilled in ancient times. Preterists go to great lengths to prove that many of them were, but their alleged "proofs" fall far short of the mark. While claiming that many of these prophesied events took place long ago, they minimize or simply ignore glaring differences between the details of the prophecies in question and the details in the testimonies of history. As an example, in "The Parousia," a book many Preterists consider a classic, the author, J. Stuart Russell, insisted that ancient Jerusalem was built on seven hills, even after admitting that Josephus spoke only of four or five such hills. [24]

The truth is that Josephus said Jerusalem was built on two hills, not four or five, much less seven. [25] Again, ten pages later in the same book, Russell argued that the ten kings mentioned in Revelation 17:12 were princes or chiefs who helped the ·Romans attack Jerusalem. This cannot be correct, for the armies that destroyed Jerusalem were the Lord's armies. In Matthew 22:7 our Lord prophetically said that **"when the king heard *about it*, he was furious. And he sent out his armies, destroyed those**

---

24. "The Parousia," by J. Stuart Russell, Grand Rapids: Baker, 1999, pg.492. Originally published London: T. Fisher Unwin, 1878. All page numbers cited are from the Baker edition.

25. "The Jewish War", by Flavius Josephus, Book 5, chapter 4, sec. 1, from "The New Complete Works of Josephus," translated by William Whiston, revised by Paul L. Maier, Grand Rapids: Kregel, 1999, pg. 851.

murderers, and burned up their city." But the ten kings of Revelation 17:12 will be the Lord's enemies, for they **"will make war with the Lamb, and the Lamb will overcome them, for He is Lord of lords and King of kings."** (Revelation 17:14) In his argument, Russell was only able to name four such chiefs; Antiochus, Sohemus, Agrippa, and Malchus. [26] He dismissed this with the comment that there were doubtless others. But then claimed that the number ten appeared to be mystic or symbolic, so there was no need to prove that there were exactly ten of them.

Russell used these arguments to prove that Jerusalem was the **"BABYLON THE GREAT"** of Revelation 17:5, whose utter destruction was prophesied in Revelation 18. But Revelation 11:8 expressly states the spiritual names of Jerusalem; **"the great city which spiritually is called Sodom and Egypt, where also our Lord was crucified."** Russell dismissed this by claiming that there was no reason why Jerusalem might not also be called Babylon. [27]

Other Preterists wrest Matthew 24:15-16, where we read, **"'Therefore when you see the** *"abomination of desolation,"* **spoken of by Daniel the prophet, standing in the holy place' (whoever reads, let him understand), 'then let those who are in Judea flee to the mountains.'"**

Some of these people pretend that the term, *"abomination of desolation,"* which we see in this passage, can legitimately be translated *"rebellion of desolation."* Because of this, we need to examine the actual Greek word translated *"abomination"* in this passage, and the actual Hebrew word used in the Old Testament passage from which Jesus quoted it.

So we first need to examine the Greek word translated *"abomination"* in Matthew 24:15. That word is βδελυγμα, *bdeluga* in our

---

26. Russell made no attempt to show that any of these came into power after the Revelation was given, as is clearly stated in Revelation 17:12.

27. Ibid, pg. 486.

alphabet, word number 946 in Strong's Greek Dictionary. This word literally means something that is *detestable*. In the Greek language, this word is derived from their word βδελύσσομαι, *be-delussomai* in our alphabet, word number 948 in Strong's Greek Dictionary, which means something *disgusting*. According to Strong's, this word, in turn, appears to be derived from the word βδεο, *bdeo* in our alphabet, which means to *stink*. So when we examine this Greek word in its derivation, we see that it indeed means *"abomination,"* and not *rebellion*.

We see this further by examining the Old Testament passage from which Jesus quoted this expression. This is Daniel 12:11, where we read, **"And from the time *that* the daily *sacrifice* is taken away, and the abomination of desolation is set up, *there shall be* one thousand two hundred and ninety days."**

Here we find that the Hebrew word translated **"abomination"** is שקוץ, *shqutz* in our alphabet, word number 8251 in Strong's Hebrew Dictionary. This word literally means something that is *disgusting* or *filthy*. It is derived from the Hebrew word שקץ, *saqat* in our alphabet, word number 8262 in Strong's Hebrew Dictionary. This word means to *be filthy*, to *loathe*, or *to pollute*. So, even as we saw concerning the Greek word used in its inspired translation in Matthew 24:15, there is simply no excuse to even pretend this word can legitimately be translated, *rebellion*. And thus we see that there is simply zero excuse for even trying to pretend that the scriptural term *"abomination of desolation"* can legitimately be translated as *"rebellion of desolation."*

So how do these pretenders come up with the notion that Jesus spoke of a *"rebellion of desolation"*? They get it from a parallel passage in Daniel, a different one than the one that Jesus quoted. For Daniel 8:13 says, **"Then I heard a holy one speaking; and *another* holy one said to that certain *one* who was speaking, 'How long *will* the vision *be, concerning* the daily *sacrifices* and** the transgression of desolation, the giving of both the sanctuary and the host to be trampled under foot?'"

The Hebrew word here translated **"and the transgression"** is והפשע, *we-phshso* in our alphabet. This is a combined word based on word number H6588 in Strong's Hebrew Dictionary, which means, as it is translated, **"and the transgression,"** but it can also be translated *"and the rebellion."* So the Hebrew phrase used in Daniel 8:13 can indeed be legitimately interpreted to mean *"and the rebellion of desolation."* But Jesus did not quote the expression from Daniel 8:13, but the one from Daniel 12:11.

This wresting of scripture was done for the sole purpose of pretending that the entire message given by Jesus in Matthew 24 was about the destruction of Jerusalem that took place in A.D. 70. This is typical of the abuse of the scriptures that is so common among Preterists. Since a Hebrew phrase that sounds like the one Jesus quoted can legitimately be translated *"the rebellion of desolation,"* they have no compunction about claiming that Jesus spoke of *"the rebellion of desolation,"* even though the phrase He actually quoted was from a completely different passage, and there is absolutely no way to even pretend that either the words Jesus used, or the phrase He quoted, mean anything other than *"**the abomination of desolation.**"*

But to Preterists, such details are abhorrent. They mock and criticize those that pont out that the details of various prophecies do not even approximately fit the historical events they claim as fulfillment of these prophecies. They refer to this as "wooden literalism." But here we see that their claims are not a rejection of "wooden literalism," but an impious pretension that the actual words used by the Holy Spirit are simply not important.

But what does the Bible say about this idea? First, we need to notice that it was concerning Bible prophecy that Jesus said, **"assuredly, I say to you, till heaven and earth pass away, one jot or one tittle will by no means pass from the law till all**

is fulfilled." (Matthew 5:18) It is a well known fact that the **"jot"** and the **"tittle"** were the two smallest marks used in writing the Hebrew language. So Jesus was here saying that, not only every word in the Bible was significant, but even the very spelling of every word. And why is the specific spelling of every word important? Because it is in the individual spellings of each word that we learn exactly what part of speech it was. The detailed spelling of a word shows whether, for instance, a verb was speaking of the past, the present, or the future, and whether it was speaking of action being done *by* the subject or *to* the subject. Likewise, the spelling of adjectives shows what they describe. All such details are critical to understanding the sentence in which a word occurs. And that is why our Lord said that **"one jot or one tittle will by no means pass from the law till all is fulfilled."**

Again, the Bible says:

"Every word of God *is* pure;
He is a shield to those who put their trust in Him.
Do not add to His words,
Lest He rebuke you, and you be found a liar."
(Proverbs 30:5-6)

And the book of Revelation, the last book of the Bible, and also the last book of the Bible to be written, ends with the solemn warning, **"For I testify to everyone who hears the words of the prophecy of this book: If anyone adds to these things, God will add to him the plagues that are written in this book; and if anyone takes away from the words of the book of this prophecy, God shall take away his part from the Book of Life, from the holy city, and *from* the things which are written in this book."** (Revelation 22:18-19)

So we see that it is a very serious thing to trifle with the exact wording of scripture, as Preterists systematically do. And

Preterism cannot be defended without such wresting of the very words of a God who cannot lie, and who never makes a mistake.

But now we need to treat one more false claim made by Preterists, which is that, in the first century, Jesus came and fulfilled all the prophecies about His coming. But this claim is simply false, and not only false, but absolutely false, and provably false.

In the first century, the Lord did not do as Jesus explicitly stated in Matthew 25:31-32, "**³¹When the Son of Man comes in His glory, and all the holy angels with Him, then He will sit on the throne of His glory. ³² All the nations will be gathered before Him, and He will separate them one from another, as a shepherd divides *his* sheep from the goats.**" Nor did He bring to pass what He explicitly promised in Matthew 19:28, saying, "**Assuredly I say to you, that in the regeneration, when the Son of Man sits on the throne of His glory, you who have followed Me will also sit on twelve thrones, judging the twelve tribes of Israel.**"

Further, at this time, He did not gather all Israel back to His "**holy mountain Jerusalem,**" as the Lord explicitly promised in Isaiah 66:15-20.) And He did not, as He explicitly promised in Ezekiel 36:1-11, cause "**all the house of Israel, all of it**" to inhabit the "**mountains of Israel,**" along with "**the hills, the rivers, the valleys, the desolate wastes, and the cities that have been forsaken.**" And He did not at that time give the nation of Israel the specific borders that were explicitly promised in Ezekiel 47:13-20. Nor was that *plot of real estate* divided up among the twelve tribes of Israel in the way explicitly stated in Ezekiel 48. Nor were the two sub-nations of Ephraim and Judah reunited under one king, as was explicitly promised in Ezekiel 37:16-22. Nor did these united Israelites go out conquering the surrounding nations, as was explicitly promised in Isaiah 11:12-14 and in Micah 5:5-6.

Again, He did not bring to pass the deaths of two-thirds of all the inhabitants of the land, with "**each one**" of the other third turning back to Himself, saying, **"The Lord is my God,"** as is explicitly stated in Zechariah 13:8-9, nor did He purge the rebels from among those returning to the land, as He explicitly stated in Ezekiel 20:33-38, saying of these rebels, that **"I will bring them out of the country where they dwell, but they shall not enter the land of Israel."** (Ezekiel 20:38b) And "**all the families that remain**" after these purges did not repent with bitter weeping, as is explicitly stated in Zechariah 12:10-14, nor **"For those of Israel who have escaped"**, was **"everyone who is recorded among the living in Jerusalem"** "**called holy,**" as is explicitly stated in Isaiah 4:2-3. Nor did the Lord at that time cause **"all"** of "**the house of Israel**" to "**known the Lord,**" "**from the least of them to the greatest of them,**" as is explicitly stated in Jeremiah 33:33-34.

And, instead of at that time causing Israel to inherit the land "**forever,**" as was explicitly promised in Isaiah 60:21, Jeremiah 7:7, Jeremiah 17:25, Jeremiah 31:40, Ezekiel 37:25, Joel 3:20, and Micah 4:7, they were soon afterwards completely cast out of the land. So it is utter nonsense to even try to pretend that all prophecy about the return of the Lord was fulfilled in the first century.

JAMES C. MORRIS

The Errors of Historicism

Like Preterism, which was discussed in the last article, Historicism relies heavily upon ancient historical records, but, again like Preterism, it systematically ignores glaring differences between the details contained in various Biblical prophecies and the historical records being cited to prove that these prophecies have been fulfilled. In both of these systems of doctrine, the critical importance of the exact wording of the Holy Scriptures is simply dismissed.

A typical example of this blatant ignoring of the differences between the historical records and the details of the prophecies, is their claim that the **"ten kings"** of Daniel 7:24 and Revelation 17:12 were ten kingdoms that became apparent when the Roman Empire collapsed in the late fifth century. But all of their various attempts to list these ten kingdoms end up including kingdoms that were specifically mentioned in the historical records of Julius Caesar's Gallic wars, which took place around two centuries before the Revelation was given. So they ignore the detail that Revelation 17:12 explicitly says that **"The ten horns which you saw are ten kings who have received no kingdom as yet."**

Historicists, like Preterists, complain about the "wooden literalism" of Dispensationalists. The main difference between Preterism and Historicism is that, while Preterists claim that all of Bible prophecy was fulfilled by the end of the first century, Historicists think that much of it is about what is now the history of the church. For that reason, this view is sometimes called the "protracted" view of Bible prophecy. But when the advocates of both of these systems of doctrine complain about the "wooden literalism" of Dispensationalists, they are forgetting the words of

THOUGHTS ABOUT PROPHETIC SUBJECTS

our Lord himself, when He said, **"For assuredly, I say to you, till heaven and earth pass away, one jot or one tittle will by no means pass from the law till all is fulfilled."** (Matthew 5:18)

Historicism basically rose from a desire to identify the Papacy as **"the Antichrist"** of Bible prophecy. Ignoring the fact that the prophetic scriptures clearly describe a specific evil individual that will appear in the end times, they make out the term, **"the Antichrist"** to mean an evil system that would continue over a long period of time.

In considering this error, we need to examine what the scriptures actually say about **"the Antichrist."** The first thing we need to notice is that the designation **"the Antichrist"** occurs only in the First Epistle of John. But then, in that passage, we need to notice that it clearly differentiates between **"the Antichrist,"** and people who are **"antichrists,"** saying, **"Little children, it is the last hour; and as you have heard that the Antichrist is coming, even now many antichrists have come, by which we know that it is the last hour."** (1 John 2:18) The two oldest Greek manuscripts of this passage omit the definite article from this term **"the Antichrist."** But essentially all modern scholars agree that both of these manuscripts, the Sinaiticus and the Vaticanus, show clear evidence of having been intentionally made different from the source texts used in their preparation. Having personally examined them, I wholeheartedly agree. So I reject the wisdom of giving *any* credence whatsoever to *any* variatiant readings in the Greek text found in these two manuscripts. But sadly, the Nestle text follows them in omitting it.

If this omission were correct, then the scriptural term **"Antichrist"** would not necessarily indicate a specific individual. But whether or not the omission was correct does not affect the fact that this scripture clearly differentiates between these two terms. The point here is that here, the Holy Spirit clearly differentiated between the future "**Antichrist**" and many people who are "**antichrists.**"

And we find an evil personage clearly presented as a specific end time individual in numerous other scriptures. The scripture where this is most clearly stated reads as follows:

> "**Now, brethren, concerning the coming of our Lord Jesus Christ and our gathering together to Him, we ask you, not to be soon shaken in mind or troubled, either by spirit or by word or by letter, as if from us, as though the day of Christ had come. Let no one deceive you by any means; for** *that Day will not come* **unless the falling away comes first, and the man of sin is revealed, the son of perdition, who opposes and exalts himself above all that is called God or that is worshiped, so that he sits as God in the temple of God, showing himself that he is God. Do you not remember that when I was still with you I told you these things? And now you know what is restraining, that he may be revealed in his own time. For the mystery of lawlessness is already at work; only He who now restrains** *will do so* **until He is taken out of the way. And then the lawless one will be revealed, whom the Lord will consume with the breath of His mouth and destroy with the brightness of His coming. The coming of the** *lawless one* **is according to the working of Satan, with all power, signs, and lying wonders, and with all unrighteous deception among those who perish, because they did not receive the love of the truth, that they might be saved. And for this reason God will send them strong delusion, that they should believe the lie, that they all may be condemned who did not believe the truth but had pleasure in unrighteousness.**" (2 Thessalonians 2:1-12)

THOUGHTS ABOUT PROPHETIC SUBJECTS

I have quoted the entirety of this rather long passage to demonstrate that it clearly indicates three things. First, that this evil personage is repeatedly spoken of as a specific individual, not as a system. And second, that this evil individual will appear in the end times, instead of a very long time before the end times. And third, that this evil individual will do things that the Papacy, as evil as it is, has never done.

In regard to the first point, we need to notice that he is repeatedly spoken of in the singular. He is called **"the man of sin," "the son of perdition,"** and **"the lawless one."** And each of these three phases specifically uses the Greek word ὁ, *ho* in our alphabet, word number 3588 in Strong's Greek Dictionary. This is the definite article, literally translating as our word *the*. And as we have often pointed out, in both Greek and Hebrew, the definite article was optional. Its omission in a sentence has no significance. But not so its usage. For, as it is optional, in the scriptures it is used mainly for stress, that is, to stress the fact that something particular is being mentioned. So the technical meanings of these three phrases is exactly what their English translations say, **"the man of sin," "the son of perdition,"** and **"the lawless one."** And finally, in this one passage, this specific individual is also called **"he"** three times and **"himself"** one more time. So there is no way this passage could even possibly be referring to an evil system that would exist over a span of many generations.

In regard to the second point, we need to notice, first, that this passage is about **"the day of Christ,"** not about the history of the church. And then, that **"the lawless one"** will not be revealed until **"He who now restrains" "is taken out of the way."** For the Historicist view to be correct, the restrainer has to be the Roman Empire. But the Papacy rose before the Roman Empire fell. Further, the restrainer is distinctly spoken of as an individual. The Greek words used here are ὁ, κατεχων, *ho katechon* in our alphabet. The Greek word "ὁ," the definite article, is in the nominative singular masculine. And the Greek word "*katechon*" is

377

a present, singular, masculine form of the word κατεχω, *katecho* in our alphabet, word number 2722 in Strong's Greek Dictionary, meaning "hold down." So these two words together distinctly represent "the restrainer" as a specific masculine person. Thus He can be none other than the **"Holy Spirit"** himself. For there is no other *person* who has the power to restrain evil on a worldwide basis.

And as to the third point, this evil end time individual will come with Satanic **"power, signs, and lying wonders."** The Papacy indeed has for many centuries wielded great power. But that power is power of a human sort, not the kind of power displayed by Satan. And it has never been able to demonstrate **"signs and lying wonders,"** although there are indeed fictitious accounts of such things being displayed by certain individuals. And finally, **"he sits as God in the temple of God, showing himself that he is God."** But Popery as evil as it is, has *never* actually claimed to *be* God. The Popes indeed claim to *represent* God, but they do not claim to actually *be* God.

So the only way to even imagine that this passage speaks of Popery is to simply ignore the details of what the Holy Spirit said. And this ignoring involves not only *some* of the details of this passage, but essentially *all* of them. For it simply does not speak of a generic evil power that would come sometime in the future, but of a specific evil individual that would not come until a specific time and would do specific things. Sadly, this callous attitude toward the precise wording of scripture runs throughout Historicist literature.

Another hallmark of Historicism is what they call the "day-year principle." From this, they insist that prophecies that speak of a specific number of days, mean that number of years. No scripture says this, but they interpret two scriptures to mean it. The first of these is Numbers 14:34, where the Lord said, **"According to the number of the days in which you spied out the land, forty days, for each day you shall bear your guilt one year, *namely* forty years, and you shall know My rejection."** But a punishment of one year for each day of their rebellion is not an indication that a day signifies a year throughout the prophetic scriptures. The second scripture they quote sounds a little more like it could mean that. For God told Ezekiel to lie on his side before a picture of Jerusalem to represent the guilt of Israel, saying:

> **"Lie also on your left side, and lay the iniquity of the house of Israel upon it.** *According* **to the number of the days that you lie on it, you shall bear their iniquity. For I have laid on you the years of their iniquity, according to the number of the days, three hundred and ninety days; so you shall bear the iniquity of the house of Israel. And when you have completed them, lie again on your right side; then you shall bear the iniquity of the house of Judah forty days. I have laid on you a day for each year."** (Ezekiel 4:4-6)

There can be no doubt that, in this case, God indeed said, and explicitly said, that each day of the prophet's symbolism would represent a year of the rebellion of His people. But that does not even so much as imply that in Bible prophecy a day *always* represents a year.

In applying this concept, Historicists make much of the 1260 days during which the **"woman"** is fed in **"the wilderness"** in Revelation 12:6 and during which the **"two witnesses"** testify in Revelation 11:3. They associate this with 1260 years which they ascribe to the power of the Papacy. But in considering this, we need to realize that it takes considerable mental gymnastics to limit the power of the papacy to 1260 years. Various Historicist writers have assigned different historical events and dates to each end of this 1260 year period to make it come out right.

But all of this neglects the indisputable fact that **"one thousand two hundred and sixty days"** of Revelation 11:3 and 12:6 is *exactly* the **"forty-two"** Hebrew, that is, Biblical, **"months"** of Revelation 11:2 and 12:5, all of which are 30 days long, making it also *exactly* three and a half Hebrew years, and thus is *exactly* the **"time, times, and half a time"** of Daniel 7:25, Daniel 12:7, and Revelation 12:14. All of these time periods are *explicitly* stated in Bible prophecy, and when we realize that they are all exactly the same length of time, we realize that, rather than being mystical symbols, all of these statements are *precise* statements of one of two specifically stated periods of time that will take place in the end times. And further, that two periods of three and a half Hebrew years make *exactly* the seventieth **"week"** of Daniel 9:27.

For Daniel 9:27 clearly says:

> **"Then he shall confirm a covenant with many for one week;**
> **But in the middle of the week**
> **He shall bring an end to sacrifice and offering.**
> **And on the wing of abominations shall be**
> **one who makes desolate,**
> **Even until the consummation, which is determined,**
> **Is poured out on the desolate."**

So the event which will take place **"in the middle of the week"** divides it into two half **"weeks,"** each of which is *exactly* **"one thousand two hundred and sixty days,"** is *exactly* **"forty-two months"** and is *exactly* **"a time, times, and half a time."** This precision of scriptural statements cannot be rationally disputed. But it clearly shows that the meaning of the 1260 days is *exactly* what it says, 1260 *days*, not 1260 *years*.

In the past, Historicists used the 2300 days of Daniel 8:14 to predict "the end off the world," which was initially calculated to come in 1844. When that did not happen, the calculations were revised several times. The ultimate failure of this prediction eventually came to be called "the great disappointment." And such is the *necessary* end of *all* false systems of interpretation of the scriptures.

THOUGHTS ABOUT PROPHETIC SUBJECTS

The Errors of British Israelism

A false doctrine that is sometimes called "British Israelism" says the modern day Jews are not Israelites at all. It says the true Israelites are Europeans, particularly the British, and through them, the Americans. It claims the so-called "lost" tribes of Israel migrated to the British Isles after Assyria was defeated. But this is contrary to well established history. It is well known to historians that the British are descended from the Celts, and that the ancestors of the Celts were the Cimmerians. But it is not so well known, although it has been proved beyond rational dispute, that the Cimmerians were the ancient nation that the Bible calls Gomer.

Biblical Gomer was called Gamer in Armenia. This can be clearly seen in the "History of the Armenians," by Moses Khorenats'i, (trans. Robert W. Thompson, Cambridge: Harvard University Press, 1978. See pages 74, 84, 86, and 92.) On page 74 this writer listed T'orgom as the son of T'iras, son of Gamer, son of Yapeth, son of Noah. Compare this with Genesis 10:1-3. "**Now this *is* the genealogy of the sons of Noah: Shem, Ham, and Japheth. And sons were born to them after the flood. The sons of Japheth *were* Gomer, Magog, Madai, Javan, Tubal, Meshech, and Tiras. The sons of Gomer *were* Ashkenaz, Riphath, and Togarmah.**"

The Assyrians called this people the Gameraaa. [28] In a book titled "The Royal Correspondence of the Assyrian Empire," this Assyrian word is translated "Cimmerians," [29] with a footnote iden-

---

28. "The Royal Correspondence of the Assyrian Empire," translated and transliterated by Leroy Waterman, Ann Arbor: University of Michigan Press, 1930. part I, pg. 74.
29. Ibed, pg. 75.

tifying them as the classical Cimmerii and Biblical Gomer. [30] [31] The Assyrian scribes described this group sufficiently to positively identify them as the people whom the Greeks called Cimmerians. Another letter in the Assyrian archives called the Gimiraa "the people of the steppe." [32] It is well known that the ancient homeland of the Cimmerians was the steppe region of southern Russia. And yet another letter in this series locates the lands of Guriania and Nagiu as between the lands of Urartu and Gamirra. [33] This was also stated in a letter contained in a different scholastic volume, [34] except that the land of Nagiu was not mentioned there. It is well known that Urartu is another name for Armenia, which was on Assyria's northern border, so we know the land of Gamirra, or Cimmeria, was significantly north of Armenia. That would place it somewhere in southern Russia. (The Scythians eventually drove them out of that region and they settled in central and western Europe. As these sources were from the Assyrian empire, this proves that Cimmeria already existed when Assyria was in power, that is, before Assyria carried away the ten northern tribes of Israel. So the Cimmerians, who are well known to be the ancestors of the Celts, and thus of the British, cannot even possibly be descended from the ten "lost" tribes of Israel.

But this notion is not only contrary to well established history. It is also contrary to scripture. For the end time prophecies in the Bible make it very clear that "Judah," that is, "the Jews," will be in their ancient homeland during the end times. We read, for instance:

"For behold, the Lord, the LORD of hosts,

Takes away from Jerusalem and from Judah

---

30. Ibid, part III, pg. 53.

31. "State Archives of Assyria, Volume V - The Correspondence of Sargon II,", ed by Giovanni B. Lanfranchi and Simo Parpola, Helsinki University Press, 1990. Part II, pg 246.

32. "The Royal Correspondence of the Assyrian Empire," op. cit., part II, pg. 361.

33. "The Royal Correspondence of the Assyrian Empire," op. cit., part I, pg 101.

34. "State Archives of Assyria, Volume V - The Correspondence of Sargon II, Part II" op. cit., pg 75.

THOUGHTS ABOUT PROPHETIC SUBJECTS

The stock and the store,
The whole supply of bread and the whole supply of water;
The mighty man and the man of war,
The judge and the prophet, And the diviner and the elder;
The captain of fifty and the honorable man,
The counselor and the skillful artisan,
And the expert enchanter.
'I will give children *to be* their princes,
And babes shall rule over them.
The people will be oppressed,
Every one by another and every one
by his neighbor;
The child will be insolent toward the elder,
And the base toward the honorable.'
When a man takes hold of his brother
In the house of his father, *saying,*
'You have clothing;
You be our ruler,
And *let* these ruins *be* under your power,'
In that day he will protest, saying,
'I cannot cure *your* ills,
For in my house *is* neither food nor clothing;
Do not make me a ruler of the people.'
For Jerusalem stumbled,
And Judah is fallen,
Because their tongue and their doings
Are against the LORD,
To provoke the eyes of His glory.

> **The look on their countenance witnesses against them,**
> **And they declare their sin as Sodom;**
> **They do not hide** *it*.
> **Woe to their soul!**
> **For they have brought evil upon themselves."**
> (Isaiah 3:1-9)

And again:

> **"The burden of the word of the Lord against Israel. Thus says the Lord, who stretches out the heavens, lays the foundation of the earth, and forms the spirit of man within him: 'Behold, I will make Jerusalem a cup of drunkenness to all the surrounding peoples, when they lay siege against Judah and Jerusalem."**
> (Zechariah 12:1-2)

We therefore understand that Judah, that is, the real Jews, will be in their ancient homeland when all this happens. Yet the ones who live in this land are not the British or the Americans, but the modern day Jews. Thus we see that this doctrine, which is sometimes called British Israelism, is contrary to both history and scripture.

Dispensational Publishing House is striving to become the go-to source for Bible-based materials from the dispensational perspective.

Our goal is to provide high-quality doctrinal and worldview resources that make dispensational theology accessible to people at all levels of understanding.

Visit our blog regularly to read informative articles from both known and new writers.

And please let us know how we can better serve you.

Dispensational Publishing House, Inc.
PO Box 3181
Taos, NM 87571

Call us toll free 844-321-4202

www.DispensationalPublishing.com

www.ingramcontent.com/pod-product-compliance
Lightning Source LLC
Chambersburg PA
CBHW071952110526
44592CB00012B/1065